Blitzed

Drugs in Nazi Germany

NORMAN OHLER

Translated by Shaun Whiteside

ALLEN LANE
an imprint of
PENGUIN BOOKS

ALLEN LANE

UK | USA | Canada | Ireland | Australia
India | New Zealand | South Africa

Particular Books is part of the Penguin Random House group of companies
whose addresses can be found at global.penguinrandomhouse.com.

First published in German by Kiepenheuer & Witsch 2015
This translation first published by Allen Lane 2016
003

Typeset in Garamond MT Std 12.5/15 pt by
Palimpsest Book Production Limited, Falkirk, Stirlingshire

Printed in Great Britain by Clays Ltd, St Ives plc

ISBN: 978-0-241-25699-2

www.greenpenguin.co.uk

MIX
Paper from
responsible sources
FSC® C018179

Penguin Random House is committed to a
sustainable future for our business, our readers
and our planet. This book is made from Forest
Stewardship Council® certified paper.

A political system devoted to decline instinctively does much to speed up that process.

Jean-Paul Sartre

Contents

I

Methamphetamine, the *Volksdroge* (1933–1938)

National Socialism was toxic, in the truest sense of the word. It gave the world a chemical legacy that still affects us today: a poison that refuses to disappear. On one hand, the Nazis presented themselves as clean-cut and enforced a strict, ideologically underpinned anti-drug policy with propagandistic pomp and draconian punishments. In spite of this, a particularly potent and perfidious substance became a popular product under Hitler. This drug carved out a great career for itself all over the German Reich, and later in the occupied countries of Europe. Under the trademark 'Pervitin', this little pill became the accepted *Volksdroge*, or 'people's drug', and was on sale in every chemist's shop. It wasn't until 1939 that its use was restricted by making Pervitin prescription-only, and the pill was not subjected to regulation until the Reich Opium Law in 1941.

Its active ingredient, methamphetamine, is now either illegal or strictly regulated,[1] but, with the number of consumers currently at over 100 million and rising, it counts today as our most popular poison. Produced in hidden labs by chemical amateurs, usually in adulterated form, this substance has come to be known as 'crystal meth'. Usually ingested nasally in high doses, the crystalline form of this so-called horror drug has gained unimaginable popularity all over Europe, with an exponential number of first-time users. This upper, with its dangerously powerful kick, is used as a party drug, for boosting performance in the workplace, in offices, even in parliaments and at universities. It banishes both sleep and hunger while promising euphoria, but in the form of crystal meth* it is a potentially destructive and highly addictive substance. Hardly anyone knows about its rise in Nazi Germany.

Breaking Bad: The Drug Lab of the Reich

Under a clean-swept summer sky stretching over both industrial zones and uniform housing, I take the suburban train south-east, to the edge of Berlin. In order to find the remnants of the Temmler factory I have to get out at Adlershof, which nowadays calls itself 'Germany's most modern technology park'. Avoiding the campus, I strike off across an urban no man's land, skirting dilapidated factory buildings, and passing through a wilderness of crumbling brick and rusty steel.

The Temmler factory moved here in 1933. It was only

---

* Methamphetamine in its pure form is less harmful than the crystal meth produced in often amateurish illegal laboratories, where it is mixed with poisons such as petrol, battery acid or anti-freeze.

one year later that Albert Mendel (the Jewish co-owner of the Tempelhof Chemicals Factory) was expropriated by the racist laws of the regime and Temmler took over his share, quickly expanding the business. These were good times for the German chemicals industry (or at least for its Aryan members), and pharmaceutical development boomed. Research was tirelessly conducted on new, pioneering substances that would ease the pain of modern humanity or sedate its troubles. Many of the resulting pharmacological innovations shape the way we consume medicine today

By now the former Temmler factory in Berlin-Johannisthal has fallen into ruin. There is no sign of its prosperous past, of a time when millions of Pervitin pills a week were being pressed. The grounds lie unused, a dead property. Crossing a deserted car park, I make my way through a wildly overgrown patch of forest and over a wall stuck with broken bits of glass designed to deter intruders. Between ferns and saplings stands the old wooden 'witch's house' of the founder, Theodor Temmler, once the nucleus of the company. Behind dense alder bushes looms a forsaken brick building. A window is broken enough for me to be able to climb through, stumbling into a long dark corridor. Mildew and mould grow from the walls and ceilings. At the end of the hallway a door stands beckoning, half open, encrusted with flaking green paint. Beyond the door, daylight peers through two shattered, lead-framed industrial windows. An abandoned bird's nest hides in the corner. Chipped white tiles reach all the way to the high ceiling, which is furnished with circular air vents.

The Temmler factory in Berlin-Johannisthal, then . . . and now.

This is the former laboratory of Dr Fritz Hauschild, head of pharmacology at Temmler from 1937 until 1941, who was in search of a new type of medicine, a 'performance-enhancing drug'. This is the former drug lab of the Third Reich. Here, in porcelain crucibles attached to pipes and glass coolers, the chemists boiled up their flawless matter. Lids rattled on pot-bellied flasks, orange steam released with a sharp hissing noise while emulsions crackled and white-gloved fingers made adjustments. Here methamphetamine was produced of a quality that even Walter White, the drugs cook in the TV series *Breaking Bad,* which depicts meth as a symbol of our times, could only have dreamed of.

Prologue in the Nineteenth Century: the Father of all Drugs

Voluntary dependence is the finest state.
Johann Wolfgang von Goethe

To understand the historical relevance of methamphetamine and other substances to the Nazi state, we must go back before the beginning of the Third Reich. The development of modern societies is bound as tightly with the creation and distribution of drugs as the economy is with advances in technology. In 1805 Goethe wrote *Faust* in classicist Weimar, and by poetic means perfected one of his theses, that the genesis of man is itself drug-induced: I change my brain, therefore I am. At the same time, in the rather less glamorous town of Paderborn in Westphalia, the pharmaceutical assistant Friedrich Wilhelm Sertürner performed experiments with opium poppies, whose thickened sap anaesthetized pain more effectively than anything else. Goethe wanted to explore through artistic and dramatic channels what it is that holds the core of the world together – Sertürner, on the other hand, wanted to solve a major, millennium-old problem which has plagued our species to a parallel degree.

It was a concrete challenge for the brilliant 21-year-old chemist: depending on the conditions they are grown in, the active ingredient in opium poppies is present in varying concentrations. Sometimes the bitter sap does not ease the pain quite strongly enough, and other times it can lead to an unintended overdose and fatal poisoning. Thrown back entirely on his own devices, just as the opiate laudanum consumed Goethe in his study, Sertürner made an astonishing discovery: he succeeded in isolating morphine, the crucial alkaloid in opium, a kind of pharmacological Mephistopheles that instantly magics pain away. Not only a turning point in the history of pharmacology, this was also one of the most important events of the early nineteenth century, not to mention human history as a whole. Pain, that irritable companion, could now be assuaged, indeed removed, in precise doses. All over Europe, apothecaries had to the best of their ability (and their consciences) pressed pills from the ingredients of their own herb gardens or from the deliveries of women who foraged in hedgerows. These homegrown chemists now developed within only a few years into veritable factories, with established pharmacological standards.* Morphine was not only a method of easing life's woes, it was also big business.

In Darmstadt the owner of the Engel-Apotheke, Emanuel Merck, stood out as a pioneer of this development. In 1827 he set out his business model of supplying alkaloids and other medication in unvarying quality. This was the birth not only of the Merck company, which still thrives today, but of the modern pharmaceutical industry as a whole. When injections were invented in 1850, there was no stopping the victory parade of morphine. The painkiller was used in the American Civil War in 1861–65 and in the Franco-Prussian War of 1870–71. Soon morphine fixes were doing the rounds as normal procedure.[2] The change was crucial; the pain of even seriously injured soldiers could now be kept within bounds. This made a different scale of war possible: fighters who before would have been ruled out for a long time by an injury were soon coddled back to health and thrust onto the front line once again.

With morphine, also known as 'morphium', the development of pain relief and anaesthesia reached a crucial climax, both in the army and in civil society. From the worker to the nobleman, the supposed panacea took the whole world by storm, from Europe via Asia and all the way to America. In drugstores across the USA, two active ingredients were available without

* The forerunners of these companies were the Christian monasteries, which produced medications on a large scale even in the Middle Ages, and exported widely. In Venice (where the first coffee house in Europe opened in 1647), chemical and pharmaceutical preparations had been manufactured as early as the fourteenth century.

prescription: fluids containing morphine calmed people down, while drinks containing cocaine, such as in the early days Vin Mariani, a Bordeaux containing coca extract, and even Coca-Cola[3], were used to counter low moods, as a hedonistic source of euphoria, and also as a local anaesthetic. This was only the start. The industry soon needed to diversify; it craved new products. On 10 August 1897 Felix Hoffmann, a chemist with the Bayer company, synthesized acetylsalicylic acid from willow bark; it went on sale as Aspirin and conquered the globe. Eleven days later the same man invented another substance that was also to become world famous: diacetyl morphine, a derivative of morphine – the first designer drug. Trademarked as 'Heroin', it entered the market and began its own campaign. 'Heroin is a fine business,' the directors of Bayer announced proudly and advertised the substance as a remedy for headaches, for general indisposition and also as a cough syrup for children. It was even recommended to babies for colic or sleeping problems.[4]

Business wasn't just booming for Bayer. In the last third of the nineteenth century several new pharmaceutical hotspots developed along the Rhine. Unlike other, more traditional industries, the chemical industry didn't require as much in terms of overheads to get business going, only needing relatively little equipment and raw material. Even small operations promised high profit margins. What was most important was intuition and specialist knowledge on the part of the developers, and Germany, rich in human capital, was able to fall back on an inexhaustible stock of excellent chemists and engineers, trained in what was at the time the best education system in the world. The network of universities and technical colleges was recognized as exemplary: science and business worked hand in hand. Research was being carried out at top speed and a multitude of patents were being developed. Where the chemicals industry was concerned, Germany was the 'workshop of the world'. 'Made in Germany' became a guarantee of quality, especially for drugs.

Germany, the Global Dealer

This didn't change after the First World War. While France and Great Britain were able to acquire natural stimulants such as coffee, tea, vanilla, pepper and other natural medicines from colonies overseas, Germany, which lost its (comparatively sparse) colonial possessions under the terms of the Versailles Treaty, had to find other ways – stimulants had to be produced synthetically. In fact, Germany was in dire need of artificial assistance: the war had inflicted deep wounds and caused the nation both physical and psychic pain. In the 1920s drugs became more and more important for the despondent population between the Baltic Sea and the Alps. The desire for sedation led to self-education and there soon emerged no shortage of know-how for the production of a remedy.

The course was set for a thriving pharmaceutical industry. Many of the chemical substances that we know today were developed and patented within a very short period of time. German companies became leaders in the global market. Not only did they produce the most medicines, but they also provided the lion's share of chemical raw materials for their manufacture throughout the world. A new economy came into being, and the picturesque Rhine Valley became a Chemical Valley of sorts. Previously unknown little outfits prospered overnight and grew into influential players. In 1925 the bigger chemicals factories joined together to form IG Farben, one of the most powerful companies in the world, with headquarters in Frankfurt. Opiates above all were still a German speciality. In 1926 the country was top of the morphine-producing states and world champion when it came to exporting heroin: 98 per cent of the production went abroad.[5] Between 1925 and 1930, 91 tonnes of morphine were produced, 40 per cent of global production.[6] Under the obligations of the Versailles Treaty, Germany reluctantly signed the League of Nations International Opium Convention in 1925, which regulated the trade. It was not ratified in Berlin until 1929. The local alkaloid industry still processed just over 200 tonnes of opium in 1928.[7]

The Germans were world leaders in another class of substances as well: the companies Merck, Boehringer and Knoll controlled 80 per cent of the global cocaine market. Merck's cocaine, from the city of Darmstadt, was seen as the best product in the world, and commercial pirates in China printed fake Merck labels by the million.[8] Hamburg was the major European marketplace for raw cocaine: every year thousands of kilograms were imported legally through its port. Peru sold its entire annual production of raw cocaine, over five tonnes, almost exclusively to Germany for further processing. The influential 'Fachgruppe

Opium und Kokain' (Expert Group on Opium and Cocaine), put together by the German drugs manufacturers, worked tirelessly on a close integration of the government and the chemicals industry. Two cartels, each consisting of a handful of companies, divided up between them the lucrative market 'of the entire world';[9] the so-called 'cocaine convention' and 'opiates convention'. Merck was the business leader in both cases.[10] The young Weimar Republic, swimming in consciousness-altering and intoxicating substances, delivered heroin and cocaine to the four corners of the world and rose to become a global dealer.

The Chemical Twenties

This scientific and economic development also resonated with the spirit of the age. Artificial paradises were in vogue in the Weimar Republic. People chose to flee into worlds of make-believe rather than engage with the often less rosy reality – a phenomenon that more or less defined this very first democracy on German soil, both politically and culturally. Many were reluctant to admit the true reasons for the military defeat and repressed the shared responsibility of the imperial German establishment for the fiasco of the First World War. The malicious legend of the 'stab in the back' gained currency, claiming the German army had only lost the war because of internal sabotage from the left.[11]

These escapist tendencies often found expression either in sheer hatred or in cultural excess, most of all in Berlin. Alfred Döblin's novel *Berlin Alexanderplatz* identified the city as the 'Whore of Babylon', with an incomparably grubby underworld, a place seeking salvation in the most appalling, barely imaginable, excesses, particularly drugs. 'Berlin nightlife, oh boy, oh boy, the world has never seen the like! We used to have a great army, now we've got great perversities!' wrote the author Klaus Mann.[12] The city on the Spree became synonymous with moral reprehensibility. When Germany's currency collapsed – in autumn 1923 one US dollar was worth 4.2 billion Marks – all moral values seemed to plummet with it as well.

Everything whirled apart in a toxicological frenzy. The icon of the age, the actress and dancer Anita Berber, dipped white rose petals in a cocktail of chloroform and ether at breakfast, before sucking them clean. Films about cocaine or morphine were showing in the cinemas, and all drugs were available on street corners without prescription. Forty per cent of Berlin doctors were said to be addicted to morphine.[13] In Friedrichstrasse Chinese traders from the former German-leased territory of Tsingtao ran opium dens. Illegal nightclubs opened in the back rooms of the Mitte district. Smugglers distributed flyers at Anhalter station, advertising illegal dance parties and 'beauty evenings'. Big clubs like the famous Haus Vaterland, on Potsdamer Platz, and Ballhaus Resi, notorious for its extravagant promiscuity, on Blumenstrasse, attracted potential fun-lovers in droves, did as smaller establishments like the Kakadu Bar or the Weisse Maus, where masks were distributed on the way in to guarantee the anonymity of the guests. An early form of sex-and-drugs tourism from western neighbours and the USA began, because everything in Berlin was as cheap as it was exciting.

The world war was lost, and everything seemed permitted: the metropolis mutated into the experimental capital of Europe. Posters on house walls warned in shrill Expressionist script: *'Berlin, take a breath / bear in mind your dance partner is death!'* The police couldn't keep up: order collapsed first sporadically, then chronically, and the culture of pleasure filled the vacuum as best it could, as illustrated in a song of the times:

Once not so very long ago
Sweet alcohol, that beast,
Brought warmth and sweetness to our lives,
But then the price increased.
And so cocaine and morphine
Berliners now select.
Let lightning flashes rage outside
We snort and we inject! [. . .]

At dinner in the restaurant
The waiter brings the tin
Of coke for us to feast upon –
Forget whisky and gin!
Let drowsy morphine take its
Subcutaneous effect
Upon our nervous system –
We snort and we inject!

These medications aren't allowed,
Of course, they're quite forbidden.

But even such illicit treats
Are very seldom hidden.
Euphoria awaits us
And though, as we suspect,
Our foes can't wait to shoot us down,
We snort and we inject!

And if we snort ourselves to death
Or into the asylum,
Our days are going downhill fast –
How better to beguile 'em?
Europe's a madhouse anyway,
No need for genuflecting;
The only way to Paradise
Is snorting and injecting![14]

In 1928 in Berlin alone 73 kilos of morphine and heroin were sold quite legally on prescription over the chemist's counter.[15] Anyone who could afford it took cocaine, the ultimate weapon for intensifying the moment. Coke spread like wildfire and symbolized the extravagance of the age. On the other hand, it was viewed as a 'degenerate poison', and disapproved of by both Communists and Nazis, who were fighting for power in the streets. There was violent opposition to the free-and-easy *Zeitgeist*: German nationalists railed against 'moral decay' and similar attacks were heard from the conservatives. Though Berlin's new status as a cultural metropolis was accepted with pride, the bourgeoisie, which was losing status in the 1920s, showed its insecurity through its radical condemnation of mass 'pleasure culture', decried as 'decadently Western'.

Worst of all, the National Socialists agitated against the pharmacological quest for salvation of the Weimar period. Their brazen rejection of the parliamentary system, of democracy, as well as of the urban culture of a society that was opening up to the world, was expressed through tub-thumping slogans directed against the degenerate state of the hated 'Jewish Republic'.

The Nazis had their own recipe for healing the people: they promised ideological salvation. For them there could be only one legitimate form of inebriation: the swastika. National Socialism strove for a transcendental state of being as well; the Nazi world of illusions into which the Germans were to be enticed often used techniques of intoxication. World-historical decisions, according to Hitler's inflammatory text *Mein Kampf,* had to be brought about in states of euphoric enthusiasm or hysteria. So the Nazi Party distinguished itself on the one hand with populist arguments and on the other with torch parades, flag consecrations, rapturous announcements and public speeches aimed at achieving a state of collective ecstasy. These were supplemented with the violent frenzies of the Brownshirts during the early '*Kampfzeit*', or period of struggle, often fuelled by the abuse of alcohol.* '*Realpolitik*' tended to be dismissed as unheroic cattle trading: the idea was to replace politics with a state of social intoxication.[16] If the Weimar

* The foundation of the NSDAP on 24 February 1920 took place in a beer hall, the Hofbräuhaus, in Munich. In the early days, alcohol played an important part in the masculine rituals of the far-right party and its SA. This book barely touches on the role of alcohol in the Third Reich, because it deserves a discussion in its own right.

Republic can be seen in psycho-historical terms as a repressed society, its supposed antagonists, the National Socialists, were at the head of that trend. They hated drugs because they wanted to be like a drug themselves.

Switching Power Means Switching Substances

... while the abstinent Führer was silent[17]

Günter Grass

During the Weimar period Hitler's inner circle had already managed to establish an image of him as a man working tirelessly, putting his life completely at the service of 'his' people. A picture was created of an unassailable leader-figure, entirely devoted to the Herculean task of gaining control of Germany's social contradictions and problems, and to ironing out the negative consequences of the lost world war. One of Hitler's allies reported in 1930: 'He is all genius and body. And he mortifies that body in a way that would shock people like us! He doesn't drink, he practically only eats vegetables, and he doesn't touch women.'[18] Hitler allegedly didn't even allow himself coffee and legend had it that after the First World War he threw his last pack of cigarettes into the Danube near Linz; from then onwards, supposedly, no poisons would enter his body.

'We teetotallers have – let it be mentioned in passing – a particular reason to be grateful to our Führer, if we bear in mind what a model his personal lifestyle and his position on intoxicants can be for everyone,' reads an announcement from an abstinence association.[19] The Reich Chancellor: ostensibly a pure person, remote from all worldly pleasures, entirely without a private life. An existence apparently informed by self-denial and long-lasting self-sacrifice: a model for an entirely healthy existence. The myth of Hitler as an anti-drug teetotaller who made his own needs secondary was an essential part of Nazi ideology and was presented again and again by the mass media. A myth was created which established itself in the public imagination, but also among critical minds of the period, and still resonates today. This is a myth that demands to be deconstructed.

Following their seizure of power on 30 January 1933, the National Socialists suffocated the eccentric pleasure-seeking culture of the Weimar Republic. Drugs were made taboo, as they made it possible to experience unrealities other than the ones promulgated by the National Socialists. 'Seductive poisons'[20] had no place in a system in which only the Führer was supposed to do the seducing. The path taken by the authorities in their so-called *Rauschgiftbekämpfung*, or 'war on drugs', lay less in an intensification of the opium law, which was simply adopted from the Weimar Republic,[21] than in several new regulations which served the central National Socialist idea of 'racial hygiene'. The term *'Droge'* – drug – which at one point meant nothing more than 'dried plant parts'* was

---

* Etymologically, the term comes from the Dutch *droog*, meaning 'dry'. During the Dutch colonial age, this referred to dried luxuries such as spices or tea. In Germany all pharmaceutically usable (dried) plants and plant parts, mushrooms, animals, minerals etc., were called *'Drogen'* (drugs), and the word later came to be applied to all remedies and medications – leading to the word *'Drogerie'*, meaning a chemist's shop.

given negative connotations. Drug consumption was stigmatized and – with the help of quickly established new divisions of the criminal police – severely penalized.

This new emphasis came into force as early as November 1933, when the Reichstag passed a law that allowed the imprisonment of addicts in a closed institution for up to two years, although that period of confinement could be extended indefinitely by legal decree.[22] Further measures ensured that doctors who consumed drugs would be forbidden to work for up to five years. Medical confidentiality

– Zentralkartei –

Nummernreiter bedeuten:

1 Händler [inländische]	10 Betrüger u. Etikettfälscher	19 Händler [internationale]
2 Verbraucher	11 Suchtgefährdete	20 Dicodidsüchtige
3 Kokainsüchtige	12 Ärzte [allgemein]	21 Kriegsbeschädigte
4 Sonstige Süchtige	13 Apotheker [allgemein]	22 Künstler
5 Rezeptfälscher	14 Apotheker [Verstoße ges. d VVO]	23 Heil-u. Pflegepersonal
6 Rezeptdiebe	15 Dolantinsüchtige	24
7 Btm.-Diebe u.-Einbrecher	16 Pervitinsüchtige	25 Berufsuntersagung
8 Pantoponsüchtige	17 Opiumsüchtige	26 Eukodalsüchtige
9 Ärzte [Vielverschreiber]	18 Morphiumsüchtige	27
		28 Selbstmörder

Farbige Reiter bedeuten:

Lila: Juden   Rot: Zur Entziehungskur Untergebrachte

Gelb: Berliner Täter aus den Jahren 1927-36   Grün: Nach 1931 Süchtig gewordene

Schwarz: In polizeiliche Vorbeugungshaft genommene Täter   Blau:

Your identity card at the Reich Central Office for Combating Drug Transgressions could be a matter of life and death. You were defined by a number (as a dealer, prescription forger, Eukodal addict, artist, etc.) and a colour (purple: Jew; red: held for drying out, etc.).

was considered breakable when it came to detecting consumers of illegal substances.[23] The chairman of the Berlin Medical Council decreed that every doctor had to file a 'drug report' when a patient was prescribed narcotics for longer than three weeks, because 'public security is endangered by chronic alkaloid abuse in almost every case'.[24] If a report to that effect came in, two experts examined the patient in question. If they found that hereditary factors were 'satisfactory', immediate compulsory withdrawal was imposed. Although in the Weimar Republic slow or gradual withdrawal had been used, now addicts were to be subjected to the horrors of cold turkey.[25] If assessment of the hereditary factors yielded a negative result, the judge could order confinement for an unspecified duration. Drug users soon ended up in concentration camps.[26]

Every German was also ordered to 'convey observations about drug-addicted acquaintances and family members, so that corrective action can be taken immediately'.[27] Filing systems were put in place in order to establish a thorough record, enabling the Nazis to use their war against drugs to feed into a surveillance state quite soon after they came to power. The dictatorship extended its so-called 'health leadership' into every corner of the Reich: in every administrative district there was an 'anti-drug consortium'. Doctors, chemists, social security authorities and representatives of the law such as the army and the police were all involved, as well as members of the National Socialist People's Welfare, establishing a full-blown anti-drug web. Its threads converged in the Reich Health Office in Berlin, in Principal Department II of the Reich Committee for the People's Health. A 'duty of health' was postulated, which would go hand in hand with the 'total containment of all demonstrable physical, social and mental damage that could be inflicted by alcohol and tobacco'. Cigarette advertising was severely restricted, and drug prohibitions were put in place to 'block any remaining breaches of moral codes in our people'.[28]

In autumn 1935 a new Marital Health Law was passed which forbade marriage if one of the parties suffered from a 'mental disturbance'. Narcotics addicts were marginalized into this category and were branded as 'psychopathic personalities' – without the prospect of a cure. This marriage prohibition was supposed to prevent 'infection of the partner, as well as hereditarily conditioned potential for addiction' in children, because among 'the descendants of drug addicts an increased rate of mental deviations' had been observed.[29] The Law for the Prevention of Hereditarily Diseased Offspring took compulsory sterilization to its brutal conclusion: 'For reasons of racial hygiene we must therefore see to it that severe addicts are prevented from reproducing.'[30]

Worse was to follow. Under the guise of 'euthanasia', those considered 'criminally insane', a category including drug users, would be murdered in the first years of the war. The precise number of those affected is impossible to reconstruct.[31,32] Of crucial importance to their fate was the assessment on their file card: a plus (+) meant a lethal injection or the gas chamber, a minus (-) meant a deferral. If an overdose of morphine was used for the killing it came from the Reich Central Office for Combating Drug Transgression, which had emerged out of the Berlin Drug Squad in 1936 as the first Reich-wide drug police authority.

Among the 'selecting doctors' a mood of 'intoxicating superiority' prevailed.[33] The anti-drug policy served as a vehicle for the exclusion and suppression, even the destruction, of marginal groups and minorities.

Anti-drug Policy as Anti-Semitic Policy

The Jew has used the most refined means to poison the mind and the soul of German people, and to guide thought along an un-German path which inevitably led to doom. [. . .] Removing this Jewish infection, which could lead to a national disease and to the death of the people, is also a duty of our health leadership.

Medical Journal for Lower Saxony, 1939[34]

From the outset, the racist terminology of National Socialism was informed by linguistic images of infection and poison, by the topos of toxicity. Jews were equated with bacillae or pathogens. They were described as foreign bodies and said to be poisoning the Reich, making the healthy social organism ill, so they had to be eradicated or exterminated. Hitler said: 'There is no longer any compromise, because such a thing would be poison to us.'[35]

In fact the poison lay in the language itself, which dehumanized the Jews as a preliminary stage to their subsequent murder. The Nuremberg Race Laws of 1935 and the introduction of the *Ahnenpass* (Proof of Aryan Ancestry) manifested the demand for purity of the blood – this was seen as one of the supreme goods of the people, and one most in need of protection. Needless to say, this produced a point of intersection between anti-Semitic propaganda and anti-drugs policy. It was not the dose that determined the poison, but the category of foreignness. Propagated as the standard work on the subject, the central, entirely unscientific thesis of the book *Magische Gifte* ('Magic Poisons') posits: 'The greatest toxic effect is always produced by narcotics alien to the country and the race.'[36] Jews and drugs merged into a single toxic or epidemiological unit that menaced Germany: 'For decades our people have been told by Marxists and Jews: "Your body belongs to you." That was taken to mean that at social occasions between men, or between men and women, any quantities of alcohol could be enjoyed, even at the cost of the body's health. Irreconcilable with this Jewish Marxist view is the Teutonic German idea that we are the bearers of the eternal legacy of our ancestors, and that accordingly our body belongs to the clan and the people.'[37]

SS Haupsturmführer Criminal Commissar Erwin Kosmehl, who was from 1941 director of the Reich Central Office for Combating Drug Transgressions asserted that 'Jews play a supreme part' in the international drug trade. His work was concerned with 'eliminating international criminals who often have roots in Jewry'.[38] The Nazi Party's Office of Racial Policy claimed that the Jewish character was essentially drug-dependent: the intellectual urban Jew preferred cocaine or morphine to calm his constantly 'excited nerves' and give himself a feeling of peace and inner security. Jewish doctors were rumoured to be 'often extraordinarily addicted to morphine'.[39]

In the anti-Semitic children's book *Der Giftpilz* ('The Poisonous Mushroom') the National Socialists combined their twin bogeymen, Jews and drugs, into racial-hygiene propaganda that was used in schools and nurseries.[40] The story was exemplary, the message perfectly clear: the dangerous poison mushrooms had to be eradicated.

While the selection strategies in the battle against drugs were directed against an alien power that was perceived as threatening, in National Socialism they almost automatically had anti-Semitic connotations. Anyone who consumed drugs suffered from a 'foreign plague'. Drug dealers were presented as unscrupulous, greedy or alien, drug use as 'racially inferior', and so-called drugs crime as one of the greatest threats to society.[41]

It is frightening how familiar many of these terms still sound today. While we have driven out other Nazi verbal monstrosities, the terminology of the war on drugs has lingered. It's no longer a matter of Jews – the dangerous dealers are now said to be part of different cultural circles. The extremely political question of whether our bodies belong to us or to a legal-social network of social and health-related interests remains a virulent one even today.

The Celebrity Doctor of Kurfürstendamm

The word 'JEW' was smeared on the plaque of a doctor's surgery on Bayreuther Strasse in Berlin's Charlottenburg district one night in 1933. The name of the doctor, a specialist in dermatological and sexually transmitted diseases, was illegible. Only the opening hours could still be

Mixing an anti-drugs campaign and anti-Semitism – even
in a children's book. 'Just as poisonous mushrooms are often
difficult to tell from good mushrooms, it is often difficult to
recognize the Jews and confidence tricksters and criminals.'

clearly seen: 'Weekdays 11–1 and 5–7 apart from Saturday afternoon'. The overweight, bald Dr Theodor Morell reacted to the attack in a way that was as typical as it was wretched: he quickly joined the Nazi Party to defuse future hostilities of that kind. Morell was not a Jew; the SA had wrongly suspected him of being one because of his dark complexion.[42]

After he had registered as a Party member, Morell's practice became even more successful. It expanded and moved into the lavish rooms of a nineteenth-century building on the corner of Kurfürstendamm and Fasanenstraße. You joined, you flourished – that was a lesson Morell would never forget, right until the end. The fat man from Hessen hadn't the slightest interest in politics. The satisfaction that made his life worthwhile came when a patient felt better after treatment, obediently paid the fee and came back as soon as possible. Morell had developed strategies over the years that gave him advantages over the other doctors on Kurfürstendamm with whom he vied for well-to-do clients. His smart private practice was soon seen as one of the most profitable in the area. Equipped with the most up-to-date technology – all originally bought with the fortune of his wife, Hanni – over time it had the whole of high society beating a path to the door of Morell, a former ship's doctor in the tropics. Whether it was the boxer Max Schmeling, various counts and ambassadors, successful athletes, business magnates, high-powered scientists, politicians, half of the film world: everyone made the pilgrimage to Dr Morell, who specialized in new kinds of treatment, or – as some mocking tongues had it – in the treatment of non-existent illnesses.

There was one field in which this modish, egocentric doctor was considered a pioneer: vitamins. Little was known at the time about these invisible helpers, which the body itself can't produce, but which it urgently needs for certain metabolic processes. Injected directly into the blood, vitamin supplements work wonders in cases of under-nourishment. This was precisely Morell's strategy for keeping his patients interested, and if vitamins weren't enough, he deftly added a circulatory stimulant to the injection mixture. For male patients he might include some testosterone with an anabolic effect for muscle building and potency, for women an extract of nightshade as an energy supplement and for hypnotically beautiful eyes. If a melancholy theatrical actress came to see him to get rid of stage fright before her premiere in the Admiralspalast, Morell wouldn't hesitate for a moment, but would reach with his hairy hands for the syringe. He was said to be an absolute master of the injection needle, and there were even rumours that it was *impossible* to feel the prick as his needle went in – in spite of the size of the implements at the time.

His reputation went beyond the boundaries of the city, and in the spring of 1936 his phone rang in the consulting room, even though he had categorically forbidden his nurses to disturb him during surgery hours. But this was no ordinary phone call. It was from the 'Brown House', Party headquarters in Munich: a certain Schaub on the line, introducing himself as Hitler's adjutant and informing him that Heinrich Hoffmann, the 'Official Reich Photographer of the NSDAP', was suffering from a delicate illness. It was the Party's wish that Morell, as a prominent specialist in sexually transmitted diseases who was well known for his confidentiality, should take on the case. They didn't want to consult a Munich doctor for such a discreet matter. The Führer, in person, had sent a plane for him, which was waiting at a Berlin airport, Schaub added.

While Morell couldn't stand surprises, he also couldn't turn down an invitation like that. Once he arrived in Munich, he was put up at state expense in the grand Regina-Palast-Hotel, treated the pyelonephritis that Hoffmann had contracted as a result of gonorrhoea – 'the clap' – and was invited with his wife to take a trip to Venice by his influential patient by way of thanks.

Back in Munich the Hoffmanns gave a dinner in their villa in the elegant district of Bogenhausen with the Morells present. There was spaghetti with nutmeg, tomato sauce on the side, green salad – the favourite dish of Adolf Hitler, who was, as this evening, often a guest at Hoffmann's house. The Nazi leader had been closely connected with the photographer since the 1920s, when Hoffmann had made considerable contributions to the rise of National Socialism. Hoffmann, who owned the copyright for important photographs of the dictator, published large numbers of picture books called things like *Hitler as No One Knows Him* or *A Nation Honours Its Führer* and sold them by the million. There was also another, more personal reason that linked the two men: Hitler's lover, Eva Braun, had previously worked as an assistant for Hoffmann, who had introduced the two in his Munich photographic shop in 1929.

Hitler, who had heard a great many good things about

the jovial Morell, thanked him before dinner for treating his old comrade, and regretted not having met the doctor before; perhaps then his chauffeur, who had died of meningitis a few months earlier, would have still been alive. Morell reacted nervously to the compliment, and barely spoke during the spaghetti dinner. The constantly sweating doctor with the full face and the thick round glasses on his potato nose knew that in higher circles he was not considered socially acceptable. His only chance of acceptance lay in his injections, so he pricked up his ears when Hitler, in the course of the evening, talked almost in passing about severe stomach and intestinal pains that had been tormenting him for years. Morell hastily mentioned an unusual treatment that might prove successful. Hitler looked at him quizzically – and invited him and his wife to further consultations at the Berghof, his mountain retreat in the Obersalzberg near Berchtesgaden.

There, a few days, later, during a private conversation, the dictator frankly admitted to Morell that his health was now so poor that he could barely perform any action. That was, he claimed, due to the bad treatment given to him by his previous doctors, who couldn't come up with anything but starving him. Then if there happened to be an abundant dinner on the programme, which was often the case, he immediately suffered from unspeakable bloating, and itchy eczema on both legs, so that he had to walk with bandages around his feet and couldn't wear boots.

Morell immediately thought he recognized the cause of Hitler's complaints and diagnosed abnormal bacterial flora, causing poor digestion. He recommended the preparation Mutaflor, developed by his friend the Freiburg doctor and bacteriologist Professor Alfred Nissle: a strain of bacteria that had originally been taken from the intestinal flora of a non-commissioned officer who had, unlike many of his comrades, survived the war in the Balkans without stomach problems. The bacteria are kept in capsules, alive, and they take root in the intestine, flourish and replace all the other strains that might lead to illnesses.[43] This genuinely effective concept convinced Hitler, for whom even processes within the body could represent a battle for *Lebensraum*, or 'living space'. Extravagantly, he promised to donate Morell a house if Mutaflor actually did cure him, and appointed the doctor as his personal physician.

When Morell told his wife about his new position, Hanni was less than enthusiastic. She commented that they didn't need it, and referred to his thriving practice on Kurfürstendamm. Perhaps she already sensed that she would rarely get to see her husband from now on, because a very unusual relationship would form between Hitler and his personal physician.

Injection Cocktail for Patient A

> He alone is responsible for the inexplicable,
> the mystery and myth of our people.
>
> Joseph Goebbels[44]

The dictator always hated being touched by other people, and refused treatment from doctors if they inquired too invasively into the causes of his ailments. He could never trust a specialist who knew more about him than he did himself. Good old general practitioner Morell, with his cosy harmless air, gave him a sense of security from the very beginning. Morell had no intention of questioning Hitler to genuinely find the root of his health problems. The penetration of the needle was enough for him; it was a substitute for serious medical treatment. If the head of state was to function, and demanded to be made imme-diately symptom-free, whatever his complaints, Morell hesitated no more than he would when treating an actress at the Metropol Theatre, but instead prepared a 20 per cent Merck glucose solution or a vitamin injection. Immediate removal of symptoms was the motto, followed not only by the bohemian circles of Berlin but also by 'Patient A', as he appeared in Morell's books.

Hitler was delighted by the speed with which his con-dition improved – usually while the needle was still in his vein. His personal doctor's argument convinced him: for the Führer, with all the tasks he had to perform, his energy consumption was so high that you couldn't wait until a substance found its way into the blood in tablet form via the digestive system. For Hitler it made sense: 'Morell wants to give me a big iodine injection as well as a heart, liver, chalk and vitamin injection. He learned in the tropics that medicine must be injected into the veins.'[45]

The busy ruler lived in constant fear of not being able to function properly, that he wouldn't be able to do everything he needed to do, and that he wouldn't be able to perform due to illness. Since he believed no one else was capable of carrying out his duties, from 1937 Morell's unconventional methods of treatment quickly gained in importance. Several injections a day were soon the norm. Hitler became used to his skin being punctured, and having what was assumed to be a potent substance flowing into his veins. Each time it happened he felt instantly better. The fine stainless steel needle that conjured up 'immediate recovery' was fully in line with his nature: his situation required constant mental alertness, physical vitality and hands-on decisiveness. Neuroses and other psychological inhibitions had to be switched off at all times, as if by the push of a button, and he himself needed to be permanently refreshed.

Soon his new physician seldom left the patient's side, and Hanni Morell's fears came true: her husband had no time for his practice any more. A locum had to be installed at Kurfürstendamm, and Morell later claimed, oscillating between pride and fatalism, that he was the only person who had seen Hitler every day, or at least every second day, since 1936.

Before every big speech the Reich Chancellor now allowed himself a 'power injection' in order to work at the peak of his capabilities. Colds, which could have kept him from appearing in public, were ruled out from the start by intravenous vitamin supplements. To be able to hold his arm up for as long as possible when doing the Nazi salute, Hitler trained with chest expanders and also allowed his body to snack on glucose and vitamins. The glucose, administered intravenously, gave the brain a blast of energy after twenty seconds, while the combined vitamins allowed Hitler to address his troops or the people wearing a thin Brownshirt uniform even on cold days without showing a sign of physical weakness. When he suddenly lost his voice before a speech in Innsbruck in 1937, Morell quickly alleviated the nuisance with an injection.

At first his digestive problems improved as well, and so the promised estate for the personal physician was given to Morell, on Berlin's exclusive Schwanenwerder island, next door to the propaganda minister, Goebbels. The elegant villa, surrounded by a hand-forged iron fence, at 24–26 Inselstrasse,* wasn't a complete gift: the Morells had to buy it themselves, for 338,000 Reichsmarks, although they did receive an interest-free loan of 200,000 RM from Hitler which was later converted into a fee for treatment. The new home didn't just bring advantages to the celebrity doctor, who had now been elevated to the highest social stratum. Morell had to employ domestic servants and a gardener, and his basic expenses soared, even though he wasn't automatically earning more. But now there was no turning back. He enjoyed his new life-style too much, as well as his immediate proximity to power.

Hitler had also become more than used to the doctor, brushing aside any criticism of the man who many people in the hard-fought-for inner circles found less than appetizing: Morell wasn't there to be sniffed at, Hitler professed, he was there to keep him healthy. To give the former society doctor a hint of seriousness, Hitler awarded him an honorary professorship in 1938.

* The building was 'Aryanized', having been previously owned by the Jewish banker Georg Solmmen.

Volkswagen – *Volksdrogen*

The first years in Morell's treatment developed into an extremely successful period for Hitler, who was cured of his intestinal cramps and, always dosed up on vitamins, was healthy and agile. His popularity grew unstintingly, chiefly due to the fact that the German economy was enjoying a boom. Economic independence became a fixed point in Nazi politics: it would produce a higher standard of living but also meant that war was inevitable. The plans for expansion were already in the desk drawers.

The First World War had made it clear that Germany had too few natural raw materials for armed conflict with its neighbours and so artificial ones had to be created: synthetic petrol produced from coal as well as 'Buna' (synthetic rubber) were at the centre of the development of IG Farben, which had gone on growing in power within the Nazi state and had consolidated its position as a global player in the chemical industry.[46] Its board described itself as the 'Council of the Gods'. Under Göring's tutelage, the economy was to become independent from all imported materials that could be produced in Germany itself. Of course, that also included drugs. While the Nazis' war on drugs brought down the consumption of heroin and cocaine, the development of synthetic stimulants was accelerated and led to a new blossoming within the pharmaceutical companies. The workforces of Merck in Darmstadt, Bayer in the Rhineland and Boehringer in Ingelheim grew and wages rose.

Expansion was also on the cards at Temmler. The head

chemist, Dr Fritz Hauschild,* had noticed how the Olympic Games in Berlin in 1936 had been influenced by a substance called Benzedrine, a successful amphetamine from the USA – and still a legal doping product at the time. At Temmler all development resources were now pooled in that direction, since the company was convinced that a performance-enhancing substance was a perfect fit for an age in which everyone was talking about new beginnings. Hauschild turned to the work of Japanese researchers who had synthesized an extremely stimulating molecule called N-methylamphetamine as early as 1887, and crystallized it in its pure form in 1919.† The drug was developed out of ephedrine, a natural substance that clears the bronchia, stimulates the heart and inhibits the appetite. In the folk medicine of Europe, America and Asia, ephedrine had been known for a long time as a component of the ephedra plant, and was also used in so-called 'Mormon tea'.

Hauschild perfected the product and in autumn 1937 he found a new method of synthesizing methamphetamine.[47] A short time later, on 31 October 1937, the Temmler factory patented the first German methylamphetamine, which put American Benzedrine very much in its shadow. Its trademark: Pervitin.[48]

---

* After the war Hauschild became one of the leading sports physiologists in the GDR, and in the 1950s he and his institute at the University of Leipzig provided the impetus for the GDR's doping programme, which made the worker-and-peasant state an athletic giant. In 1957 the inventor of Pervitin was awarded the National Prize of the GDR.
† It was on sale there under the trademark Philopon/Hiropon, and later used by kamikaze pilots in the war.

The molecular structure of Pervitin.

The molecular structure of this pioneering material is similar to adrenalin and so it passes easily through the blood and into the brain. Unlike adrenalin, however, methamphetamine does not cause sudden rises in blood pressure, but works more gently and lasts longer. The effect occurs because the drug tickles out the messenger substances dopamine and noradrenaline from the nerve cells of the brain and pours them into synaptic gaps. This puts the brain cells in excited communication with each other and a kind of chain reaction takes place. A neuronal firework explodes and a biochemical machine gun starts firing an uninterrupted sequence of thoughts. All of a sudden the consumer feels wide awake and experiences an increase in energy; the senses are intensified to the extreme. One feels livelier, energized to the tips of one's hair and fingers. Self-confidence rises, there is a subjectively perceived acceleration of thought processes, a sense of euphoria, and a feeling of lightness and freshness. A state of emergency is experienced, as when one faces a sudden danger, a time when an organism mobilizes all its forces – even though there is no danger. An artificial kick.

Methamphetamine does not only pour neurotransmitters into the gaps but also blocks their reabsorption. For this reason the effects are long-lasting, often more than twelve hours, a length of time which can damage the nerve cells at higher doses as the intracellular energy supply is drawn into sympathy. The neurons run hot and brain chatter can't be turned off. Nerve cells give up and die off irrevocably. This can lead to a deterioration in the ability to find words, in attention and concentration, and a general depletion in the brain where memory, emotions and the reward system are concerned. The lack of stimulation once the effect fades away is a sign of empty hormone stores, which have to fill up again over the course of several weeks. In the meantime fewer neurotransmitters are available: the consequences can include a lack of drive, depression, joylessness and cognitive disturbances.

The sugar-coating room at Temmler.

Although such possible side-effects have been investigated by now, further in-depth research was put on the back-burner at the time because Temmler were over-eager, bursting with pride over their new product. The company smelled a roaring trade and contacted one of the most successful PR agencies in Berlin to commission an advertising campaign the like of which Germany had never seen. Their publicity model was the marketing strategy for another rather stimulating product, produced by none other than the Coca-Cola Company, which – with the catchy slogan 'ice cold' – had enjoyed enormous success with their brown brew.

In the first weeks and months of 1938, when Pervitin was beginning to go from strength to strength, posters appeared on advertising pillars, the outsides of trams and on the buses and local and underground trains of Berlin. In a modern, minimalist style they mentioned only the trademark and referred to its medical indications: weakness of circulation, low energy, depression. It also showed the orange and blue Pervitin tube, the characteristic packaging with curved lettering. At the same time – another trick by this branch of business – all the doctors in Berlin received a letter from Temmler saying bluntly that the company's aim was to persuade the doctors personally: what people like themselves they also like to recommend to others. The envelope included free pills containing 3 milligrams of active ingredient as well as a franked postcard to be returned: 'Dear Doctor, Your experiences with Pervitin, even if they were less than favourable, are valuable to us in helping to limit the field of indication. So we would be very grateful to you for a message on this card.'[49]

A substance in its test phase. Just like the old dealer's trick: the first dose is free.

Representatives of the Temmler factory visited large-scale practices, hospitals and university clinics all over the country, delivered lectures and distributed this new confidence- and alertness-boosting drug. The company's own account said, 'reawakening joy in the despondent is one of the most valuable gifts that this new medication can give to patients.' Even 'frigidity in women can easily be influenced with Pervitin tablets. The treatment technique is as simple as can be imagined: four half-tablets every day long before bedtime ten days a month for three months. This will achieve excellent results by increasing women's libido and sexual power.'[50] On the Patient Information Leaflet it also said that the substance compensated for the withdrawal effects of alcohol, cocaine and even opiates. It was marketed as a kind of counter-drug to replace all drugs, particularly illegal ones. The consumption of *this* substance was sanctioned. Methamphetamine was regarded as a kind of panacea.

The substance was also claimed to have a system-stabilizing component: 'We live in an energy-tense time that demands higher performance and greater obligations from us than any time before,' a senior hospital doctor wrote. The pill, produced under industrial laboratory conditions in consistently pure quality, was supposed to help counteract inadequate performance and 'integrate shirkers, malingerers, defeatists and whiners' into the labour process.[51] The Tübingen pharmacologist Felix Haffner even suggested the prescription of Pervitin as a 'supreme commandment' as it amounted to 'the last effort on behalf of the whole': a kind of 'chemical order'.[52]

An advertisement for the supposed panacea Pervitin.
It stimulates the psyche and the circulation and has an
undefined impact on depression, hypotonia,
fatigue, narcolepsy and post-operative depression.

Germans, however, didn't need an order to take the buzzy substance. The hunger for powerful brain-food was already there. Consumption wasn't decreed from above and it wasn't top-down, as you might have expected in a dictatorship; it was entirely bottom up.[53] This so-called 'speedamin' landed like a bomb, spread like a virus, sold like sliced bread and was soon as much of a fixture as a cup of coffee. 'Pervitin became a sensation,' one psychologist reported. 'It soon gained acceptance in a very wide range of circles; students used it as a survival strategy for the exertions of exams; telephone switchboard operators and nurses swallowed it to get through the night shift, and people doing difficult physical or mental labour used it to improve their performance.'[54]

Whether it was secretaries typing faster, actors refreshing themselves before their shows, writers using the stimulation of methamphetamine for all-nighters at the desk, or hopped-up workers on conveyor belts in the big factories raising their output – Pervitin spread among all social circles. Furniture packers packed more furniture, firemen put out fires faster, barbers cut hair more quickly, nightwatchmen stopped sleeping on the job, train drivers drove their trains without a word of complaint, and long-distance lorry-drivers bombed down freshly constructed autobahns completing their trips in record time. Post-lunchtime naps became a thing of the past. Doctors treated themselves with it, businessmen who had to rush from meeting to meeting pepped themselves up; Party members did the same, and so did the SS.[55] Stress declined, sexual appetite increased, and motivation was artificially enhanced.

A doctor wrote: 'Experimenting on myself, I also observed

that both physically and mentally one may receive a pleasant boost in energy, which for six months has allowed me to recommend Pervitin to manual and clerical workers, fellow colleagues who are temporarily short of time, and also speakers, singers (with stage fright) and examination candidates. [. . .] One lady likes to use the medication (c. 2 x 2 tablets) before parties; another successfully on particularly demanding working days (up to 3 x 2 tablets daily).'[56]

Pervitin became a symptom of the developing performance society. Boxed chocolates spiked with methamphetamine were even put on the market. A good 14 milligrams of methamphetamine was included in each individual portion – almost five times the amount in a Pervitin pill. 'Hildebrand chocolates are always a delight' was the slogan of this potent confectionery. The recommendation was to eat between three and nine of these, with the indication that they were, unlike caffeine, perfectly safe.[57] The housework would be done in a trice, and this unusual tidbit would even melt the pounds away, since Pervitin, a slimming agent, also curbed the appetite.

Another part of the highly effective campaign was an essay by Dr Fritz Hauschild in the respected *Klinische Wochenschrift*. In this, and again in the same journal three weeks later, under the headline 'New Specialities', he reported on the extremely stimulating effect of Pervitin, its ability to increase energy and boost both self-confidence and decisiveness.[58] Associative thought became much faster and physical work easier. Its multiple applications in internal and general medicine, surgery and psychiatry seemed to give it a wide field of indication, and at the same time to stimulate scientific research.

Hildebrand-Pralinen erfreuen immer

Making housework more fun: methamphetamine chocolates: 'Hildebrand chocolates always delight'.

Universities all over the Reich pounced on these investigations. First to engage was Professor Schoen from the Polyklinik in Leipzig, who reported 'psychic stimulation lasting for several hours, sleepiness and weariness disappearing and making way for activity, loquacity and euphoria'.[59] Pervitin was fashionable among scientists, perhaps not least because at the start there was so much pleasure involved in taking it yourself. Self-experimentation was only common courtesy, after all: 'First of all we may report on our personal experiences based on self-experimentation after repeated consumption of 3–5 tablets (9–15 mg) of Pervitin, which were what enabled us to draw conclusions about its psychical effects.'*[60] More and more advantages came to light. Possible side-effects remained in the background. Professors Lemmel and Hartwig from the university in Königsberg testified to greater focus and concentration and advised: 'In these eventful times of conflict and expansion it is one of the doctor's greatest tasks to maintain the performance of the individual and where possible to increase it.'[61] A study by two brain researchers from the southern town of Tübingen claimed they had demonstrated an acceleration of the thought process through Pervitin, along with a general increase in energy. Inhibitions of the decision-making process, inhibitions generally and depressive conditions had been ameliorated. An intelligence test had demonstrated a distinct improvement. A Munich-based Professor Püllen released data from 'many hundreds of

* This is approximately the quantity taken in a typical contemporary dose of crystal meth.

44

cases' supporting these statements. He reported a generally stimulating effect on the cerebrum, the circulation and the autonomic nervous system. He had also, with a 'high dose of 20 milligrams administered once only, established a distinct reduction in fear'.[62] Hardly a surprise that Temmler should have supplied doctors with these positive results by mail, and ensured that they were regularly updated.

Pervitin was a perfect match for the spirit of the age. When the medication conquered the market there actually seemed to be a reason for thinking that all forms of depression had come to an end. At least those Germans who profited from the Nazis' tyranny thought so, and that was most of them. If, in 1933, many had still believed that the new Chancellor's career would be short-lived, and didn't think him capable of very much, a few years later everything looked very different. Two miracles had occurred, one economic and one military, covering the two most urgent problems for Germany in the 1930s. When the Nazis took power there were six million unemployed and only 100,000 poorly armed soldiers; by 1936, in spite of a continuing global crisis, almost full employment had been achieved, and the Wehrmacht was one of the most powerful military forces in Europe.[63]

Successes in foreign policy mounted up, whether it was a matter of the remilitarization of the Rhineland, the annexation of Austria or 'bringing the Sudeten Germans home to the Reich'. The Western powers did not punish these breaches of the Versailles Treaty. Quite the contrary, they made greater and greater concessions because they hoped to prevent a new war in Europe. But diplomatic successes didn't mollify Hitler. 'Like a morphine addict who can't give up his drug, he couldn't give up his plans for new seizures of power, new surprise attacks, secret marching orders and grand parades,' the historian Golo Mann wrote, describing the character of the emperor from Braunau.[64] The Allies misjudged the situation: Hitler would *not* be mollified by diplomatic success. Hitler was *never* content. Boundaries had to be crossed in every respect and at all times, and state borders in particular. From the German Reich to the Greater German Reich to the planned Teutonic World Reich: the constant hike in doses was in the nature of the National Socialist cause, and this lay first and foremost in the hunger for new territories. The slogans 'Home to the Reich' and 'A People without Space' summed it up.

Dr Morell, the personal physician, was even directly involved with the defeat of Czechoslovakia. On the night of 15 March 1939 the Czech president, Emil Hácha, in poor health, attended a more or less compulsory state visit to the new Reich Chancellery. When he refused to sign a paper that the Germans laid in front of him, a *de facto* capitulation of his troops to the Wehrmacht, he suffered a heart attack and could no longer be spoken to. Hitler urgently summoned Morell, who hurried along with his case and his syringes and injected the unconscious foreign guest with such a stimulating medication that Hácha rose again within seconds, as if from the dead. He signed the piece of paper that sealed the temporary end of his state. The very next morning Hitler invaded Prague without a fight. During the following years, Hácha sat at the powerless head of the 'Protectorate of Bohemia and

Moravia', to which parts of his country had been reduced, remaining Morell's loyal patient. In that respect, pharmacology worked as a way of continuing politics by other means.

During those first months of 1939, the last months of peace, Hitler's popularity reached a temporary peak. 'Look at everything this man has achieved!' was a standard proclamation, and many of his countrymen also wanted to put their potential to the test. It was a time when effort seemed to reap rewards. It was also a time of social demands: you *had* to be part of it, you *had* to be successful – if only so as not to arouse suspicion. The general upturn also produced a concern that you might not be able to keep up with the new rapid pace. The increasingly schematic nature of work placed fresh demands on the individual, who became a cog in the works. Any help was welcome when it came to putting yourself in the mood – even chemical help.

Pervitin made it easier for the individual to have access to the great excitement and 'self-treatment' that had supposedly gripped the German people. The powerful stuff became a sort of grocery item, which even its manufacturer didn't want to keep stuck just in the medical section. 'Germany, awake!' the Nazis had ordered. Methamphetamine made sure that the country *stayed* awake. Spurred on by a disastrous cocktail of propaganda and pharmaceutical substances, people became more and more dependent.

The utopian ideal of a socially harmonized, conviction-based society, like the one preached by National Socialism, proved to be a delusion in terms of the competition of real economical interests in a modern high-performance society. Methamphetamine bridged the gaps, and the doping mentality spread into every corner of the Reich. Pervitin allowed the individual to function in the dictatorship. National Socialism in pill form.

2

Sieg High! (1939–1941)

Music is sometimes really a great consolation to me (not forgetting Pervitin, which provides a wonderful service – particularly during air raids at night).

Heinrich Böll[1]

The man writing home from the frontline to his parents was later a Nobel Laureate for literature. He couldn't go without the 'wonderful service' of methamphetamine even after the war had ended and he was sitting back at his desk. He became dependent on it as a soldier in order to be able to endure the exertions of war and carry on functioning: 'Please remember to send me, at the next opportunity, an envelope containing Pervitin. Father can pay for it out of what he lost to me from our bet,' he says in another letter from the war.[2]

Heinrich Böll speaks of his Pervitin consumption with a matter-of-factness that lets us conclude that he was aware of the effect, but not of the dangers: 'If next week goes as quickly as last, I'll be glad. Send me more Pervitin if you can; I can use it on my many watches; and a bit of

Gunner Heinrich Böll was an enthusiastic early
consumer of the drug.

bacon, if possible, to fry up with potatoes.'[3] His mentions of the upper, as short as they are frequent, suggest that his family was familiar with it and did not disapprove of its use. 'Dear parents and siblings! Now I have time to write to you, and more importantly the peace to do so. Of course I am dog-tired, because last night I only slept for two hours, and tonight again I won't have more than three hours of sleep, but I've just got to stay awake. The Pervitin will soon start working, by the way, and help me over my tiredness. Outside the moonlight is unusually bright, there's a clear, starry sky and it's very cold.'[4] Again and again sleep seems to be Böll's great adversary: 'I'm exhausted and now I want to knock off. If possible send me some more Pervitin and some Hillhall or Kamil cigarettes.'[5] And elsewhere: 'Duty is strict, and you must understand if in future I write only every 2–4 days. Today I'm mostly writing to ask for Pervitin!'[6]

Is Heinrich Böll unique? Or did soldiers also engage in widespread substance abuse, as was happening in civil society? Were hundreds of thousands of German fighters waging their campaigns under the influence of methamphetamine? Did this addictive drug influence the course of the Second World War? A trip into the depths of the archives begins.

Looking for Clues at the Military Archive

The Bundesarchiv–Militärarchiv in Freiburg is surrounded by a barbed-wire fence and guarded by a doorman with a strong Saxon accent. Anyone who can prove a genuine

Osnabrück, den 9.4.39.
7 Uhr 0,5 aus

Liebe Eltern und Geschwister!

Eure beiden Briefe und Vaters Karte habe
ich heute erhalten. Recht herzlichen Dank
dafür. Ich bin immer recht froh, wenn ich
von zu Hause etwas höre. Besuche habe
vorläufig keinen Sinn, denn wir kommen
aus der Kaserne nicht raus (wahrscheinlich —
sind die ersten vier Wochen) und zivilisierte
Dinge natürlich nicht ~~rein~~ rein. Ich
möchte aber auch — ~~Vorstell Dir recht~~
keinen Besuch hier empfangen, denn
kann man einmal wirklich die Atmosphäre
der Heimat gespürt hat, wird es schwer,
und so habe ich mich schon gut gewöhnt.
Der Dienst ist schwer, und Ihr müßt ver-
stehen, wenn ich spärlicher und alle 3–4
Tage schreibe. Heute schreibe ich hauptsäch-
lich über

Pervitin!

Wir haben einen sehr anständigen, wirklich vernünftigen und menschlichen Leut-
nant, der fand vielleicht gegen

One of the many Pervitin letters by the future Nobel
Laureate for literature. 'Dear parents and grandparents . . . today I am
writing mostly about Pervitin!'

research interest will have the steel gates opened to him by photoelectric sensor, and subsequently be drawn into the meticulously tidy study rooms. Their computers provide access to store rooms full of documents, stacked from floor to ceiling. Millions of dead have left behind millions of files, and here is where you can research the drama of the wars that shook the twentieth century

At least, in theory. A lot has been stored, but navigating the clutter isn't easy. The headings of each folder only describe minimal aspects of its content. An additional complicating factor is that the keywords were chosen decades ago, when researchers were focused on different areas. In the immediate post-war years, for example, less importance was placed on medical-history details than today. Therefore access to the past, although it is supported by the latest technology, is based on an outmoded understanding of history.

The German Army Discovers a German Drug

The rise of methamphetamine in the Wehrmacht is inseparably connected with an ascetic-looking senior staff doctor with a narrow face and dark-brown eyes, which appear worryingly intense in the few photographs that survive of him. Prof. Dr Otto F. Ranke was thirty-eight years old when he was appointed director of the Research Institute of Defence Physiology – a key position even though no one would have thought so at the time.

Back then, physiology was a marginal discipline in medicine. A holistic approach towards understanding an organism, it treats the interactions between the physical and biochemical processes of cells, tissue and organs. *Defence* physiology, in turn, dealt with the specific burdens of soldiers with the aim of boosting the performance of the army in the face of excessive demands and a stressful environment. The military was starting to see itself as a modern organization and soldiers were described as 'animated engines'.[7] Ranke's task was to protect them against 'wear', meaning incapacity. He was to oil the cogs of the machine, and functioned as a kind of performance coach for the German army, as well as a gadget inventor. Over the years Ranke developed a sighting device for spotting artificial green (camouflage uniforms within a forest, for example), new anti-dust goggles for motorcyclists, tropical helmets that were both bulletproof and sweat-permeable for the Afrika Korps, and directional microphones to help the counter-intelligence service listen in on its targets.

Ranke's Research Institute of Defence Physiology was a section of the Military Medical Academy on Invalidenstrasse in Berlin. A large building in eighteenth-century neo-Baroque style, it is now home to the Federal Ministry for Economic Affairs and Energy. Curved gold letters read 'SCIENTIAE HUMANITATI PATRIAE' in a relief on the mansard roof above the main door: 'To Science – to Humanity – to the Fatherland'. From 1934 until 1945 this was where the army trained its rising medical officers. The Prussian elite institution, known as the MA for short, had the biggest medical and scientific library in Europe and a two-storey laboratory building fully equipped with the latest technology, several big auditoria, reading rooms, a hall of honour with busts of Virchow, von Helmholtz, von Behring and other doctors and researchers who had, it was said, each performed an immortal service for science. The complex also included the most modern gymnasiums and swimming pools, as well as a five-storey residential block with comfortable double rooms for the 800 trainee medical officers. These were known as *Pfeifhähne,* a complex Berlin play on the word 'Pépin', a derivative of 'Pépinière', the former training institute for military doctors under the Prussian kings, which had turned out the cream of medical scientists in the nineteenth century. In their wake, the MA students confidently wore the Reich eagle and the swastika on their smart uniforms. There were also a riding stable with ninety horses, several racing tracks, and nursing stables for sick horses, veterinary officers and a smithy.

The scientific departments were housed in the big block to the rear of the inner courtyard: the Institute for Pharmacology and Army Toxicology, the Laboratory for Serum Conservation and the Aeronautical Medical Research Institute directed by Prof. Hubertus Strughold (who would pioneer American space travel after the war along with Wernher von Braun), as well as the Research Institute of Defence Physiology, run by Otto Ranke, which in 1938 consisted only of an additional auxiliary doctor, three medical interns and a few civilian clerical staff. But the ambitious Ranke wanted to build up his department very quickly. He planned to do this through something he promoted for the Wehrmacht – a small molecule about to have a grand career.

From Brown Bread to Brain Food

Ranke, the leading defence physiologist in the Third Reich, had one main enemy. It wasn't the Russians in the east or the French or the British in the west. The adversary he was determined to defeat was fatigue – a strange antagonist, hard to grasp, one that regularly knocked out fighters, put them on the ground and forced them to rest. A sleeping soldier is a useless soldier, incapable of action. Fatigue causes your coordination to deteriorate, you fire randomly and you lose the capacity to drive motorbikes, cars or tanks. In Ranke's words: 'Relaxing on the day of fighting can decide the battle. [. . .] Often in combat perseverance in that last quarter of an hour is essential.'[8]

Ranke declared the war on exhaustion to be his main concern. In the spring of 1938, a year and a half before the outbreak of war, he read the Temmler chemist Hauschild's hymn of praise to Pervitin in the *Klinische Wochenschrift* and his ears pricked up. A claim preyed on his mind: supposedly this substance helped subjects achieve a 20 per cent increase in lung capacity and absorb greater amounts of oxygen – standard measurement parameters at the time for increased performance. He decided to explore the subject in depth, testing a rising number of medical officers – ninety at first, then 150; he organized voluntary blind tests, giving them Pervitin (P), caffeine (C) or placebos (S, for *Scheintablette*). Test subjects had to solve maths and logic problems through the night until 4 p.m. the following day. The results seemed unambiguous; at around dawn the 'S men' had their heads on their desks, while the 'Pervitin gang' were still manically working away, 'fresh-faced, physically and mentally alert', as the experimental record has it. Even after over ten hours of constant concentration they still felt 'that they wanted to party'.[9]

But after the test sheets were evaluated, not all of Ranke's findings were positive. Procedures that demanded greater abstract achievements from the cerebellum were not performed well by consumers of Pervitin. Calculations might have been carried out more quickly, but they contained more mistakes. Neither was there any increase in capacity for concentration and attention during more complex questions, and there was only a very small increase during less high-level tasks. Pervitin kept people from sleeping, but it didn't make them any cleverer. Ranke concluded without a trace of cynicism that this made it ideal for soldiers, according to results gathered from what was probably the first systematic drug experiment in military history: 'An excellent substance for rousing a weary squad [. . .] We may grasp what far-reaching military significance it would have if we managed to remove natural tiredness using medical methods. [. . .] A militarily valuable substance.'*[10]

---

* It was also cheap: the military average dose, Ranke calculated, came to four tablets per day, which at chemists' purchase price amounted to 16 pfennigs, while coffee worked out at about 50 pfennigs a night – 'So these stimulants are more economical.'

400Uhr 3.5.39. Müdigkeit der S-Leute.

415 Uhr Krampfhaftes Wachhalten der S-Leute.

540 Uhr 26.4.39. Teilnahmslosigkeit der S-Leute.

520 Uhr Schlafen und Teilnahmslosigkeit der S- Leute.

In the first systematic drugs tests in military history,
the guinea-pigs were given placebos ('S'),
Benzedrine ('B'), caffeine ('C') or Pervitin ('P').

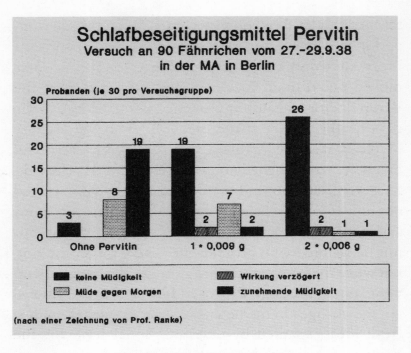

Pervitin in the fight against sleep:
'a valuable substance for the military'.

Inspired by this result, Ranke suggested a larger series of tests be carried out on regular units.[11] To his surprise, the request fell on deaf ears. In the Bendlerblock office complex, the seat of the General Army Office (and today the Federal Ministry of Defence), the possibilities, and dangers, of the drug, were ignored. While the ambitious scientist Ranke was already imagining the soldier of the future whose equipment would also include synthetic alkaloids – which attacked the centre of the brain in a way that wasn't yet understood[12] – his superiors, military bureaucrats in the medical inspection unit, hadn't quite reached this level of sophistication. They were still wondering whether it was better to give the troops brown bread or white bread – while Ranke had long since moved on to brain food. He had predicted what the Berlin doctor and author Gottfried Benn, trained in the days of the Kaiser at the predecessor to the Military Medical Academy, wrote a few years later: 'Powerful brains are strengthened not with milk, but with alkaloids. Such a small organ, and so vulnerable, that has managed not only to comprehend pyramids and gamma rays, lions and icebergs, but to produce and to imagine them, cannot be watered with groundwater like a forget-me-not, not while there's so much that's already stagnant.'[13] Benn wrote this in his essay 'Provoked Life': 'the provocations' are the changes in the neuronal streams: new thoughts, fresh ideas, sparked by unconventional food for the brain.

Knowledge of Pervitin and its striking effects spread fast through the young medical officers. Under severe pressure in their difficult medical studies, they soon expected genuine miracles from the supposedly performance-enhancing substance, and began to take more and more. This made them forerunners of the students of today at universities all over the world, among whom the use of performance pills like Ritalin and amphetamine derivatives is widespread. It was only when Ranke found out about this trend, which he had sparked in part with his tests, and learned that a room had had to be set out at Munich University for so-called 'Pervitin corpses' (fellow students who had overdosed and had to rest till they came round), that he became aware of the danger. He was forced to acknowledge that the consumption of high doses was already common in the run-up to exams at his Military Medical Academy. The results from those under the influence left much to be desired, and a concerned colleague wrote: 'In the cases in which an admission of drug assistance was made, the result of the examination was extraordinarily poor.'[14]

Ranke hastily cancelled another Pervitin experiment planned for 1939, and sent a letter to the other Institute directors at the Academy warning about possible dangers of addiction and urging them to forbid Pervitin completely at the Academy.[15] But Ranke couldn't get rid of the ghosts he had summoned up: methamphetamine spread like wildfire and would pass through every barracks gate over the next weeks and months.

The last few days of peace passed. The medical officers were preparing themselves for their approaching deployment in Poland, and bought up everything in the chemist's shop, as Pervitin wasn't officially supplied by the Wehrmacht, or at least not yet. Ranke could only look on. Less than a week before the start of the war he wrote to a military general surgeon at High Command: 'Of course it's a double-edged sword, giving the troops a different medicine which cannot be restricted to emergencies.'[16] The warnings came too late. An uncontrolled large-scale test began: without instructions as to the correct dosage of the upper, and supplied with huge quantities of it, the Wehrmacht fell upon its unsuspecting eastern neighbour.

Robots

'I am the driver of a hospital train and am often exposed to great stress. Your pills have proved their worth with both me and my staff.' – 'Difficulties seem easier to overcome.' – 'Now I am fresh again.'[17]

The reports by the medical service on methamphetamine use in the attack on Poland, which began on 1 September 1939 and sparked the Second World War, fill whole dossiers in the Freiburg Military Archive. A jumble of garbled depictions, the records hold no claims to being complete or representative. But they were all that Ranke, who had been appointed advisory defence physiologist of the Army Medical Inspection Service at the beginning of the war, had to work on. There was no planned investigation – because the substance had not been deployed in a planned way, but randomly, according to the whim of the relevant commander, medical officer or individual soldier.

When crossing the grand river Vistula in Poland, the 3rd Panzer Division swerved at Grudziądz in the direction of East Prussia and advanced from there towards Brest-Litovsk, reporting the following: 'Often there is euphoria, an increase in attention span, clear intensification of performance, work is achieved without difficulty, a pronounced alertness effect and a feeling of freshness. Worked through the day, lifting of depression, returned to normal mood.'[18]

War was seen as a task that needed to be worked through, and the drug seemed to have helped the tank units not to worry too much about what they were doing in this foreign country, and instead let them get on with their job – even if the job meant killing: 'Everyone fresh and cheerful, excellent discipline. Slight euphoria and increased thirst for action. Mental encouragement, very stimulated. No accidents. Long-lasting effect. After taking four tablets, double vision and seeing colours.' Even slight hallucinations, clearly perceived as pleasant, enchanted the men, soon to be heady with victory. 'The feeling of hunger subsides. One particularly beneficial aspect is the appearance of a vigorous urge to work. The effect is so clear that it cannot be based on imagination.'[19]

One senior lieutenant reported on his own good experience of the substance: 'No side-effects, no headache, no roaring in the ears, intellect wide awake.'[20] For three days and three nights, in a convivial mood, he engaged in negotiations with the Russians in Brest-Litovsk. It was a matter of dividing up the country. When he encountered Polish defenders on the way back the methamphetamine put him 'particularly on the ball'.[21]

For many soldiers, the drug seemed to be an ideal companion on the battlefield. It switched off inhibitions, which made fighting easier – whether it was night marches, before which the upper was consumed by 'all drivers and leaders at midnight to sharpen their attention', removing stuck tanks, shooting or 'performing other automatized manoeuvres'.[22]

In every aspect of the attack, which led to the deaths of 100,000 Polish soldiers and, by the end of the year, 60,000 Polish civilians, the drug helped the aggressors to work 'without any sign of tiredness until the end of the mission'. It provided that extra portion of energy which made everything that much easier. A medical officer from the IX Army Corps raved: 'I'm convinced that in big pushes, where the last drop has to be squeezed from the team, a unit supplied with Pervitin is superior. This doctor has therefore made sure that there is a supply of Pervitin in the Unit Medical Equipment.'[23]

```
Sanitätskompanie 2/59              O.U., den 30.12.1939
-----------------------
Bezug: Div.-Arzt 8.Pz.-Div. v.28.12.39
Betr.: Verwendung von Pervitin als Stärkungsmittel.

    Dem
    Div.-arzt der 8. Panzer-Division
    B i e l e f e l d
    -------------------

    Eigene Erfahrungen sehr günstig. Wirkung bei allge-
    meiner Unlust, deprimierter  Stimmung ausgezeichnet.
                    ------------
    Bei der Kpmpanie wurde Pervitin mehrmals an Einzelpersonen aus-
    gegeben. Truppenversuch fand nicht statt. Die gemachten Erfah-
    rungen sind sehr günstig. 1 Tablette hält von dem Fahrer Ermü-
    dungserscheinungen fern. Selbstbeobachtung bei Ärzten ergab
    Verschwinden von deprimierter Stimmung und Auftreten eines
    subjektiven Frischegefühls. Überdosierungserscheinungen (Herz-
    klopfen) treten erst bei Einnahme von 2 Tabletten auf.
                            gez. Dr. Wirth
                            Stabsarzt
```

A medical report from the 8th Panzer Division on using Pervitin as a stimulant: 'Own experience very favourable . . . Effect on depressed mood excellent'.

'An increase in performance is quite evident among tank drivers and gun operators in the long-lasting battles from 1 to 4 September 1939 and the reconnaissance division, which has used this substance with great success on tough long journeys at night, as well as to maintain and heighten attentiveness on scouting patrol operations,' another report read: 'We should particularly stress the excellent effect on the working capacity and mood among severely taxed officers at divisional headquarters, all of whom acknowledged the subjective and objective increase in performance with Pervitin.'[24]

This 'heightened attention' didn't only apply to tank drivers. One senior military doctor wrote: 'Motorcyclists were expected to make quite enormous efforts in great heat, severely dusty conditions and on bad roads, on prolonged journeys which lasted from early in the morning until late in the evening, and from Silesia through Bohemia–Moravia and Slovakia almost as far as Lemberg [Lwów] in Poland. The tablets were distributed without indication of their purpose, but their striking effects soon made it clear to the crews what purpose they were supposed to serve.'[25] Teutonic Easy Riders with drugs from Temmler and goggles by Ranke.

If Pervitin was unavailable, it was assumed that the soldiers in question faced a greater threat. A senior staff medic reported regretfully: 'Among the drivers many accidents, mostly attributable to excessive fatigue, could have been avoided if an analeptic such as Pervitin had been administered.'[26] Crystal meth to avoid road accidents? Really?

There were critical voices too. The army doctor for the 6th Army (which was later to perish at Stalingrad) assembled several reports from subordinate medical officers and wrote to Ranke: 'These contradictory reports make it clear beyond any doubt that Pervitin is not a harmless medication. It does not seem at all appropriate for it to be handed out at random to the troops.'[27] So some people clearly held reservations about the use of this stimulant. Still, curiosity had been awakened. The concluding sentence of the report from the IV Army Corps states: 'To continue the experiments [. . .] a larger quantity of Pervitin tablets is required.'[28]

Burn-out

Britain and France declared war on Germany on 3 September 1939, after the invasion of Poland. Initially no shots were fired in the west. Instead the adversaries watched each other, motionless, for months. No one wanted to fight. The shock of the First World War, with millions of soldiers slaughtered, was still lodged in the memory. Banners were hung at the frontlines: 'We won't shoot unless you shoot first'.[29] It would be wrong to speak of belligerence or nationalist pride on either side, unlike the situation in 1914. 'The Germans started the war,' the historian Golo Mann writes, 'but they weren't keen on it, not the civilians, not the soldiers, least of all the generals.'[30]

One person saw things differently. Hitler wanted to attack France as quickly as possible, ideally in the autumn of 1939. But there was one problem: the Western Allies clearly had superior equipment and greater armed forces. Contrary to what Nazi propaganda told the outside world, the Germans did not have superior armies. Quite the opposite – after the Polish campaign their equipment urgently had to be renewed. Most divisions had poor equipment, barely half of it suitable for use.[31] The French army, on the other hand, was considered the strongest in the world, and Great Britain, through its global empire, had access to infinite resources for its war economy.

The figures spoke volumes: on the German side there were just three million soldiers, while the Allies had a good million more. In many categories the Allies outclassed the Wehrmacht.[32]

A general rule of thumb in military strategy is that an attacker must be superior by 3:1 to be able to carry out a successful invasion. No wonder then that the Wehrmacht High Command struggled to devise a successful plan. Hitler refused to acknowledge these realities and was convinced the Aryan warrior's soul would achieve dominance against the odds. Again and again, mistakenly inspired by the military's doped performance on the Polish campaign, he spoke of 'miracles of courage of the German soldier'.[33]

In fact, even the dictator was clueless. The French and British declaration of war had caught him off guard; until the last moment he had hoped the West would react to the invasion of Poland in the same way as it had reacted to the absorption of Czechoslovakia. But that was not the case, and suddenly, unprepared, Germany had to fight a war against the whole of Western Europe. Hitler had manoeuvred the Reich into an impossible situation, and his back was against the wall. His Chief of the General Staff, Franz Halder, warned: 'Time, generally speaking, will work against us if we don't exploit it as much as we can. Economic means on the other side are stronger.'[34] What was to be done? Apart from rashly facing his opponents down, Hitler had no ideas. The Wehrmacht High Command, given to sober, mathematical planning, was horrified. The Bohemian lance corporal with his erratic ideas and volatile intuitions was not well thought of among the Prussian Chiefs of the General Staff, and was often dismissed as a military dilettante. An inadequately prepared attack could only lead to another defeat, as in the First World War. So strongly was this felt that a coup was even planned against the dictator to prevent his rushing into war: von Brauchitsch and Halder decided to arrest their Führer if he gave an order to attack. After Georg Elser's unsuccessful attempt on Hitler's life on 8 November 1939 in the Munich Bürgerbräukeller, there was a general crack-down and tightening up of security and these plans would be dropped.

Then, in the autumn of 1939, a crucial meeting was held between two senior officers. They came up with a daring concept. Erich von Manstein, a 52-year-old general from Berlin with an irascible temperament and permanently flushed cheeks, had a discussion with an East Prussian tank general, Heinz Guderian. The Wehrmacht's only chance, they reasoned, might lie in pushing a lightning armada of tanks through the supposedly impassable Belgian Ardennes mountains to reach the French border city of Sedan within a few days, and then charge all the way to the Atlantic coast. As the Allies were anticipating an attack further to the north and were massing their forces there, such a *Sichelschnitt* ('sickle cut' was how Churchill later referred to it) might outsmart and encircle most of the defending forces.

Among the German General Staff the foolhardy suggestion prompted only a shaking of heads. Tanks were still seen as ungainly monsters which might come to the aid of other branches of the armed forces, but could not lead a moving attack in autonomously acting units, particularly through difficult, mountainous terrain. The sketched invasion plan was seen as simply insane, and in order to thwart the risk-taking von Manstein, the General Staff moved him to the Baltic port of Stettin, far from the potential battle zone. Hitler's Chief of the General Staff kept coming up with new excuses in response to Hitler's constant pressure to begin fighting. The bad weather alone was mentioned dozens of times as a reason for not attacking. The Wehrmacht Oberkommando argued that it only had what was called 'fine weather weaponry'– and it needed a cloudless sky for the Luftwaffe.

So at first the Western Front fell into an enchanted slumber. When Ranke visited the baroque town of Zweibrücken, close to the border with Lorraine, anti-tank obstacles loomed, but the squaddies spent most of their time playing card games, smoking their cigarette rations – seven a day – kicking footballs about, helping with the potato harvest and practically lulling the French, only a few kilometres away, into a false sense of security with their peaceful bearing.

But that didn't mean that the Germans weren't ready to switch to a different tempo at any moment. In their trouser pockets they had always had their pep pills at the ready. Ranke quickly established that 'a very large proportion of officers carries Pervitin on their person. [. . .] The favourable effect was confirmed by all those asked, both motorized troops and members of other parts of the troops.'[35] They knew that the fighting could begin at any moment. When that happened they had to be on top form and wide awake. No wonder they already practised extensively with meth.

*

Alarmed at its prophylactic use, Ranke wrote: 'The question is not whether Pervitin should be introduced or not, but how to get its use back under control. Pervitin is being exploited on a mass scale, without medical checks.' He urged the introduction of guidelines and an instruction leaflet, to regulate application of the drug and 'make the experiences of the east [Polish campaign] lessons for the west'.[36] However, none of these measures were enacted.

How casually Pervitin was thought of, and how widespread its use was, is also apparent in the fact that Ranke himself took it regularly and freely reported the fact in his wartime medical diary as well as in letters. He eased an average working day with two Temmler tablets, using them to overcome his work-related stress and improve his mood. Even though he knew about the dangers of dependency, he, the self-appointed expert on Pervitin, drew no conclusions about his own use of the substance. For him it remained a medication that he took in whatever quantities he saw fit. If he experienced side-effects, he did not acknowledge them as such, but deluded himself: 'In spite of Pervitin, from eleven o'clock in the morning I increasingly suffer from headaches and digestive problems.' He wrote bluntly to a colleague: 'It distinctly revives concentration and leads to a feeling of relief with regard to approaching difficult tasks. It is not just a stimulant, but clearly also a mood-enhancer. Even at high doses lasting damage is not apparent. [. . .] With Pervitin you can go on working for thirty-six to fifty hours without feeling any noticeable fatigue.'[37]

Staying awake for two days and two nights in a row became the norm for the defence physiologist. He constantly worked at high speed during the first few months of war. Between the front, where he delivered lectures on Pervitin, and the capital, where he was enlarging his institute, he found no time to rest. His workload was getting too much for him, and he took the drug more and more regularly so as not to fall behind in his performance. It wasn't long before Ranke was on the brink of a classic case of burn-out – though the term didn't yet exist. In his diary he reported bravely: 'Personal matter: my depression has been overcome. I've been ready for work again since midday on 8.11.'[38] But often he only went to bed very late at night, where he spent an 'abundantly sleepless night', and complained the following day: 'Nearly collapsed.' His slow descent into dependency is exemplary. He tried to use chemicals to keep pushing against his own limits, even when he was completely exhausted. It didn't always work: '19.11.39. General inability to work under the pressure of imminent discussion and inspection.'[39] Ranke wasn't the only one squashed between the stress of war and Pervitin consumption. His correspondence from those days shows that more and more officers were using the drug to keep up with their duties.

Outside of the military the addiction was also growing. In 1939 Pervitin fever was rife in the Third Reich, whether it was housewives going through the menopause who 'wolfed down the stuff like sweets',[40] young mothers who took methamphetamine to ward off the baby blues, or widows who were looking for 'Elite partners' through the marriage bureau, and who took high doses to combat inhibitions during their first meeting. To help with childbirth, to fight seasickness, vertigo, hay fever, schizophrenia, anxiety neuroses, depressions, low drive, disturbances of the brain – wherever the Germans hurt, the blue, white and red tube was at the ready.[41]

As coffee had hardly been available since the start of the war, methamphetamine was often added as a substitute to pep up ersatz versions of the drink. 'Pervitin could, rather than being pumped into bomber pilots and bunker pioneers, be used deliberately for cerebral machinations in higher-education colleges,' Gottfried Benn wrote of these times.'It may sound deviant to some people, but it is only the natural continuation of an idea of humanity's progress. Whether it is rhythm, drugs or modern autogenic training – it is the ancient human desire to overcome tensions that have become unbearable.'[42]

In late autumn 1939 the Reich Health Office reacted to this trend, which could be overlooked no longer. Leo Conti, the 'Reich Health Führer', tried to prevent, however belatedly, 'an entire nation becoming addicted to drugs'. He pointed out that 'the disturbing after-effects fully obliterate the entirely favourable success achieved after use'. To toughen the legal situation, he approached the justice ministry and expressed his 'concern that the emergence of a tolerance to Pervitin could paralyse whole sections of the population. [. . .] Anyone who seeks to eliminate fatigue with Pervitin can be quite sure that it will lead to a creeping depletion of physical and psychological performance reserves, and finally to a complete breakdown.'[43]

In a personal proclamation he appealed in a typical Nazi manner to all honorary affiliates in the battle against drugs: 'The serious nature of the times should forbid all German men and women from devoting themselves to questionable pleasures. The personal example of the rejection of drugs is more necessary and appropriate today than it has been in the past. [. . .] I ask you to help, through your work, to protect and strengthen German family life where it is threatened by the use of drugs. By doing so you will increase the inner resilience of our people.'[44]

In November 1939 he made Pervitin available 'on prescription only, in every case'[45] and a few weeks later delivered a speech in the Rathaus in Berlin to members of the National Socialist German Association of Doctors, warning against the 'big, new threat of addiction, with all its side-effects, which faces us all'.[46] But his words were not taken seriously and consumption continued to rise. Many chemists stuck only loosely to the new prescription regulation and even gave their customers hospital packs of the drug without prescription. It was still easy for a citizen to get hold of several Pervitin ampoules or hundreds of pills from chemists' shops every day.[47]

This was also true of soldiers. The regulation concerning prescriptions applied only to civilian society and not to the military. But Conti also had the military in his sights. A war on drugs was waged against the background of the real war when the Reich Health Führer challenged the Wehrmacht to take a position on the 'use and abuse of drugs and its possible damage', as he had observed 'that our young soldiers look extraordinarily ill, often grey and sunken-cheeked'. But Conti's Reich Health Office was a civilian authority, and the military promptly resisted his interference: 'The Wehrmacht cannot renounce a temporary increase in performance or a defeat of fatigue, even through the use of medication,' Army Medical Inspector Waldmann wrote back, coolly and clearly.[48]

Anweisung für den Sanitätsoffizier über das Weckmittel Pervitin

1. Wirkungsweise.

Pervitin ist ein Arzneimittel, das durch zentrale Erregung das Schlafbedürfnis beseitigt. Eine Leistungssteigerung über die Wachleistung hinaus kann nicht erzielt werden. Bei richtiger Dosierung ist das Selbstgefühl deutlich gehoben, die Scheu vor Inangriffnahme auch schwieriger Arbeit gesenkt; damit sind Hemmungen beseitigt, ohne daß eine Herabsetzung der Sinnesleistungen wie bei Alkohol eintritt. Bei Überdosierung tritt hinzu Schwindelgefühl und Kopfschmerz sowie gesteigerter Blutdruck. Rund in $1/10$ der Fälle versagen die Weckmittel auch bei richtiger Dosierung.

2. Dosierung.

Zur Überwindung der Müdigkeit nach eingenommener Mahlzeit genügt gewöhnlich 1 Tablette mit 0,003 g Pervitin. Bei starkem Schlafbedürfnis nach Anstrengung besonders in der Zeit zwischen 0 Uhr und dem Morgengrauen sind vorbeugend 2 Tabletten kurz nacheinander und nötigenfalls weitere 1—2 Tabletten nach 3—4 Stunden einzunehmen. Weckmittel sind überflüssig, solange die Kampferregung anhält.

Werden 0,04 g = etwa 12 Tabletten und mehr auf einmal einverleibt, ist mit Vergiftung zu rechnen.

3. Anwendungsbereich.

Die Weckmittel dürfen nicht eingenommen werden, solange unvorhergesehene Rasten zum Schlaf ausgenutzt werden können. Die Anwendung verspricht in erster Linie Erfolg beim Kolonnenmarsch mot. Verbände bei Nacht sowie bei übermüdeten Personen nach Wegfall der Kampferregung. Nur in zwingenden Ausnahmefällen darf mehr als 24 Stunden lang der Schlaf durch Weckmittel verhindert werden.

4. Ausgabe.

Nur auf Anweisung eines San. Offiziers wird durch das San. Personal nur je eine Tagesmenge ausgegeben. Der Verbrauch ist zu kontrollieren.

5. Wirkungszeit.

Die volle Wirkung tritt bei leerem Magen 15 Minuten nach der Einnahme, bei vollem Magen nach etwa ½—1 Stunde ein. Die schnelle Aufnahme bei leerem Magen führt gelegentlich zu rasch vorübergehenden Überdosierungserscheinungen.

6. Darreichung.

Zweckmäßig in einem Schluck nicht zu heißen Getränkes gelöst, notfalls auch als trockene fast geschmacklose Tablette.

7. Wirkungsdauer.

Einmal 2 Tabletten beseitigen das Schlafbedürfnis für 3—8 Stunden, zweimal 2 Tabletten gewöhnlich für etwa 24 Stunden. Bei starker Übermüdung ist die Wirkung verkürzt und vermindert.

8. Gegenanzeige.

Bei Nervösen und Vagotonikern (langsamer Ruhepuls) können die Weckmittel zu harmlosen aber leistungsmindernden Erregungszuständen mit Kopfschmerzen und Herzklopfen führen. Wer einmal so auf diese Weckmittel anspricht, soll keine Weckmittel mehr nehmen. Bei Anlage zu Nierenkrankheiten, Herzkrankheiten und schweren Blutgefäßkrankheiten sowie bei allen fieberhaften Erkrankungen sind Weckmittel verboten. Im Alkoholrausch sind sie unwirksam.

'Stimulant decree' of 17 April 1940: the instruction pamphlet for Wehrmacht drug use. '[. . .] Pervitin is a medication that removes the need to sleep by stimulating the central nervous system. Performance enhancement beyond waking performance cannot be attained [. . .] In overdoses, there is also a feeling of vertigo and headache, as well as increased blood pressure. In about $1/10$ of cases the stimulants fail even at the correct dose [. . .]'

On 17 February 1940 – the same day as Conti wrote his letter of protest to the army medical authority – there was a fateful meeting between Hitler and the generals Erich von Manstein and Erwin Rommel, who had recently been appointed commander of a Panzer Division. Von Manstein, hands plunged deep in his pockets as always, was able to set out in great detail his risky plan of attack, which no one at senior command was willing to hear. But Hitler, who was known for constantly interrupting his generals, listened spellbound as Manstein delivered his lecture about how he wanted to push through an impossible region of forested crags to wrong-foot the French and the British.[49] Although Hitler couldn't stand the general, with his brazenly arrogant way of displaying his military expertise – 'Certainly a very clever mind with operational gifts, but I don't trust him'[50] – he was immediately convinced by his surprise-based strategy. The success of the operation would depend on time, speed and a daring idea, not just equipment. The material inferiority of the Germans suddenly didn't need to hinder an attack. Hitler didn't hesitate, clutching at this last straw: 'The Führer gave his agreement to these propositions. A short time later the new and definitive deployment instruction was issued,' Manstein's note on the discussion concludes proudly.[51]

The question remained as to whether a quick push through the Ardennes could be achieved at all. There was a strong possibility of getting stuck in the rough terrain and being halted by enemy forces, however weakly positioned they were. The Allies should have had enough time to rush in with reinforcements from both north and south and catch the Germans in a pincer action. The 'sickle cut' only had a chance if the Germans could drive day and night. No stopping, and, above all, no sleeping. Hitler swept all doubts aside. Of course a German soldier could be constantly ready by force of will if the situation called for it. Hadn't it been true for him in the Flanders trenches, as a despatch runner in the First World War?

In fact it wasn't the superhuman will that counted. This is what Pervitin was for, after all. In army High Command they were working feverishly on the new deployment instruction. This also included planning for medical support, and Ranke's tests at the MA were remembered. On 13 April 1940, three weeks before the attack in the west, Army Medical Inspector Waldmann submitted a document to Field Marshal von Brauchitsch, the army's commander-in-chief: 'The Pervitin question. Decree concerning careful, but necessary use in a special situation.'[52] Ranke was summoned for discussions and drove several times from the MA on Invalidenstrasse to the Bendlerblock on the Landwehrkanal. He had to quickly write a lecture for the General Staff, and also a tailor-made Wehrmacht instruction leaflet for Pervitin.[53]

On 15 April, he received a letter from the corps medic of the Panzer Group von Kleist, which was to lead the thrust through the Ardennes. The group was already engaged in heavy consumption: 'Pervitin seems ideally suited as a stimulant for counteracting signs of fatigue after great physical and mental efforts, particularly among brain-workers and soldiers [. . .], who have special demands made on their mental freshness and their capacity for absorption and concentration as well as their judgement, and who must reduce their need for sleep. Some of the observations [. . .] were carried out during the Polish campaign, some on drill marches and training trips, on crews and also in self-examination tests carried out by many medical officers and company-grade officers.'[54] The countdown was running, and Ranke demanded Temmler increase production. Two days later, on 17 April 1940, a document was making the rounds of the Wehrmacht, one with no parallel in military history.

The so-called 'stimulant decree' was sent out to a thousand troop doctors, several hundred corps doctors, leading medical officers and equivalent positions in the SS. The first paragraph was as dry as it was controversial: 'The experience of the Polish campaign has shown that in certain situations military success was crucially influenced by overcoming fatigue in a troop on which strong demands had been made. The overcoming of sleep can in certain situations be more important than concern for any related harm, if military success is endangered by sleep. The stimulants are available for the interruption of sleep. Pervitin has been methodically included in medical equipment.'[55]

The text was by Ranke, and signed by the army's commander-in-chief, Walther von Brauchitsch. The recommended dosage was one tablet per day, at night two tablets taken in short sequence and if necessary another one or two tablets after three to four hours. In exceptional cases sleep could be 'prevented for more than twenty-four hours' – and was an invasion not an exceptional case? One possible negative side-effect according to the decree was 'a belligerent mood'. Should that be seen as a warning or an inducement? 'With correct dosage the feeling of self-confidence is clearly heightened, the fear of taking on even difficult work is reduced; as a result inhibitions are removed, without the decrease in the sensory function associated with alcohol.'[56]

The Wehrmacht was thus the first army in the world to rely on a chemical drug. And Ranke, the Pervitin-addicted army physiologist, was responsible for its regulated use. A new kind of war was on the way.

Modern Times

At the Temmler factory dozens of women workers sat at circular machines that looked like mechanical cakes. Steel slides pressed finished tablets on to running belts, tire-lessly, thousands of them, where they suddenly began to dance, shaken up ready for manual inspection: women's fingers in pale gloves moved like bees' feelers, slipping through the snow-white splendour of the skipping pills, sorting them out: bad ones cast aside, good ones straight into the special packages for the medical supply bags, into the army's collapsible boxes, the boxes in cases with the Reich eagle on them. Everyone worked overtime, because of Ranke's demands.

833,000 tablets could be pressed in a single day. An adequate amount; the Wehrmacht had ordered an enormous quantity for the army and the Luftwaffe: 35 million in all.[57] Heinrich Böll would never again have to ask his parents for extra supplies.

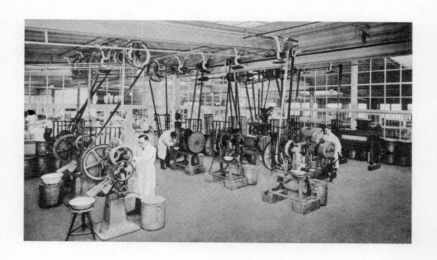

A large order at Temmler . . . 35 million methamphetamine doses for the army and Luftwaffe.

Time is War

> Success lies in speed. The important thing is to keep
> surprising the defender.
>
> From Panzer Group von Kleist's order to attack [58]

Phosphorus strips hanging on oak trees illuminated the
path which was freshly beaten through the undergrowth.
In the middle of the forest stood the map-house, a
wooden shed hardly wider than an arm's span furnished
with a plain table and a single wicker chair. A relief map
of Flanders hung on the wall, all the more vivid when
you looked out of the window to the hilly landscape of
the Eifel and the Ardennes beyond. Reich photographer
Hoffmann, Morell's old buddy, had positioned himself
outside, frantically snapping Patient A within.

Hitler's headquarters at Felsennest ('cliff nest'), near the
old sand-track-and-half-timbered village of Rodert, 10 May
1940, seven o'clock in the morning: Major General Jodl
was setting out the military situation. During the night
German paratroopers, launched from Cologne, had taken
the strategically important Belgian fort of Eben-Emael.
But this was just a decoy attack to reinforce the Allies'
conviction that the assault was going to happen in the
north of Belgium. In fact most of the Wehrmacht were
massing in a completely different area, near the border with
Luxembourg, much further south. There the tanks were
rattling into position in uninterrupted succession. Slightly
ahead of these stood General Guderian's medium-sized
radio armoured car, with its striking circular system of

aerials. The mood among the troops was still anything but belligerent. 'Wherever you went there was an oppressive feeling of calm, and a deep sense of dejection,' one officer reported.[59]

The uncertainty and confusion that prevailed among the aggressors is revealed in the fact that the German deployment, which had been in preparation for such a long time, seemed at points to be permanently stuck. Rather than setting off in good time and taking advantage of the crucial moment of surprise, there was unholy confusion and a complete collapse of traffic while still on German soil. The reason for this was that the horse-drawn vehicles of the infantry kept flowing into the broader roads that were actually needed for the tanks, and soon everything ground to a standstill. Wheel to wheel and bumper to bumper stood the vehicles of Panzer Group von Kleist, the biggest motorized unit ever assembled in military history, with a total of 41,410 vehicles, including 1,222 tanks. The avalanche of iron and steel was stuck in a 250-kilometre traffic jam, backed up all the way to the Rhine. It was the longest snarl-up in European history, and the Allies could easily have destroyed the whole lot with a handful of bombers, nipping the German deployment in the bud. But an attack from this bottleneck wasn't expected, and the monstrous traffic jam went unnoticed. French enemy reconnaissance couldn't see what was coming.

The cause of the German confusion lay in the fact that High Command still didn't recognize tanks as being capable of leading an invasion and had assigned too few roads to them, and no zones of action of their own. No one had yet mentioned the notion of '*Blitzkrieg*'; nobody really had any idea what it was – apart from a few generals, Guderian leading the way. Over his radio, he desperately tried to persuade the infantry to free up the lanes, but the infantry saw the tanks as rivals and wanted to lead the advance themselves, as they always had done. Their flatbed trucks, horse-drawn carts and marching soldiers, many of them carrying the same rifles as their fathers had shouldered in the First World War, continued to block the roads. But when the tanks were finally able to manoeuvre themselves out of the muddle and immediately rumble off through the narrow valleys and along the bending, climbing roads through the range of hills ahead of them, making up for lost time, they showed what they were capable of. Nothing would halt them, all the way to the English Channel. Well, almost nothing.

'Think Big'[60]

Perhaps France died in 1940: their defeat against the Germans came after only eleven days, the country has never recovered from that humiliation.

Frédéric Beigbeder[61]

'The task is a very difficult one,' General Halder, chief of the OKH General Staff, noted in his diary. 'In the given terrain [Maas] and with the given strength of the forces – particularly in terms of artillery – it cannot be solved. [. . .] We have to resort to unusual means and bear the associated risk.'[62] Methamphetamine was one such unusual means, and the men desperately needed it when General Guderian ordered: 'I demand that you do not sleep for at least three days and nights, if that is required.'[63] And required it was. Only if the French border city of Sedan was reached during that time and the border river Maas (or Meuse) was crossed, would the Germans be in northern France sooner than most of the French army itself, which was either still in northern Belgium, or inside the Maginot Line further south.

The Wehrmacht were well prepared. The quartermasters had ordered the pills in time. General Graf von Kielmansegg (who became NATO Commander-in-Chief of Allied Land Forces in Central Europe in the 1960s) ordered 20,000 for his 1st Panzer Division, and during the night between 10 and 11 May it was taken en masse.[64] Thousands of soldiers took the substance out of their field caps or were given it by their medical officers.[65] It was laid on their tongues and gulped down with a swig of water.

Twenty minutes later the nerve cells in their brains started releasing the neurotransmitters. All of a sudden dopamine and noradrenalin intensified perception and put the soldiers in a state of absolute alertness. The night brightened: no one would sleep, lights were turned on, and the 'Lindworm' of the Wehrmacht started eating its way tirelessly towards Belgium. The listlessness and frustration of the first few hours made way for new and rather strange feelings. Something started happening, something that later no one could readily explain. An intense chill crept across scalps, a hot feeling of cold filled everyone from within. There were as yet no storms of steel, as there had been in the First World War, but instead a storm of chemicals broke out, punctuated by euphoric flashes of mental lightning, and the level of activity reached its peak. The drivers drove, the radio operators' decoding machines, like futuristic typewriters, radioed, gunners in black combat trousers and dark grey shirts crouched behind their weapons, ready to fire. There were no more breaks – an uninterrupted chemical bombardment had broken out in the cerebrum, the body released greater quantities of nutrients, boosting its sugar production so that the machine was running at maximum output, and the pistons were going up and down exponentially. The average blood pressure increased by up to 25 per cent, and hearts thundered in the cylinder chamber of the chest.

The first battle began in the morning. The Belgian defenders had entrenched themselves near Martelange, a small border community, in bunkers on a hillside. In front of them lay a slope, several hundred metres of open terrain: impossible to take except by a frontal attack, which was apparent suicide. But that's exactly what the pepped-up infantrymen of the Wehrmacht did. The Belgians, shocked by this fearless behaviour, retreated. Rather than securing their position, as military practice would normally have decreed, the completely uninhibited attackers immediately chased after them and set their enemies unambiguously to flight. This first clash was symptomatic.

After three days the division commander reported that they had reached the French border. Sedan lay in front of the Germans; many of them had not shut their eyes since the start of the campaign. And they still couldn't rest: the German artillery fire was scheduled for 4 p.m. on the dot, and the massive wave of dive bombers was rolling in from the sky. Whenever the pilots of the Luftwaffe began their breakneck plunge and hurtled vertically down, they turned on their wailing sirens, the so-called horns of Jericho, which were followed by mighty explosions. Windowpanes rattled with the blasts and the houses of the border city shook. Meth unleashed charge after charge in German brains, neurotransmitters were released, exploded in the synaptic gaps, burst and dispersed their explosive cargo: neuronal paths twitched, gap junctions flared, everything whirred and roared. Down below the defenders cowered, their bunkers shaking. The siren wail of the plunging planes drilled into their ears and left their nerves bare.[66]

In the course of the hours that followed, 60,000 Germans, 22,000 vehicles and 850 tanks crossed the river: 'We felt a kind of high, an exceptional state,' one participant reported. 'We were sitting in our vehicles, covered in dust, exhausted and wired.'[67] In a rush they had never experienced before, the Germans took the French border city. 'The pugnacious desire to defeat the enemy in chivalrous combat will never fade,' says the official Wehrmacht report.[68] In fact Pervitin made an enormous contribution to putting the soldiers in a warlike mood.

French military reinforcements arrived a few crucial hours too late. The Germans had already crossed the Meuse. The dam was broken. Until their capitulation the French were no match for Germany's chemically enhanced dynamism. They kept acting too slowly, were surprised and overrun, and continually failed to grab the initiative.

A Wehrmacht report dryly states: 'The French must have been thrown into such confusion by the sudden appearance of our tanks that their defence was carried out very weakly.'[69]

The French historian Marc Bloch, who fought for his country in May and June 1940, analyses the breakdown of French troops as a 'mental defeat': 'Our soldiers were baulked, they allowed themselves to be thwarted much too easily, because our thinking was too slow.' The French brains were not dominated by the same euphorically tinted exceptional situation. 'We encountered the Germans everywhere, they were criss-crossing the terrain,' Bloch writes, describing the crazed confusion that the attackers were sowing: 'They believed in action and unpredictability. We were built on immobility and on the familiar. During the whole campaign the Germans maintained their terrible habit of appearing precisely where they shouldn't have been: they didn't stick to the rules of the game. [. . .] Which means that certain, hardly deniable, weaknesses are chiefly due to the excessively slow rhythm that our brains have been taught.'[70]

French losses through bombing were relatively small on this first day in Sedan, with fifty-seven dead. It was more the psychological effects provoked by the attack of the unfettered Germans that were so devastating. This was a campaign that was decided in the psyche. A French investigative report described the quick crossing of the Meuse by the Germans and the failure of the French defence as a *'phénomène d'hallucination collective'*.[71]

Time is Meth

Blitzkrieg was guided by methamphetamine. If not to say
that *Blitzkrieg* was founded on methamphetamine.

Dr Peter Steinkamp, medical historian[72]

Where an invasion is concerned, the advantages of stimulants are obvious: war is played out in space and time.
Speed is crucial. One exception to this was the First World
War, where minimal territorial gains were won over four
whole years of fighting. But if, for example, Napoleon
had been able to lead his troops out into the field two
hours earlier at the Battle of Waterloo, things might have
turned out very differently.

In the Wehrmacht report the methamphetamine-soaked
advance of Guderian is described like this: 'The General
drives alone along the southern bank of the Maas [Meuse]
in his off-road vehicle and heads off towards Donchery
[. . .], engines firing, without rest or peace, day and night,
as far as his fuel allows.'[73] The reality is less harmless than
these lines suggest. Thousands of people died in this invasion of France, which served as a blueprint for later
campaigns, waged as it was in an innovative, unparalleled
fashion.[74] Guderian – with his grey moustache and his
trademark binoculars around his neck – spoke of a miracle, but in fact he was the one who had during those days
and nights invented the *Blitzkrieg*. In less than a hundred
hours the Germans gained more territory than they had
in over four years in the First World War. In planning the
operation, Panzer Group von Kleist, of which Guderian

was also part, had been given operational freedom as long as they could move fast enough and drive the front ahead of them. As soon as the tanks faltered, the Group would be integrated into the structure as a whole. This instruction was now revealed to be a clever piece of planning: the squad developed the ambition *never* to falter and therefore be absorbed into the rest. Quite the contrary, they refused to be stopped and kept advancing, like the tip of a lance.

From Sedan onwards Guderian was practically autonomous, out in front in his armoured radio car, flanked by his ordnance officers in motorcycle combinations. His intention was no longer to secure the position and then to set up the bridgehead in an orderly fashion, following the rules. After taking the border city he charged on even though he was given a strict order to stop. In the rush of the campaign he became wholly insubordinate. He no longer needed flank protection; it was a matter of being faster than anyone who could have come at him from the side. He didn't worry about supplies; he already had everything his unit needed. An ingenious supply system guaranteed that even the furthest forward tanks always had enough fuel, and Pervitin was distributed by the Main Medical Park, the Wehrmacht's wholesale chemist.[75]

Four days went past, and the Allies were still being completely taken by surprise. They couldn't adjust to this unpredictable invader, who didn't act methodically, but was simply focused on reaching the Atlantic coast as quickly as possible, to make the encirclement perfect. The journey there would be achieved through a kind of ad hoc planning, in which methamphetamine played a crucial part.

'We drive as fast as convoy travel permits. The General has his men run the operation as smoothly as possible. We covered huge distances today. Two officers from a French supply column are presented to the General: "Oh, the Germans very fast – *très, très vite*." They are flummoxed at suddenly having been caught. They had no idea where and when we were coming from. [. . .] On we progress to Montcornet. All the vehicles on this stretch are going at full speed. The General has to assign new roads for us to travel along. It's all so incredibly fast',[76] as the report on Guderian's advance has it. 'In the market square the French are still getting out of their trucks, for a stretch they travel along in our column. No one has had time to take care of the town. The General stops at the church and regulates the traffic with his adjutant. One division off to the right, the other to the left. Everyone is chasing along as if in a race.'[77]

The *Blitzkrieg* had unleashed itself and became autonomous – and in those hectic spring days of May 1940 it embodied the evolving modern age, bursting all its bonds, crossing every boundary. From now on, uppers were indispensable.

The Crystal Fox

Erwin Rommel, later by some way the best known of all the German generals, wasn't an expert on tanks, but came from the infantry, the rank and file of the army. But it was his ignorance of the steel giants and their possible movements which helped him advance in a completely unconventional way. He led his 7th Panzer Division intuitively, like a shock troop. Instead of waiting until the assault engineers had built pontoons, he put his massively heavy vehicles onto ferries across the rivers of France – and it worked. Winston Churchill, named British Prime Minister on the day of the German invasion, was rarely wider off the mark than when he tried to reassure his French colleague, the Prime Minister, Reynaud: 'All experience shows that the offensive will come to an end after a while. [. . .] After five or six days, they have to halt for supplies, and the opportunity for counterattack is presented.'[78]

Rommel didn't halt. Too nimble to offer a target, he drove and drove and drove, taking advantage as Guderian had done of the excellent German logistics and becoming a kind of deadly joker, always playing high and wild, becoming unpredictable, uncontrollable, unstoppable. They admired him at headquarters: 'I'd like to go right to the front like General Rommel. He's the greatest daredevil, always in the first combat vehicle of his division!'[79] Even his superior, General Hoth, couldn't issue him with orders, because by the time these written documents arrived on the battlefield, Rommel was already miles away and out of radio contact. He had no apparent sense of danger – a typical symptom of excessive methamphetamine consumption. Even in the middle of the night he stormed on and attacked solid positions while still in motion, firing all barrels like a sort of berserker, constantly catching his adversaries on the back foot. The French despaired at the sight of the unleashed monsters coming at full speed towards their artillery. What on earth were they supposed to do? There were no instructions on how to defend yourself in that situation; they'd never practised it in manoeuvres.

Towards the end of that first week of the attack there was a ghostly scene that casts a sharp light on the German advance: in the early hours of 17 May 1940, Rommel, no longer answerable to any of his superiors, tore along the road from Solre-le-Château, right in the north of France, towards Avesnes. As chance would have it, the 5th Infantry Division, parts of the 18th Infantry Division and the 1st Infantry Division of the French army had struck their bivouac on that very spot. Rommel didn't hesitate for a second. He dashed through them, crushing everyone and everything, fired broadsides, and over the next ten kilometres he pushed hundreds of vehicles and tanks, along with the dead and wounded, into the ditches on either side and rattled on with blood-smeared tracks, standing between two officers from his staff in the armoured command post vehicle, his cap pushed to the back of his head, leading the attack.[80]

The *Blitzkrieg* by the Germans, who no longer had to sleep, had breached all boundaries. The seed was sown for future orgies of violence. There was an impression that these soldiers could be stopped by nothing and no one, and they gradually appeared to believe their own propaganda, which claimed they were truly superior. Methamphetamine, which encourages arrogance, supported this false assessment of the situation. The first rumours of the 'unconquerable Wehrmacht' started doing the rounds. The French war minister, Daladier, in the Élysée Palace, wouldn't have it, and yelled his disbelief down the receiver when his commander-in-chief, Gamelin, told him of the defeat on 15 May at 8.30 p.m. 'No! What you're telling me is impossible! You must be mistaken! It's impossible!' The *boches* were already 130 kilometres from Paris – and there were no French reserves to protect the capital. Everything had gone so fast. 'Is that supposed to mean that the French army is beaten?' Daladier's expression was one of utter dejection.[81] 'I was dumbfounded,' Churchill recorded in his memoirs. 'I admit that this was one of the greatest surprises in my life.'[82]

The Germans had won the war in Europe after only a few days. Well, almost.

Hitler Doesn't Understand the *Blitzkrieg*

At the moment it looks like the greatest military disaster in history.

General Edmund Ironside, Chief of the Imperial
General Staff, about the situation of the Allies on 17
May 1940[83]

A most ungratifying day. The Führer is extremely nervous. He is afraid of his own success, doesn't want to risk anything and would ideally like to stop us.

Franz Halder, head of the Army General Staff, also on
17 May 1940[84]

He rages and roars, he's on the way to spoiling the whole operation and exposing himself to defeat.

Halder, a day later[85]

The rapid progress of events surprised everyone in the General Staff. The military departments worked day and night, collected telephone messages about the various sections and constantly corrected the position of the front. At midday and in the evening Major General Jodl delivered the situation report in the Felsennest headquarters. But the restless and impatient sleepwalker Hitler got up from his couch in the middle of the night, left his bunker, which was protected with reinforced concrete walls a metre and a half thick, and found his bearings from the luminous phosphorus strips, tapping his way through the dark oak grove to the map-house, where Jodl's adjutant had already drawn a new battle line, further to the west. The dictator sat down in the wicker chair until dawn, and only the constant motion of his jaws revealed his inner agitation and paradoxically bad mood.

The Führer wasn't leading this campaign. Instead he was panting along behind his headstrong, independent tank generals. Even though they were successful, the dictator could not cope with the fact that he had effectively handed over control. Was this still 'his' war? Had the senior officers, who had been opposed to the attack for so long, now seized the initiative, and were they charging along faster than the planning in the map-house allowed? Hitler's fear of the highly specialized military officers, all better educated than him, a simple lance corporal, rushed to the forefront. He sensed problems where none existed, and accused the generals of being drunk on victory, of not covering their flanks, making themselves vulnerable to attack: what if the Allies coming from Belgium and the south carried out a pincer attack on the extended front? In fact, because of the unholy confusion on the opposing side this had never been a possibility. But Hitler didn't recognize reality. He was guided instead by his own anxieties, fuelled by a latently smouldering inferiority complex.

So in the spring of 1940, in the forest in the Eifel, the hopelessly overtaxed supreme commander made a crucial mistake when he decided to halt the full-throttle, whipped-up brain of the Wehrmacht. He had made his secret decision: he would disempower the army leadership as the locus of the war, whatever the cost. He just didn't know how to do it yet. Everyone was going to see who was in control. He was firmly convinced that the physical resilience of a genius like himself was enough on its own to give him victory over his adversaries. When all the others lost their nerve he, and he alone, would be the one still standing. Physically he felt as strong as an ox and thought he could take on the whole world. So why not his own army command?

Hitler's personal physician also paradoxically experienced these days of heady success as a personal setback and defeat. He was constantly at the ready, but his services were barely used. He wrote to his wife: 'Asked the Führer a few days ago if he had any complaints. He said no. He is really fit as a fiddle. He is fresh and cheerful. Medically there's hardly anything for me to do here.'[86] As a useless civilian Morell remained a hopeless outsider in the military command post, with its round-the-clock staff rotations. He was in everyone's way, and many people felt repelled by both his presence and his role. It didn't do him any good that he had himself made a fantasy uniform based on his own designs, with gold rods of Asclepius on its light-grey and green collar, so that he didn't have to go walking around in plain clothes any more. His ridiculous outfit only earned him mockery from the generals. When he added an SS buckle to his black belt, objections were raised immediately because he wasn't a member of the SS, and he had to get rid of it. He then, rather helplessly, chose a gold buckle that looked like something out of an operetta. He was envious of his rival, Hitler's surgeon, who had a proper Wehrmacht rank: 'From today Dr Brandt wears the epaulettes of a lieutenant colonel (army).'[87] In response, Morell tried to acquire his own regular rank as a military doctor, but his attempts fell on deaf ears. Even Hitler didn't support him in his project. That was precisely the appeal of his personal physician: it was only if he remained an outsider, without a position in the Party, the Wehrmacht or any other mass organization, that he couldn't be manipulated or abused – and he belonged to him, the Führer, alone.

While the tanks were trundling over the enemy, in his isolation in the Felsennest Morell became plagued by fears for his livelihood. Others in Hitler's inner circle, such as the photographer Hoffmann, profited greatly from the successes of the Third Reich, and a kind of modern robber-baronhood had spread among the leadership clique. Morell, however, only received a basic income of 3,000 Reichsmarks a month for his treatments of Hitler, including medical treatment of his adjutants. 'As all the other gentlemen are less free, I always sit on my own. [. . .] If it were not for the Führer, I would sometimes be glad to be at home. I'm about to turn fifty-four,' he complained in a letter to his wife, lamenting that his villa in Schwanenwerder 'can only be maintained with a large steady income, so I must either earn a great deal from medicine or get myself an income from chemicals/pharmaceuticals'.* It was the latter course of action that he would take in the end, with wide-ranging effects, not only for his patient.

The Miracle of Dunkirk – A Pharmacological Interpretation

> We shall have lost almost all our trained soldiers within the next few days – unless a miracle appears to help us.
> General Edmund Ironside, Chief of the Imperial General Staff[88]

On Tuesday, 20 May 1940, a courier aircraft from the propaganda ministry landed at the Felsennest, bringing the latest issue of the *Wochenschau*, the weekly newsreel produced under Goebbels's instructions. Hitler walked down the hill to Hack, the village pub. There he sat down in the side room, watched the reel three times in a row and dictated the changes he wanted. Then he showered in the bath-house opposite and was driven back to his headquarters.[89] The next morning the broadcast went back to Berlin, and from ten o'clock on Thursday morning it

---

* Morell's income was later increased to 60,000 Reichsmarks per annum. He also received tax favours for his business undertakings.

flickered across the screens of all the premier cinemas on the Kurfürstendamm. Of course, the *Wochenschau* edition of 22 May 1940 wasn't about pep pills. It was about the 'German sword, which is writing a new page of history', about 'the indomitable Aryan fighting spirit'.[90]

By now Guderian had occupied Abbeville, a major town on the Somme river. All French, British and Belgian troops north of the 'sickle cut' were thus cut off from all the units stationed further south, and there was only one open Atlantic port, one last chance of escape: Dunkirk. Again Guderian worked faster than his enemies. It would take him no more than a few days to block the last escape route and thus encircle a million Allied soldiers. These squaddies were in fact a good hundred kilometres away, fighting the 6th and 18th Armies, exposed without protection to the deadly danger behind them. After only ten fighting days the British Empire was close to its downfall.

That morning Göring was a guest of Hitler's at the Felsennest. Following the stomach injury that he had received during the storming of the Munich Feldherrenhalle in 1923, the second most important man in the state had developed a severe morphine addiction.[91] Before he left his bedroom, 'Möring', as he was secretly nicknamed, took his craftsman-made syringe with its gold ring out of its light-brown deer-hide case, pulled it open as usual, drew back the sleeve of his green velvet dressing gown as he always did, bound his arm, narrowed his eyes to find the right spot and gave himself a massive injection. It took only a few seconds for the morphine to enter his blood. A huge ruby brooch glittered spectacularly on his chest. Göring's eyes were now big and gleaming, pierced with pinprick pupils. The world lay at his feet, and in his blissfully opium-soaked brain he decided that the glorious victory over the Allies should under no circumstances be left to the arrogant leaders of the army. The German generals, Göring feared, would otherwise win such respect among the people that they might undermine his own position as well as Hitler's. It also seemed to be a praiseworthy task for the Luftwaffe: defeating enemy troops from above. His pilots just needed an open target – the Wehrmacht tanks had to retreat a bit to stay out of the danger zone. Göring nodded at this idea, which struck him as quite brilliant. As an indescribable feeling of well-being from the morphine rushed through him, he replaced his red pointed slippers with black high-sided boots and stamped out into the forest.

Beneath blossoming maple trees Hitler listened to his deputy's idea over porridge, muesli and apple tea. The two former fellow comrades trusted each other blindly. Hitler felt he was on the same wavelength with 'Möring', in a way that he wasn't with the Pervitinated generals. For him, the 'National Socialist Luftwaffe' was philosophically superior to the 'Prussian army'. So he agreed with his Reich Marshal's haphazard suggestion and used the opportunity to eliminate the army supreme command as planned and impose his 'Führer principle'. That morning he flew to Charleville, to the headquarters of Army Group A. At 12.45 an order was issued which still puzzles historians even today. It is the ominous Dunkirk 'Halt Order', which cannot be explained rationally.

When the British noticed that German tanks were stopping, they could hardly believe their luck. An unparalleled evacuation situation began straight away, and everyone hurried towards Dunkirk. Within a very short time hundreds of rescue ships arrived: Royal Navy destroyers and other warships, launches, even packet steamers and confiscated private yachts, Thames barges: a colourfully assorted armada ceaselessly coming and going. The Allied troops crossed makeshift bridges made of lorries with planks laid on the top and made their getaway through the miraculous loophole of Dunkirk.

Guderian could only stand and watch. Through his binoculars he observed what was going on in the port town, into which the unstoppable stream of British and French soldiers was flowing. But he couldn't advance, even though Göring's high-handed plan to snatch victory from the air was a failure from the very beginning. The Reich Marshal had overestimated himself in his morphine dream. Now his Stukas were sinking over a thousand of the British rescue boats, but at the end of May clouds had gathered and obstructed their view. The Royal Air Force, whose bases were much closer, also played their trump card now: suddenly Spitfires appeared from above and conquered the sky. The commander-in-chief of the army, von Brauchitsch, stood in the map-house of the Felsennest, about to have a nervous breakdown. He devoutly implored Hitler to be allowed to strike again and bring the campaign to an end. But the dictator refused to budge. He would show the army. *He* and no one else would wage this war.

Over 340,000 British, French and Belgian soldiers escaped in this way. At the very last second the Allies averted a total defeat. Von Manstein, the inventor of the 'sickle cut', later called it a 'lost victory'. When Guderian was finally able to enter Dunkirk at 9.40 on 4 June, after ten days of incomprehensible waiting, all he found was the equipment that the British left behind: vast numbers of cars, trucks, and motorcycles, 475 tanks, many artillery pieces, huge quantities of ammunition and handguns – as well as the 80,000 French soldiers who did not get a spot on the British ships. What was also left was a bombed-out, smoking silhouette, a charred black carcass of a town that seemed to be laughing at him. The British had got their heads out of the noose.

The battle for Flanders was over, the first phase of the western campaign at an end, finished. Contrary to later accounts, it had never been conceived consistently as a *Blitzkrieg*, but had, after the breakthrough at Sedan, boosted by the large-scale use of Pervitin on the German side, developed a dynamic of its own that was countered only by Hitler, who didn't understand its speed. Regardless, the dictator claimed the victory as his own personal triumph. In future, in spite of his Halt Order, with its far-reaching consequences, he would see himself as infallible, and his entourage acted out this farce with varying degrees of enthusiasm. In the German press the campaign was presented as 'the most astonishing event in all of military history, because in fact something was made possible that had, not without reason, been considered impossible'.[92] Wilhelm Keitel, head of Wehrmacht High Command, described Hitler, after this 'greatest military victory of all time', as the 'greatest commander of all time' (*'grösster Feldherrn aller Zeiten'*), which later, when Hitler's startling weaknesses as supreme commander became all too obvious, was mockingly shortened to *Gröfaz*.[93]

The Dealer for the Wehrmacht

I had ordered you not to sleep for forty-eight hours. You
kept going for seventeen days.

Heinz Guderian[94]

Berlin, 6 June 1940: pale rain cut the deep-black stormy
sky into strips, bounced off the bodywork of the cars,
buses and taxis, the raincoats of the pedestrians, pearled
on caps, hats and umbrellas. The forced euphoria of a
news announcer rattled from the loudspeaker of the
brand-new car radio, a Telefunken T655, announcing
that the German troops were on the edge of Paris. 'Ich
bin wie ich bin' by Arne Hülphers and his orchestra
now rang out inside the official car, while outside the
advertising slogan 'Persil bleibt Persil', in bright-green
neon letters, glittered in the dancing puddles.

At 10.52 p.m. Ranke's train set off for the west from
Anhalter station; he had decided to drive to the front to
investigate Pervitin use and to bring fresh supplies. His
war diary for the next few weeks, preserved in the
Freiburg Military Archive, gives an unadorned insight
into the second phase of the campaign, concerned with
the French heartland, the operation called '*Fall Rot*' (Case
Red). Often Ranke's sentences are chopped and the
descriptions over-hasty, full of abbreviations. They always
involve a considerable quantity of methamphetamine:
'14.6.40 Friday 9 a.m.: discussion with Lieutenant Colonel
Kretschmar about military situation. Knows precisely,
takes 2 tabs *c*. every 2nd day, finds it fabulous, is fresh

afterwards without subsequent tiredness, no mental under-achievement on Pervitin, expressly confirmed in response to question from me.'[95]

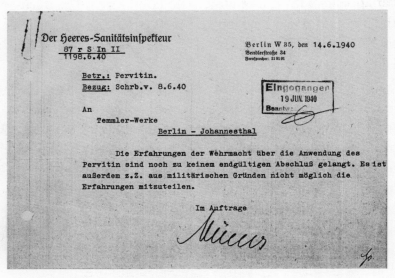

A typically cagey note to the Temmler Works from the Army during the Battle of France: 'The Wehrmacht's experience of using Pervitin has not yet reached any definitive conclusions. For military reasons it is also currently impossible to communicate these experiences.'

On Ranke's personal Tour de France, in the course of which he covered over 4,000 kilometres, travelled along the sea, through the cities and over the mountains, drugs played the decisive part. It is telling that he accompanied the most senior army officers, the *Blitzkrieg* inventors of Panzer Group von Kleist: Guderian and Rommel. Ranke was always wherever the most methamphetamine was being taken, where everyone was hopped up and needed him – because he had a serious quantity of hard drugs on him, which he willingly distributed:

'16.6.40 Sunday: just before the planned departure my car appears with driver Holt, who couldn't find us during the night. Hurrah. Packing 40,000 Pervitin. Set off 11 a.m. to XIV Army Corps, first chocolate (me at wheel), in Lormes market square 1 cup coffee, on to Montesauche. I ate only a box of biscuits all day.'[96]

Often on his explorations Ranke had his camera at the ready. His most frequent subject is initially surprising. He took pictures of sleeping people: soldiers stretched out on the grass beside a utility vehicle, slumbering drivers in their cars, officers who have fallen asleep in armchairs, a staff sergeant in a deck chair under a tree. The pictures seem to want to prove that Morpheus, Ranke's arch-enemy, still hadn't been defeated, but had to be caught in the crosshairs . . . with Pervitin, of course.

The external enemy caused fewer problems: when Paris fell into German hands in mid-June, the French army put up no resistance. The picture that France presented during those days was a gruesome one: 'fields of rubble, charred cars and dead horses in big squares surrounded by singed trees. Burned-out tanks and houses. On the retreat routes of the British and the French there lay a motley jumble of equipment, including abandoned gun mounts, defective tanks etc. and on either side of the road retreating men, mostly on bicycles, packed with the bare minimum of belongings.'[97]

Ranke's superior, Army Medical Inspector Waldmann, also travelled to the war zone and praised Pervitin without directly specifying it: 'Maginot front broken through.

Extraordinary marching achievements: 60–80 km! Extra supplies, increased performance. Evacuation – all much better than 1918.'[98] In this war the German troops dashed over the summer countryside with unparalleled speed. Rommel, who by now was avoiding roads to go round the last French defence positions, often drove cross-country, and on 17 June 1940, travelling 240 kilometres, established a kind of 'military world record'. The head of the Luftwaffe staff noted: 'The marching achievements are incredible.'[99]

In mid-June, Guderian reached the Swiss border at Pontarlier. The remaining half a million French soldiers standing on the Maginot Line were now also encircled, and the German Reich's victory over its neighbour definitive. Only Hitler didn't understand the speed with which everything was happening: 'Your message is a mistake,' he cabled his general. 'It must mean Pontailler-sur-Saône.' Guderian had to clarify: 'No mistake. I myself am in *Pontarlier* on the Swiss border.'[100] The speed of the thrust is clear from the account of a German war reporter. 'The tanks, the artillery, the anti-aircraft guns, the supply columns come rolling in without interruption. Even at night we feel our way along the country road. No one thinks of sleep. A little piece of chocolate replaces lunch. On we head! We've now driven 300 kilometres in convoy, some of it across cornfields, meadows and ploughed land. Only the people behind the wheel can say what that means. Really, our drivers have done some incredible things over the last few days. We were so fast, the French population had no time to get away. "You Germans dash across the country like a whirlwind," said one civilian. "A few days

After seventeen days awake: sleeping after the *Blitzkrieg*.

ago in Calais, and now in the South of France already."
He could only shake his head.'[101]

It wasn't just chocolate that replaced lunch, as the
Berliner Lokal-Anzeiger claimed. It was also the little round
pills from Temmler; they drove away the feeling of hunger. Ranke, who was driving with Guderian, and who had
travelled over 500 kilometres in just three days, was given
confirmation by a medical officer of the Panzer troop
that units were using between two and five Pervitin tablets
per driver per day. German propaganda, however, tried
to depict the surprisingly fast victory as proof of the
morale of the National Socialists, but this had little bearing on reality. Ranke's military medical diary is proof that
other forces were involved, chemical ones: 'Senior Staff
Doctor Krummacher has experience with Pervitin. He
introduces me to Colonel Stockhausen. [. . .] Signed out
with Lieutenant Colonel Kretschmar, who insistently
requests Pervitin. [. . .] Since the start of the campaign he
has used a tube of 30 tabs apart from 6 tabs.'[102]

Ranke wrote of Kretschmar, the senior quartermaster
of Panzer Group von Kleist, who was responsible for
supplies, that he 'was allowed several times by Pervitin to
go on working in spite of being tired. He emphasized the
positive effect on the mood, and also stressed that he
always carried out difficult work that required strong concentration.'[103]

Mostly it was the 'General Staff officers [. . .] who knew
and valued Pervitin and asked me for it'. With Rommel's
leading medical officer, Senior Physician Baumeister,
Ranke had 'a detailed and gratifying conversation about
Pervitin, science'. The Waffen-SS, who liked to boast of

their fighting ability, couldn't do without the medication either: 'Set off 10 o'clock via the reconnaissance route of the 10th Panzer Division. Took pictures of the SS, very disciplined in spite of long journey. Dropped off 2000 Pervitin there with troop doctor.'[104]

Side-effects of the pharmacological mass abuse were also observed, but Ranke himself didn't notice them – or he decided not to mention them in his notes. Older officers from the age of forty felt the effects of the use of meth on their hearts. One colonel with the 12th Panzer Division who was known to 'take a lot of Pervitin'[105] died of a heart attack while swimming in the Atlantic. One captain also had a cardiac arrest after using Pervitin at a stag party. A lieutenant general complained of fatigue during long periods of fighting and took Pervitin before driving to the front to join the infantry, against medical advice. There he suffered a collapse. A lieutenant colonel with Panzer Ersatz Division 1, who during the battles had 'for four weeks taken daily 2 times 2 tabs Pervitin', complained of heart pains and stressed in his report that his 'blood circulation had been perfectly normal *before* the use of Pervitin'. He describes the prescribed mass drug use in critical terms: 'Pervitin was delivered officially before the start of the operation and distributed to the officers all the way down to the company commander for their own use and to be passed on to the troops below them with the clear instruction that it was to be used to keep them awake in the imminent operation. There was a clear order that the Panzer troop had to use Pervitin.'[106]

Another staff officer made it known that he had taken four tablets of Pervitin on each of his thirty-three days of fighting within a month and a half. After that he was unfit for duty because of 'chronic high blood pressure'.[107] Dependencies also came to light. More and more men were fighting with the after-effects of the drug, which could include low drive and depression. The longer they spent on meth, the less dopamine and serotonin was released in the brain. The worse the individual felt, the more he took to balance it out.

Ranke ignored all of this. The scientist, considered unimpeachable at his institute at the Military Medical Academy, whitewashed the inquiries into the stimulant prepared for Berlin. At the same time he revealed his own, very personal inadequacy: he knew the drug better than anybody, and he was aware of its dangers, but he had become dependent upon it and played down the negative effects both to himself and to others. A classic case of an addicted dealer.

War and Vitamins

In the rush of the victorious campaign Morell's thoughts turned to his role as a vitamin pioneer, and he set about manufacturing a combination preparation called 'Vitamultin'. His pan-European marketing strategy was as simple as it was striking: he just had to persuade the great commander, his Patient A, to swear by his product, and everyone else was bound to follow. To heighten the appeal to Hitler, Morell had the Hamburg firm Nordmark, of which he owned 50 per cent, manufacture the so-called 'Nobel-Vitamultin'. They were meant for one person only, wrapped in glittering gold paper and stamped 'SF' – *Sonderanfertigung Führer* ('special product for the Führer'). Somewhat less glamorous than the packaging were the contents, which consisted of rosehip powder, dried lemon, yeast extract, skimmed milk and refined sugar.[108]

Even though Hitler didn't suffer from a lack of vitamins, since he hardly ate anything but fruit, vegetables and salads, he pounced on the tablets as if they were the apples of the Hesperides. After all, additional vitamins could never hurt. Soon he was consuming several of these gilded gifts every day, and Morell advised the Engel-Apotheke, a kind of court chemist's near the Reich Chancellery, 'always to keep a small store of about 50–1000 Vitamultin-F bars. [. . .] You must ensure that there is never a gap in supplies.'[109] He kept the recipe strictly under lock and key, and instructed the chemist only to supply the product to him in person or to Hitler's valet.

Now came the second step in Morell's marketing strategy. For the senior officers of the Wehrmacht and important members of the staff he made a brand stamped 'SRK' – *Sonderanfertigung Reichskanzlei* ('special product for the Reich Chancellery') – wrapped not in gold but in silver. Soon the senior officers were fighting over the moderately tasty sweets, which were ostentatiously consumed at military briefings. Morell wrote contentedly from the Führer's headquarters to his wife: 'Vitamultin is proving a great success here. All the gentlemen are very appreciative of it, and recommend it to their families at home.'[110]

This success laid the foundation for large-scale deals

with the mass organizations of the Third Reich. Shamelessly exploiting his influence as Hitler's personal physician, Morell won over the German Labour Front (DAF) for several 'Vitamultin operations'. Huge quantities were ordered: sometimes 260 million, then even 390 million. Overall the DAF took almost a billion tablets. The goal was to heighten the performance of munitions workers and increase their resistance to infectious diseases. The doctor also approached the SS, who received 100,000 free Vitamultin biscuits, as 'an affectionate gift'. These were supposed to get the Mountain Corps in Norway hooked. At a personal discussion with Himmler, the head of the SS, Morell touted the usefulness of Vitamultin in Scandinavia: it was demonstrably clear that an increased intake of vitamin C improved night vision, and up there it was often dark.[111] The SS seemed pleased with the result and ordered more, hundreds of millions in all. The product even received a special edition branding of its own and bore the label 'SS Vitamultin'.[112]

The commercially focused doctor also fixed his sights on the ground troops: 'Mustn't we offer Vitamultin to the army again?' he wrote in a letter.[113] But when he approached Otto Ranke, the dealer for the Wehrmacht, he found he was banging his head against a brick wall. The advisory defence physiologist, used to stronger stuff, wasn't impressed by a mere vitamin preparation, and refused to pack the bars in the troops' equipment.

But the Vitamultin business worked without the army. Morell could even cope with a rejection by the Luftwaffe, although he did take it personally, and plotted against Dr Erich Hippke, leader of the Luftwaffe medical service:

'On the basis of false data the *Generalstabsarzt* [Senior Staff-Surgeon General] is trying to disavow a valuable preparation and circulating a letter seeking to defame me,' Morell wrote to Hippke's superior, the Reich aviation minister, Hermann Göring. 'I can't calmly accept such a mode of behaviour, which has happened on duty. If it had happened in private life, I would go to court so I ask you, my dear Reich Marshal, to be so kind as to make a just judgement. In deepest respect for you, Herr Reich Marshal, I remain yours, *Heil Hitler*.'[114] Göring reacted, and Hippke had to go. This was a triumph for the physician. His own rise to becoming a pan-European pharmaceutical entrepreneur was off to a good start.

Flying High: The Battle of Britain

After the fiasco of Dunkirk, for which the blame was laid at his door, Göring, 'the Fat Man', tried desperately to appear as the radiant lordly figure he imagined himself to be when under the effects of morphine. 'Operation Sea Lion' was planned: the invasion of Great Britain with ground units. For the precarious sea journey of thousands of German soldiers across the Channel, air supremacy also had to be achieved so as not to risk the troops. This was Göring's job, as well as his great opportunity to impress Hitler and justify his great power as well as the extravagant lifestyle that went with it.[115]

The Battle of Britain was beginning. To force Britain to its knees from the air, Göring first bombed logistical air force targets: aerodromes, hangars, landing strips, planes. This successful strategy was changed, however, after the British bombed the Berlin districts of Kreuzberg and Wedding in a night raid on 25 August 1940. Hitler ordered an attack on London for 4 September, to demoralize its population – a severe tactical error, because it meant that enemy airfields were no longer the prime target. Consequently, the British were able to strengthen their defences.

Bombs fell on the British capital and other towns. Over 40,000 civilians had lost their lives by the end of the campaign. These were the first systematic terror attacks of the war. On the island there was a grim comment: 'London can take it.'[116] The RAF struck resolutely back: countless German planes were shot down over England, and the British flew retaliatory attacks against German cities. The clash escalated. Soon it became too dangerous for the Luftwaffe to operate by day. One bomber pilot describes the situation: 'The launch was very often late, ten o'clock, eleven o'clock, and then you were over London or some other English city at about one or two in the morning, and of course then you're tired. So you took one or two Pervitin tablets, and then you were all right again. [. . .] I had a lot of night operations, you know. And, of course, the commander always has to have his wits about him. So I took Pervitin as a precautionary measure. Imagine the commander being tired in battle! Uh, yes, please, that's not going to work. [. . .] One wouldn't abstain from Pervitin because of a little health scare. Who cares when you're doomed to come down at any moment anyway!'[117]

This certainly wasn't a one-off remark. There are no statistical studies of Pervitin among the Luftwaffe, and by historiographical standards there is little supporting evidence of the comprehensive use of the 'speedamin' among pilots, apart from Ranke's original order of 35 million doses for the army and the Luftwaffe together.

Control of the skies was essential to win the war, and to do that you need the right materials: steel and manpower. Both must function perfectly and keep going longer than the enemy can. While Messerschmitts were technically inferior to Spitfires, the Luftwaffe's use of drugs was far ahead of that in the RAF. Pervitin had several nicknames that indicated its use: 'pilot salt', 'Stuka pills', 'Göring pills'. One commodore reports from the Mediterranean: 'In my knee pocket there is a hand-length strip of linen covered with cellophane, with five or six milk-white tablets stuck to it, the size of a chocolate bar. The label reads: "Pervitin". Tablets against fatigue. I open the bag and tear first two, then three of these tablets from the pad, take the breathing mask off my face for a moment and start chewing the tablets. They taste repellently bitter and floury, and I've got nothing to wash them down with.'[118]

After a while the effect kicks in: 'The engine is running cleanly and calmly. I'm wide awake, my heartbeat thunders in my ears. Why is the sky suddenly so bright, my eyes hurt in the harsh light. I can hardly bear the brilliance; if I shield my eyes with my free hand it's better. Now the engine is humming evenly and without vibration – far away, very far away. It's almost like silence up here. Everything becomes immaterial and abstract. Remote, as if I were flying above my plane.'[119]

After landing, reality was a strange world for the zonked

pilot: 'I kept my course precisely, in spite of my euphoric indifference and my seemingly weightless state. Upon landing, I find the place in a state of complete stasis. Nothing moves, there's no one to be seen, rubble of the hangars forlornly looms [. . .] between the bomb craters. As I roll on to the squadron's stand my right tyre bursts. I've probably driven over a bomb splinter. Later I meet Dr Sperrling and ask him in passing what kind of "crap" this Pervitin really is, and whether it mightn't be better to warn pilots in advance? When he learns that I've taken three tablets, he nearly faints, and forbids me to touch a plane, even from outside, for the rest of the day.'[120]

As hopped up as the Germans might have been, this couldn't give them the advantage over the Royal Air Force, which was plainly better run. The Battle of Britain was lost by the Reich – Germany's first defeat in this war. Hitler had to call off Operation Sea Lion and thus an invasion of Britain, and looked for a new theatre for his war.

Consequences weren't drawn from this new failure on Göring's part. He still held court in the huge building of the Reich aviation ministry, built of pale stone blocks on Wilhelmstraße. Red Reich war flags emblazoned with a swastika fluttered confidently above, as if to point out unequivocally that even the winds were subject to the power of this government and particularly to that of the Reich Marshal. But anyone who passed through the big cast-iron gate and crossed the broad forecourt stepped into a realm of chaos, of unbridled alcohol and drug abuse, of intrigues and of general mismanagement. The conditions in Göring's 3,000-room fortress (which today houses the Federal Ministry of Finance) were symptomatic of the regime's loss of political reality and the wrong track that Germany had set off on.

An officer describes the Reich Marshal's appearance: 'We struggled to keep a straight face. He dons a white silk, blouse-like shirt with flowing sleeves, and over it a yellow, sleeveless, fur-lined suede jacket. With this he sports long medieval looking bloomers, and around his waist a broad, gold studded leather belt, with a short Celtic sword jangling from it. Long silk stockings and golden-yellow Saffiano leather sandals complete the picture.'[121]

The face of the powerful minister was covered in make-up, and his fingernails were painted red. Often during discussions Göring, once the opium content of his blood had dropped, felt so deranged that he would leave the room abruptly without a word of explanation, and not come back until a few minutes later, plainly much refreshed. A general describes one such surprising trans-formation: 'Göring had the air of being new-born, he looked magnificent and fixed his sparkling blue eyes on us. The difference in his whole appearance between the first and second parts of our conference was notable. For me it was clear that he had been taking some form of stimulant.'[122]

These frequent escapes from reality didn't help Göring's official duties. Soon the precondition for holding a sen-ior post in his office was not so much one's qualifications as one's entertainment value.[123] He swept aside criticisms of one of his closest colleagues, Bruno Loerzer, whom Göring himself described as his laziest general, with the remark: 'I need someone I can drink a bottle of red wine with in the evening.'[124] Similar considerations may also have played a part in the appointment of Ernst Udet as so-called 'Generalluftzeugmeister', or General Master of Aircraft, one of the most influential positions in the Third Reich. Admittedly, after the Frenchman René Fonck, Udet was very popular as the most successful surviving fighter pilot of any nation in the First World War. But this exceptionally gifted flyer and bon viveur, who enjoyed his cameo appearances in Leni Riefenstahl films, struggled with his desk job at the top level of the leadership. Göring couldn't care less, however, and his treatment of Udet was a particularly impressive example of how capriciously he ran his ministry, where the concept of administrative supervision was unheard of.

A lot of alcohol, even more Pervitin: General Luftzeugmeister Ernst Udet (centre).

When the Reich aviation minister and his General-luftzeugmeister talked together, they liked to reminisce about the good old days, when they had fought aerial battles together in the First World War, high on cocaine.[125] On the other hand they were less keen on talking about current armament problems, the complex process of developing new types of aircraft and other similarly intricate matters. At his opening speech at the ministry Udet admitted, his face cloudy and terribly hungover, that it would be unwise to expect him to perform many administrative duties. The only problem was that he was now in charge of up to twenty-four different offices, which were soon in a state of indescribable chaos. Udet, who was known to serve cognac at meetings throughout the day, and to take methamphetamine in enormous quantities to balance out the effects of the alcohol, was notorious for extraordinary mismanagement even within the inefficient Reich aviation ministry.

It's possible that Göring was referring to Udet when he observed: 'There are departments you have no idea about, but all at once they appear, and promptly some mess happens. [. . .] And swiftly you discover: there's been a department there for years, and no one knows anything about it. In all seriousness: it's happened a few times. There are people who have been thrown out three times, and then they reappear in a different department, and become bigger and bigger.'[126]

Udet particularly liked to spend his days drawing caricatures, often enough of himself. Whenever possible, he crept off home, where he ran a small private bar decorated with trophies from his world travels, and always surrounded himself with friends because he couldn't bear to be alone. Although he just wanted to be sitting in a plane stunt flying, there was no time for that now; Udet was imploding under the burden of his constantly increasing responsibilities. In the course of 1941 he shovelled Pervitin into his mouth in dangerous quantities to keep himself capable of functioning. In that way he personified the hubris of German warfare, which had overstretched itself and lost contact with reality long ago. 'Our defeat was caused by Udet,' Hitler, of all people, would later claim. 'That man concocted the most nonsensical state of affairs ever seen in the history of the Luftwaffe.'[127] And that was saying something.

In the German theatre play most often performed after the war, *The Devil's General*, the dramatist Carl Zuckmayer gave his friend Udet far too flattering a monument in the figure of the honourably tragic, nonchalant swashbuckler, Air Force General Harras. Udet is not worthy of such a heroic status. At best one might say in his favour that he unwittingly might have done great damage to the system through his incompetence and drug addiction. So he is no more and no less than a buffoon, a historical curiosity, and he embodies those deviant qualities that historians usually ignore.[128]

On 17 November 1941 a report from the German news service came over the ticker: 'Generalluftzeugmeister Air Chief Marshal Udet [. . .] while testing a new weapon suffered such a severe accident that he died of his injuries on the way to hospital. The Führer has ordered a state funeral for an officer who was lost so tragically while carrying out his duty.'[129] In fact Udet had fired a bullet into his head at his grand villa on Stallupöner Allee in Westend, Berlin's most exclusive residential area, and at a stroke delegated all the thousand technical and organizational problems of the Luftwaffe back to his old fellow soldier from the First World War, Göring. Just before he brought his intoxicated life to an end with a bang, Udet had scribbled one last message beside his deathbed: 'Iron man, you have deserted me.'

The suicide of the self-aggrandizing Udet anticipated the downfall of the Third Reich. As Göring walked behind the coffin at the state funeral, with a metallic, morphine-doped expression and muttered something about 'one of the greatest heroes in German history', the Wehrmacht was getting stuck in Russia. Just behind the Military Medical Academy, in the Invalidenfriedhof, only a few steps from the place where Otto Ranke had tested Pervitin for the Wehrmacht, Udet's grave can still be seen today.[130]

Just What the World was Waiting For

On 13 September 1940 the Milan daily *Corriere della Sera* reported on a 'courage pill' used by the Germans, which had gone from medicine to secret weapon. The military effectiveness of this 'pillola di coraggio', the article said, wasn't a match for a Stuka bomb, but it did guarantee the German General Staff the uninterrupted operational capability of its soldiers.

Britain went on to study and eventually use Benzedrine (which has fewer side-effects than Pervitin) as a result of the Milan piece.[131] The article provided the reassuring explanation that the Germans' relentless fighting power could be explained chemically rather than ideologically. The BBC immediately produced a feature on the provision of Pervitin to German pilots. As a result, a controversy at the highest level of the civil service broke out in Berlin.

Leo Conti, the Reich Health Führer, who was critical of Pervitin, wrote to the Army Medical Inspector: 'I would be grateful if you could tell me in what quantities and with what degree of success Pervitin is actually being administered to members of the Luftwaffe. I would also like to know your attitude towards this issue. [. . .] I cannot approve the prescription of Pervitin. After repeated declarations of the harmfulness of this substance, I have wondered whether stricter regulations should be introduced concerning the prescription of Pervitin, perhaps identifying it as an intoxicating drug. Heil Hitler!'[132]

This letter made little impression on the army. It was not until a month later that their new Army Medical Inspector, Prof. Siegfried Handloser, wrote: 'British propaganda has claimed several times that the German Wehrmacht is only capable of its achievements thanks to drugs. The fallacy of these reports by London radio is apparent from the fact that they also have German Panzer divisions in France marching on drugs. The fact is that Pervitin was only used at that time by individuals and in vanishingly small quantities.'[133] A clear lie, because Handloser must have been aware of both the 35 million tablets ordered for the western campaign and Ranke's report from France.

Conti wouldn't leave the matter alone. Stubbornly he fought for his ideological ideas of a poison-free Aryan nation. At the same time he misjudged the realities of the geopolitical competition of the Second World War, and its crying need for doping. In an act of desperation he engaged a scientist friend to write, under the headline 'The Pervitin problem', the first major critical piece on the favourite drug of the Germans, regarding the dangers of the stimulant and its violently addictive properties. In typical Nazi terminology he called for Pervitin to be 'eradicated wherever we find it', and stressed that anyone who was addicted to it was 'degenerate'.[134]

In fact the article touched a nerve in scientific circles, and cases of Pervitin dependency were now discussed more and more frequently, whether it was doctors who consumed several doses a day or medical students who took a similar number of tablets and were then unable to sleep for nights, scratching their skin bloody looking for imaginary vermin.[135]

In Germany the use of the substance now ran to over a million doses per month.*[136, 137] In February 1941 Conti again delivered a warning, this time in an internal memo to the Party: 'I am following up with mounting concern the terrible abuse being practised in the widest circles of the population. [. . .] This is an immediate danger to the health and future of our people.'[138]

At last the Reich Health Führer acted – or at least attempted to – and on 12 June 1941 made Pervitin subject to the Reich opium law. By doing so he officially declared

---

* These are conservative estimates, because the official figures often refer to 'units'. If these refer not to individual tablets but for example the well-known Pervitin tubes (each containing thirty tablets), then consumption was even higher. Also, the additional consumption of (higher-dosed) ampoules for injections cannot be reconstructed.

the people's drug to be an intoxicant.[139] This act, however, did not lead to a restriction in its use. In fact it meant only a formal victory for Conti and his ideologically motivated officials. The Reich Health Führer, once one of the most powerful men in the National Socialist state, waged a lonely battle and went on to lose more and more influence. The population was less concerned with Conti's campaign against drugs than it was with the mounting strains of the war, which were easier to endure with the help of the chemical stimulant, even if that meant becoming dependent on it. The Germans barely took any notice of the rigorous prohibition, let alone observed it. Civilian use even increased, by over 1.5 million units a year.[140] In this way the drug revealed the internal contradictions of the National Socialist state and played a part in the process of its gradual self-dissolution. It wasn't long before a total of over 100 million doses had reached German stomachs and bloodstreams.

Where use by the military was concerned, the date chosen for the ban on Pervitin was more than risky, because Germany was due to attack the Soviet Union ten days later, and the soldiers had developed a high tolerance by now. The Wehrmacht High Command, along with the Reich Ministry for Arms and Ammunition, endorsed by Göring, had even classified Pervitin as 'decisive for the outcome of the war'.[141] There was no trace of restriction. Drug use wasn't the only thing about to explode in the summer of 1941.

Reichsstelle "Chemie"   Berlin W.35, den 7.5.41.
                                         Sigismundstr. 5
                                         Dr.Hy/Küs.

                B e s t ä t i g u n g
                -.-.-.-.-.-.-.-.-.-.

Der Firma Temmler-Werke, Berlin-Johannisthal. . . . . . .

. . . .

wird für ihre Erzeugnisse
  pharmazeutische Produkte gemäß der Ihnen erteilten Produktionsaufgabe

hiermit bestätigt, dass diese gemäss Erlass des Reichswirtschaftsministeriums II Chem. 27 742/41 vom 2.4.1941 im Einvernehmen mit dem
Oberkommando der Wehrmacht und dem Reichsministerium für Bewaffnung
und Munition als kriegsentscheidend erklärt worden sind.
Der Herr Reichsarbeitsminister sowie die Vorsitzenden der Prüfungs-
kommissionen sind hierüber unterrichtet worden.
Diese Massnahme erfolgte gemäss Ziffer F 5 der Ausführungsbestimmun-
gen (ADFW) vom 21.12.1940 zu dem Erlass des Vorsitzenden des Reichs-
verteidigungsrates, Ministerpräsident Reichsmarschall Göring, über
Dringlichkeit der Fertigungsprogramme der Wehrmacht vom 20.9.1940

Die Sicherung der kriegsentscheidenden Fertigungen hat gemäss
Erlass des Reichswirtschaftsministeriums S 1/1098/41 vom 22.3.1941
zu erfolgen.
Ein Missbrauch dieser Bestätigung durch Weitergabe bei Unterlieferun-
gen für oben nicht angegebene Erzeugnisse wird auf Grund des Straf-
erlasses des Reichsmarschalls vom 20.9.1940 nach Massnahme der Ziffer
II der zweiten Verordnung zur Durchführung des Vierjahresplans vom
5.11.1936 bestraft.

                              Der Reichsbeauftragte:

44

Six weeks before the attack on the Soviet Union.
'[. . .] in agreement with Wehrmacht High Command and the
Reich Ministry for Arms and Ammunition [. . .] Pervitin has been
declared "crucial to the war".'

3

High Hitler: Patient A and His Personal Physician (1941–1944)

The doctor's task in peace and war – if it is done correctly
– is always one of leadership in the truest sense of the
word. [. . .] The relationship of trust between doctor and
patient must be made in such a way that the doctor always
and at all times has the feeling of standing over the patient.
[. . .] Being a doctor means being the stronger of two.

From the text of a speech by Theo Morell[1]

The sometimes rather obscure guild of Hitler researchers
is united by a desire finally to decipher the enigma of the
dictator, probably the worst criminal and psychopath of
all time. It looks like there is little progress. The public
events have been grasped by biographers for decades; a
wide range of literature of all kinds is fully available. Even
though more has been written, and is still being written,
about this person than about anyone else in the world,
even though 'the psychopathography of Adolf Hitler' is
a psychiatric subject in its own right, which deals exclusively with notional psychological diseases of the man

from Braunau, no one seems to have come to grips with the mystery; the dubious mythology burns on.

Could it be that in the literature on Hitler there is a blind spot, however diverse the research might have become? I am intervening here in a sort of trial based on circumstantial evidence, over which scholars have been arguing for years – and which has also led to massive scandals and famous forgeries such as the so-called 'Hitler Diaries' published in *Stern* magazine a few decades ago. We should always remain suspicious of some sources. I cannot present a definite solution to the enigma, but will offer a particular reading of the issues involved.

Anyone who wishes to approach Hitler should take a detour via Morell, the fat doctor in the light-brown gabardine coat. It was, after all, in the autumn of 1941 – the point where the dip in Hitler's performance became obvious, and where all the books on him reveal a vacuum because they can't adequately explain that dip – that Morell ceases to be the curious, marginal figure of most historical accounts. In Joachim C. Fest's 900-page biography, *Hitler*, the physician is mentioned only seven times – the first instance no earlier than on page 535. The author's accurate description of Hitler's 'narcotic trance'[2] remains unexplained, and when Fest speaks of him becoming 'fatally drug-dependent',[3] the extent and symptoms of that addiction are not touched upon. Fest claimed that nothing new about Hitler could possibly come out after the publication of his own work in 1973, because it had been proven that 'we can expect no further material which could even begin to modify the picture of the era and its protagonists'.[4] This has now been proved premature.

Even if history is attempting to shift the focus away from details about Hitler's life to historical processes that influenced his rise and made him what he was, beside those quite reasonable endeavours there remains a vacuum that needs to be filled. It isn't enough to speak blandly about 'Dr Morell's colourful pills'.[5] And when the British historian Ian Kershaw, himself an author of a famous Hitler biography, maintains that 'the increased number of pills and injections provided every day by Dr Morell – ninety varieties in all during the war and twenty-eight different pills each day – could not prevent Hitler's physical deterioration', he possibly confuses cause and effect.[6]

For the German historian Dr Henrik Eberle matters are less ambiguous. He comes to the conclusion that the head of the German state was not at all addicted to drugs, and Morell had acted 'entirely responsibly'. However, the doctor himself seems to contradict this statement. In his notes he records a conversation with his patient in the following terms: 'I always had to carry out short treatments with high doses, and had to go to the boundaries of the permissible, even though many colleagues might have condemned me for it, but I did and can bear the responsibility, because if treatment had been suspended at the present time, Germany would have been brought to its knees.'[7]

So what did Hitler really take, and what is its significance? Can historical events and developments be linked to pharmacological preparations? For years Morell painstakingly recorded the medications he used to keep his patient constantly on the go. Meticulous records were required in case anything happened to Hitler, in which case Morell would have had to hand over his detailed reports to the Gestapo. This gave rise to an immense bundle of papers, unique in medical history, and overflowing with details. Anyone with the desire to decipher the collection will have to visit several sites to put together the various fragments of the doctor's estate. A chunk is in the Federal Archive in Koblenz, another part in the Institute of Contemporary History in Munich – and a third, significant, portion in Washington DC.

On-site Visit: National Archives, Washington DC

Reminiscent of an ancient temple, the monumental archive building stands on Pennsylvania Avenue, in the innermost administrative district of the victorious power of the Second World War. The White House, on the same street, is just a stone's throw away. Words are chiselled into pale stone beside the entrance: 'What is past is prologue'.

Inside there is an overwhelming sense of confusion. Finding documents isn't easy; there are simply too many of them. Like an enormous vacuum cleaner, the armed forces and intelligence services of the United States sucked up mountains of files from the German Reich and deposited them in Washington and College Park in Maryland – the biggest archive building in the world. To help you find your way through the holdings, there are catalogues, computer hubs and, most importantly, the personal help of archivists, who effortlessly manage to cope with such complicated German specialist terms as *Reichssicherheitshauptamt*.

From the very outset Paul Brown, who helps me with my Morell research, dampens my hopes of finding *everything* about Hitler's personal physician here. He compares my investigations at the archive with skipping flat pebbles over the water. Total access, complete immersion doesn't exist, he reckons. You simply cannot exhaust the whole of the National Archives, this vast belly of documents. History, in Brown's view, always remains one thing: speculation drawing on the most relevant possible facts. Historical truth isn't something he can offer me.

So much quickly becomes clear: soon after the end of the war Theo Morell was subject to investigations by the US secret service, some of which were made accessible only a few years ago by the Nazi War Crimes Disclosure Act.[8] The Americans tried to find out what part the doctor had played, whether he was involved in Hitler's medical decline, which progressed rapidly from the autumn of 1941 onwards, or whether he had even tried to poison Hitler. The handling of addictive drugs was the focus of their inquiry. Might we find simple answers here to something that was so difficult to understand? Or did the doctor put himself in the wrong by artificially doping up his patient?

From the summer of 1945 Morell was interrogated for two years, and according to his own account tortured – purportedly his toenails were pulled out to retrieve his secrets. But the US military didn't get much out of their prisoner. The secret files reveal the frustration of the interrogators, who report contradictory statements. In

Morell's Medical Assessment file it says: 'He is communicative, often gets lost in meaningless trivia when making his statements, and tries to replace the very obvious gaps in his memory with fictions, which often leads to contradictory information. [. . .] At different times the patient's psyche shows a completely different picture. [. . .] In the case of Professor Morell this is plainly a mild form of exogenous psychosis, caused by the fact of his imprisonment. This in no way limits his accountability. On the other hand, his credibility should not be viewed as complete because of the presence of memory gaps which he attempts to bridge with fictions.'[9] Morell, according to the file, was not willing or able to explain the relevance of his activities.

The statements of three German pharmacologists and doctors who were brought in as experts right after the war weren't any help either.[10] One of the investigations devoted to Morell, Special Report No. 53, entitled 'The Rumored Poisoning of Hitler' came to the conclusion that the doctor gave his patient neither enough poison nor enough narcotics to damage his health. Hitler's astonishing physical and psychic decline was presumed to be due only to a huge amount of stress and his largely vegetarian diet.

Is this assessment correct? Or should it at least be read with caution, due to its proximity to the events, as well as its incomplete study of source material? The US authorities had aimed to receive information to dispel the countless myths that had built up around Hitler.[11] In these terms they – ostensibly – failed with Morell.

On closer examination the answers actually lie in

Morell's notes – although they are hidden and not always easy to interpret. Morell's posthumous papers are a chaotic mass, consisting of scribbled pages from his prescription pads, file pages scattered with cryptic abbreviations, note-books with barely legible handwriting, diaries filled from cover to cover, loose sheets of paper with observations and descriptions, countless business and personal letters. Entries are repeated, slightly changed, appear again in notebooks, on envelopes, on notes from a telephone pad.

From August 1941 until April 1945 the doctor treated his patient on a more or less daily basis. There are accounts for 885 of these 1,349 days. Medications were recorded 1,100 times, as well as almost 800 injections, about one per recorded day. Every now and again the needles themselves are cleanly stuck on to the notes, as if to give an outward appearance of transparency and conscientious documentation. Morell was afraid of the Gestapo; he knew that personal physicians have always lived dangerously.

The result is a chaotic record, a jungle that is almost impossible for outsiders to penetrate, particularly if they have an imperfect command of the German language. Precisely in the alleged over-precision much remains sketchy, and on an attentive reading it becomes clear that some visits are not recorded. Was Morell, who normally kept his business papers meticulously in order, trying to hide something with this confused representation of events, which was incomplete while simulating complete-ness? Was he trying to keep a secret that he alone knew, and of which even his patient was unaware? When the war took a fateful turn for the Third Reich, what really happened between Hitler and his personal physician?

The Bunker Mentality

Whenever I was allowed to stay with you more often in headquarters last year, these visits have given me more than you, my Führer, can begin to guess. I have done everything within my power to pass on the abundance of strength that you conveyed to me to as many people as possible.

Joseph Goebbels [12]

This entirely unique process cannot be understood with traditional concepts and moral categories.

Percy Ernst Schramm[13]

To approach the truth of Hitler's drug consumption it helps to imagine the place where he spent most of his

Searching for traces: the former Führer Headquarters known as the Wolf's Lair.

time between the summer of 1941 and the autumn of 1944. A search for clues in eastern Poland: colossal exploded bunkers lie like crash-landed concrete spaceships in the light-drenched Masurian forest. This is the 'Wolfsschanze', the Wolf's Lair. Moss has climbed over everything and birch trees grow on the undulating roofs. Everywhere there are wide cracks you can climb into. Steel reinforcements jut and bend from the crumbling concrete. On every corner yellow signs have been set up in Polish, German, English: UWAGA!!! ACHTUNG!!! DANGER!!! Still the many tourists from all over the world, numbering almost a thousand a day, aren't deterred. They clamber into gaping black holes, force their way into chinks, take videos and selfies . . . as if they're searching for something.

In the summer of 1941 the Wolfsschanze looked very different. The fortress, protected by mines in a ring between fifty and 150 metres wide, near the East Prussian town of Rastenburg, had just been established and was going into operation. Its core was initially formed by ten bunkers, the backs of which lay under two metres of concrete. This was where the sleeping areas were. The front was relatively less protected and was where the work spaces were set up. The mess hall where officers ate formed the middle of the camp, and resembled an ugly village pub. A revolutionary star was soon hung behind an ungainly wooden table that sat twenty people: a captured Red Army flag. Hitler arrived on the evening of 23 June 1941, one day after the start of the German invasion of the Soviet Union. It was from the Wolf's Lair that he would direct 'Operation Barbarossa', factoring in no more than three months for its victorious conclusion. The soldiers didn't even bring winter uniforms.

Because of this hubristic assessment, the location of the headquarters for the Russian campaign had been chosen more or less on a whim. They wouldn't be staying long anyway, it was thought – just like they didn't stay long in the previous headquarters, the Felsennest. This time, they would pay the price for their arrogance.

Even in the very first days there were complaints about the Wolfsschanze: it was hard to think of a less hospitable place than this boggy soil between stagnant lakes and marshy ponds. The Führer's abode was soon decried as an airless, lightless camp in the forest, often swathed in fog, the ground contaminated with petrol that had to be sprayed around the compound to keep the plague of mosquitoes down. A minor official wrote to his wife: 'It would be difficult to come up with a more stupid spot. Damp, cold bunkers in which we shiver pitifully at night because of the constant roar of the electric air ventilation system, which causes a terrible draught. We sleep badly and wake up with a headache in the morning. Our linen and uniforms are always cold and damp.'[14]

'Bunker damp and unhealthy,' Morell recorded shortly after moving in. He was staying in cramped bunker number 9. A fan rotated on the ceiling but didn't create any fresh air, just swirled the mustiness around: 'Ideal temperature for the breeding of mould. My boots are mildewed, clothes clammy. Stenocardia, anaemia, bunker psychosis.'[15]

Hitler didn't seem to be bothered by any of that. He had already enjoyed the cave-dwelling life in the Felsennest, but it was with the Wolf's Lair that he reached his dream destination: a remote retreat where his life was reduced entirely to the military events at the front. Over the next three years the Wolf's Lair became the centre of his life and grew to over a hundred different residential and administrative buildings as well as massive, reinforced-concrete bunkers, its own rail connection and airport. Over 2,000 officers, private soldiers and civilians remained there permanently. No one actually enjoyed the location except the man who was also known as the Boss. He claimed to feel perfectly at home in his bunker. The temperature was always cool and even, fresh air was pumped in. Morell also had an oxygen tank set up for him, 'for inhalation and possible release into the bedroom. Führer *very* content, one might even say enthusiastic.'[16]

Artificial oxygen supply, protective bunker walls: if it outwardly appeared as if the German supreme commander was somewhat close to the action on the front, he was indeed further removed from the realities of war than ever before. This determination to hide himself away (nothing unusual really, for dictators) would have disastrous consequences. Over the previous years the world had always bent to Hitler's will, helping him to achieve incredible victories that had further reinforced his position of power. But as soon as he encountered genuine Russian resistance that couldn't be removed with a sweep of the hand, 'the greatest commander of all time' retreated further and further into his world of make-believe. The microcosm of the Wolf's Lair was nothing more than a bubble made of concrete and steel.

The Soviet Union, as was already clear in July 1941,

defended itself bitterly against Hitler's megalomaniac fantasies. Even though the Germans conquered huge amounts of territory in the early weeks of the murderous campaign, and took hundreds of thousands of Red Army soldiers prisoner, as more and more space opened up in front of the Wehrmacht, more and more Russian reserves were coming in. Sure: Hitler's troops were winning one battle after another, and advanced quickly, encircling the enemy on a huge scale and causing comprehensive chaos, just as planned. But the Red Army simply behaved as if it hadn't even noticed these setbacks. That 'sickly house of cards', Hitler's term for Russia, refused to collapse. Battles were fought ruthlessly on both sides from the very beginning, and for the first time in this war the Germans suffered great losses within a very short time.

Even the doping which had been deployed for this gigantic *Blitzkrieg* advance wasn't much help. The drugs had been delivered to the tank troops, and one army group alone consumed the crazy amount of almost thirty million tablets within only a few months.[17] But Pervitin didn't bring about a quick victory. Soon the spoonful of time was paid for dearly. The Germans eventually had to rest – while the Red Army brought in new divisions from its massive hinterland.

During this crucial early phase, in August 1941, Hitler fell ill for the first time in years. As he did at eleven o'clock every morning, his valet Heinz Linge, already permanently pallid from life in the bunker, knocked at the door of bunker number 13. But Hitler stayed in bed. He had fever and diarrhoea, was shivering and had severe pains in his limbs. Dysentery was presumed.

'Summoned by telephone to come to the Führer *straight away*. Sudden dizziness.'[18] The news of his patient's collapse reached Morell through telephone line 190 in the so-called 'drone barracks', a claustrophobically cramped, practically unlit working space which he had to share with the son of Hoffmann, the Reich photographer. The doctor quickly looked around for his black bag – the room was full of medications and photographic equipment – stepped outside and hurried to Hitler, whom he found slouched in his bed, collapsed in on himself like a marionette. He was demanding immediate relief from his pain, because he wanted to go to the briefing and had serious decisions to make.

This time vitamins and glucose didn't work as they had done before. Nervously and with excessive haste Morell prepared a mixture of Vitamultin and calcium, and combined it with the steroid glyconorm, a hormone preparation that he had manufactured himself, which consisted of extract of cardiac muscle, adrenal cortex, and the liver and pancreas of pigs and other farm animals. It was a doping agent. The injection did not go as smoothly as usual: 'Bent needle during jab.'[19] To combat the stinging pains caused by the mishap Hitler was given twenty drops of dolantin, an opioid whose effects are similar to those of morphine.* But the dysentery-like diarrhoea persisted. Patient A had to keep to his bed and didn't appear during the military briefing held in Keitel's and Jodl's bunker at twelve o'clock. Dictator unfit for service: a sensation in operational headquarters.

---

* Natural alkaloids from the poppy plant are called opiates. So-called opioids are the synthetically produced derivatives based on them.

'Führer very irritable,' Morell wrote that evening, describing his failure. 'Have never experienced such hostility towards myself.'[20] Undeterred, the physician stuck to his pharmacological refresher course, and soon the injections started working; the dysentery was vanquished. The very next day Hitler took part in the meetings with the generals again, and was immediately determined to make up for his one-day collapse. The old conflict between him and the General Staff, which had used his absence to act on its own initiative, flared up again. It concerned the continued thrust of the attack. Unlike their leader, the generals saw Moscow as their paramount goal. They planned to take the Russian capital in a decisive battle, and win the war by that means. But the freshly cured Hitler had a different strategy. He divided the troops up to conquer Leningrad in the north, cutting the Soviet Union off from the Baltic, while at the same time Army Group South was to advance via the Ukraine into the Caucasus to take the oil resources that were of crucial importance to the war economy.

This crisis deeply affected the doctor and his concept of 'immediate recovery'. So that Patient A didn't end up in the sick bay again and fall behind, Morell administered a harder course of prophylactic injections. Morell became a typical proponent of polypragmasia, and went on to prescribe more and more remedies in ever-changing concentrations.[21] He barely made any diagnoses, but instead constantly added to his 'basic medicinal treatment'.*

* Things were quite different in Moscow, for example. Stalin had his own clinic at the Kremlin with the best specialists – who weren't, of course, allowed to make any mistakes.

This soon included such diverse substances as Tonophosphan, a metabolic stimulant made by Hoechst, chiefly used nowadays in veterinary medicine, the hormone-rich and immune-system-boosting body-building supplement Homoseran, a by-product of uterine blood,[22] the sexual hormone Testoviron to combat declining libido and vitality, and Orchikrin, a derivative of bulls' testicles, which is supposed to be a cure for depression. Another substance used was called Prostakrinum, and was made from seminal vesicles and the prostates of young bulls.

Even though he didn't eat meat, Hitler surely could no longer be considered vegetarian. From autumn 1941 onwards, more and more highly concentrated animal substances began to circulate in his bloodstream. The purpose of these supplements was to compensate for states of psychological and physical exhaustion, or to prevent them in advance by reinforcing the body's defences; however, as a result of the constantly changing applications and the rising doses that followed, Hitler's natural immune system was soon replaced by an artificial protective shield. This made Morell increasingly indispensable.

This approach to the dictator's health could be compared to using a sledgehammer to crack a walnut. In the few walks that Hitler still took in the fresh air of Restricted Area 1 at the Wolf's Lair, the doctor always went with him, and a few steps behind followed an assistant with the doctor's bag. The consistency with which this long-term medication was applied is apparent from a train journey in August 1941. Hitler and Mussolini were on their way to the front: a twenty-four-hour journey through Eastern Europe where mass murder was ubiquitous. They passed close by Kamianets-Podilskyi in western Ukraine, where over 23,600 Jews had just been shot by the SS and a German police battalion – it was the first murder of all the Jews belonging to a whole region.

So that Patient A did not have to miss a single injection en route, the Führer's special train stopped in the open countryside, as no injection could be given on the juddering train. The armed anti-aircraft wagon was immediately put at the ready, Morell quickly opened his fat-bellied medical bag, took out the set of ampoules wrapped in black leather, removed their napped metal plates, opened the zip fastener of the case in which the syringe was kept, tipped the first ampoule over, stuck in the needle and drew out the fluid. He swiftly bound Hitler's snow-white, almost hairless arm, wiped the sweat from his own forehead and jabbed in the syringe: first in the vein, then, quickly, a second intramuscular injection. Morell proudly described the unusual pit stop: 'Train stopped mid-journey for glucose i.v. then Tonophosphan forte and Vitamultin Calcium i.m. to the Führer. All done in eight minutes.'[23]

Such a process was not a one-off event; it was the norm. The injections increasingly determined the course of the day: over time the Führer's medical mixture was enriched by over eighty different, and often unconventional, hormone preparations, steroids, quack remedies and balms.*[24]

* An alphabetical list giving the German names clearly demonstrates the madness of the treatment (the psychoactive, consciousness-changing drugs are italicized: Acidol-Pepsin, Antiphlogistine, Argentum nitricum, *Belladonna Obstinol*, Benerva forte, Betabion, Bismogenol, *Brom-Nervacit*, *Brovaloton-Bad*, *Cafaspin*, Calcium Sandoz, Calomel, Cantan, *Cardiazol*, *Cardiazol-Ephedrin*, Chineurin, *Cocaine*, *Codein*, Coramin, Cortiron, Digilanid Sandoz,

There was psychological importance in the fact that the combination of injections changed every day. It meant that Hitler never had the impression of becoming dependent on a particular substance. It was Morell's overall package that he could no longer do without. In his personal physician he had found a perfect tool for self-medication and self-adjustment that he increasingly began to abuse.

This polytoxicomania, which developed in the second half of 1941, sounds bizarre, even for an age in which steroid and hormone research could not begin to guess the effect of the complex interactions of these highly potent substances on the human constitution. Hitler understood less than anyone what was going on in his body. He had always been interested in medication but had never acquired any medical knowledge. As a drug consumer, as well as a general, he remained an eternal dilettante, and allowed himself to be guided by spontaneous suggestions without first understanding basic

Dolantin, Enterofagos, Enzynorm, *Esdesan*, Eubasin, Euflat, *Eukodal*, Eupaverin, Franzbranntwein, Gallestol, Glucose, Glyconomr, Gycovarin, Hammavit, Harmin, Homburg 680, Homoseran, Intelan, Jod-Jodkali-Glycerin, Kalzan, Karlsbader Sprudelsalz, Kissinger-Pills, Kösters Antigas-Pills, Leber Hamma, Leo-Pills, Lugolsche Lösung, Luizym, *Luminal*, Mitilax, Mutaflor, Nateina, Neo-Pycocyanase, Nitroglycerin, Obstinol, Omnadin, *Optalidon*, Orchikrin, Penicillin-Hamma, Perubalsam, *Pervitin*, *Profundol*, Progynon, Prostakrin, Prostophanta, Pyrenol, *Quadro-Nox*, Relaxol, Rizinus-Oil, Sango-Stop, *Scophedal*, Septojod, Spasmopurin, Strophantin, Strophantose, Suprarenin (Adrenalin), Sympatol, Targesin, Tempidorm-Suppositories, Testoviron, Thrombo-Vetren, Tibatin, Tonophosphan, Tonsillopan, Trocken-Koli-Hamma, Tussamag, Ultraseptyl, Vitamultin, Yatren.

principles. This was to prove disastrous in the end, for him at least. His natural intuition, which had served him well so often until the beginning of Operation Barbarossa, left him when the injections began to throw his body into chaos. Tolerances build up with intense consumption and the body accustoms itself to substances; doses have to be increased or the effect declines, and the dictator couldn't bear declining effects.

In this respect Morell didn't help the patient in his care. The doctor doesn't seem to have given much thought to problematic interactions – a failure in medical responsibility. An opportunist, a sycophant like so many others, he was too insecure to threaten his advantageous position by imposing a critical form of care on his leader. While in these autumn months of 1941 the systematic murder of the Jews took its course and the Wehrmacht waged a criminal war of annihilation in Russia that would cause millions of casualties, the National Socialist reign of terror was slowly poisoning itself from within.

Eastern Rush

My findings have given me the deepest impression that the Führer is in good health.

Joseph Goebbels[25]

On 2 October 1941 the war diary of Wehrmacht High Command records: 'At dawn Army Group Middle went on the offensive in fine autumn weather.'[26] Now the attack on the Russian capital was belatedly under way. In a huge battle at Vyazma, half-way between Smolensk and Moscow, a staggering 670,000 Red Army soldiers were taken prisoner. In the Wolf's Lair some were already declaring victory. But the Germans had lost valuable time and squandered their efforts too much in other theatres of war to be able to take Stalin's power centre in a swift operation. When the weather got worse, the advancing soldiers got stuck in the morass: 'Persistent rain, fog. Serious deterioration in the tracks, making all movements and supplies more difficult,' the German army leadership reported at the end of October.[27] The possibility of defeat was suggested for the first time.

Hitler reacted stoically to the critical situation. When the Red Army launched a counter-offensive with fresh Siberian elite divisions in the early winter, he ignored all appeals from generals to let the troops fall back to avoid further defeats. Instead, on 16 December 1941, he issued a fateful order, which had disastrous long-term effects: *Hold the line at all costs.* Any form of retreat without his express permission was forbidden from now on. The German military, formerly feared because of its unpredictable dynamism, had lost all spontaneity. The astonishing successes of the mobile combat that opened the war were a thing of the past. It is telling that Guderian (who in the spring of 1940 had been partly responsible for the western campaign victory thanks to his unconventional, consistent disobedience) was now accused by Hitler of standing too close to events when the Panzer general tried to persuade his supreme commander to take back the frontlines close to Moscow.

Hitler's only prescription at this point was 'fanatical resistance', with no regard for casualties – and with no regard in fact for the reality of the front. In this first winter of the eastern war the Wehrmacht was therefore severely beaten, and in Moscow the church bells rang confidently. Orthodox priests hurried from house to house, from hut to hut, in full regalia and with raised crucifixes, to drum up men and women, young and old, to make the ultimate sacrifice for sacred Russian soil. All over the Soviet Union pictures flickered across screens showing Red Army soldiers putting on quilted clothing and shoes made of felt, while German prisoners without coats or gloves performed a macabre dance, barefoot on the icy ground, to try to keep from freezing to death.

Hopeless situations accumulated for the aggressors. Often the only thing that helped was Pervitin. One of many examples: in the fishing village of Vzvad, on the southern shore of Lake Ilmen, between Moscow and Leningrad, the Germans were encircled, their accommodation set on fire, rations arriving only sporadically from the ice-cold air. One last, tiny window of escape was open, and 500 exhausted men loaded with heavy bags and machine-guns over their shoulders began a fourteen-hour night march through waist-deep snow. Soon many men were, as the official Wehrmacht report has it, in 'a state of extreme exhaustion. [. . .] The snowfall had stopped from around midnight, and the sky was filled with stars. Enervated soldiers wanted to lie down in the snow; in spite of energetic pep talks their will-power could not be revived. Such men were each given

2 Pervitin tablets. After half an hour the first men confirmed that they felt better. They marched in an orderly fashion again, back in line.'[28] This reveals that by now the uppers were not used primarily for storming and conquering, but above all for endurance and survival.[29] The tide had turned.

A Former Medical Officer Speaks

'I always had lots of it,' Ottheinz Schultesteinberg, who trained at the Military Academy between 1940 and 1942, reports on his deployment as a medical officer in Russia: 'The stuff was just doled out. The motto was, *come and get it!*' The 94-year-old, who now lives on Lake Starnberg near Munich, remembers the war that took him to Stalingrad as if it were yesterday. We meet on the terrace of a Croatian restaurant in the town of Feldafing: 'I didn't take Pervitin myself, or at least not often, just once to try it. To know what I was prescribing,' he says. 'And I can tell you: it worked. It kept you awake, mercilessly. We knew it was addictive, and that it had side-effects: psychoses, nervous excitement, a loss of strength. And in Russia, it was a war of attrition, positional warfare. In such circumstances Pervitin was no use: it just exhausted you. You eventually had to catch up on the rest you'd missed. Sleep deprivation simply didn't bring any tactical advantages any more.'[30]

They knew about these problems in Berlin. The Reich Health Führer, Leo Conti, and his 'Reich Central Office for Combating Drug Transgression' was still attempting to draw up a complete record of all drug-dependent soldiers. He issued a directive to the Wehrmacht and the SS to the effect that all fighters who had been discharged were to be graded according to their possible affinity for drugs, to decide whether they should be given compulsory therapy or whether they should be 'expeditiously identified as unregenerate or incurable'.[31] That sounded both drastic and menacing, so the Wehrmacht neglected to comply: it reported such cases rarely or not at all. The intense military situation did not lead to punishment for drug consumption, and the army even deliberately recruited staff from Conti's office to fight at the front – which further hindered his anti-drug campaign.

In the Führer's headquarters it dawned on some at the end of 1941 that victory was no longer possible. The Chief of Staff, Halder, summed up the situation: 'We have reached the end of our strength.'[32] The *Blitzkrieg* strategy had tried to reverse the existing power relations through surprise, and this had failed, along with Hitler's whole concept of war, built from the very beginning on the sand of speculation. The Germans could not survive lengthy attritional warfare against the Russians, who were both superior in numbers and by now also increasingly better equipped. It was a sobering realization with new conclusions to be drawn. But the Führer was in denial. He had severed relations with geopolitical reality; more and more poor decisions followed. If the supreme commander had enjoyed successes before the autumn of 1941, his fortunes had now changed.

As if reality could be duped by simply refusing to acknowledge the obvious facts, in December 1941 an exhausted Germany, already fighting on several fronts, irrationally declared war on the well-rested industrial giant, the USA. Hitler, wildly overestimating himself, had assumed supreme command of the armed forces, thus expropriating von Brauchitsch's task. Ceasing to understand the world, he was plainly no longer able to consider the matter in a sober fashion. In his own words, with Operation Barbarossa he felt as if he were 'pushing open a door to a dark room never seen before, without knowing what lies behind it'.[33] Hitler was also plunged into *literal* darkness, as Morell wrote: 'On top of everything, a life in a bunker without daylight.'[34] In this murkiness nothing could touch the unhinged dictator and he could ignore reality completely. The only thing that penetrated his mental armour now was the needle of his personal physician injecting hormonal doping agents into his bloodstream. 'Tragic that the Führer is closing himself off from life like this, and leading such a disproportionately unhealthy existence,' Goebbels wrote in his diary: 'He no longer gets any fresh air, he doesn't take any kind of relaxation, he just sits in his bunker.'[35]

In January 1942, at the Wannsee Conference in Berlin, the preconditions for the 'final solution of the Jewish question' were drawn up. Hitler's method now became rigidly fixated on genocide. There was a convincing reason for the frantic insistence on refusing to give up any conquered territory: to keep the chimneys of the extermination camps of Auschwitz, Treblinka, Sobibór, Chełmno (Kulmhof), Majdanek and Bełżec smoking for as long as possible: to hold all positions – until all the Jews were dead. Patient A, who was radically distancing himself from the human conventions of living, was determined to bring his war on the defenceless to a satisfactory conclusion.

Planet 'Werwolf'

I envy you for being able to experience the great world-
historical events in the Führer's headquarters. The Führer's
genius, his timely intervention and the structuring of our
Wehrmacht, thought through with the greatest precision
in every direction, ensure that we can look into the future
with great confidence. [. . .] May it be granted to him to
preserve perfect health, so that he receives the strength
to achieve even his last goals for his people.

From a letter to Theo Morell[36]

In July 1942 the geographical reach of the Third Reich
extended from the North Cape in Norway to North Africa
and the Middle East. The plateau of the National Socialist
expansion trip had been achieved – while the signs were
already pointing to defeat. That summer saw the beginning
of 'Operation Reinhard', the systematic killing of over
two million Jews and 50,000 Sinti and Roma in occupied
Poland. At the same time a large-scale move was taking
place: the Nazi leadership shifted from the Wolf's Lair to
brand-new headquarters, a few kilometres from Vinnytsia,
a small city in rural western Ukraine.

The change of location was something of an ostenta-
tious display, little more than a farce designed to convince
the leadership that they were moving closer to the front,
closer to the action. But the main line of battle was still a
comfortable distance of hundreds of kilometres from this
camp of huts, which had been quickly assembled in the
forest. Here the power circle was even safely removed from

the massive bombing raids on German cities by the British – Lübeck, Rostock, Stuttgart and above all Cologne had already suffered severe attacks. Hitler's avoidance of the political and social realities was perfectly in line with this new central command post, this non-place in nowhere, this high-tech location in the sticks where he could more easily dope himself up and remove himself from reality. There hadn't been a solid home in his life, like his former flat on Prinzregentenplatz in Munich, for quite some time.

The newly appointed armaments minister, Albert Speer, described the new headquarters in the Ukraine as an 'arrangement of bungalows, a small pine forest, a park-like garden'.[37] The stumps of the felled trees were painted green to match the landscape, the car parks were shadily protected in the undergrowth. It almost sounds like a holiday in the countryside, a rest home. But it was from these two handfuls of log cabins and barracks surrounded by tall oaks that a war was waged, more cruel than any waged before. Hitler christened his new headquarters for mass murder 'Werwolf', or Werewolf, a somewhat suitable name for this zone of unreality. Monstrous events were planned and ordered from here while its inhabitants remained secluded from the world, and stuck strictly to their ritualized daily routine.*[38] Here Hitler, with billions of crazed bacteria in his gut, could go on fearing microbes while his soldiers in the steppes and marshes of Russia

* 'Any association with civilians is forbidden, as is staying in the houses of the local population.' It was widely suspected that these houses contained vermin which could transmit diseases. Warnings were issued about flies – dysentery! – bugs and lice – typhus! – and Ukrainian rats, as potential carriers of plague.

became acquainted with infectious diseases from Volhynia fever to tularaemia and malaria.

By now Morell was essential to the dictator, and wouldn't leave him even at military briefings, even though as a civilian doctor he had no business there and received sceptical looks from the generals. At these meetings, which were held twice a day, the world was abstracted into procedures and military maps. Even in fine weather the windows were closed and the curtains drawn. In spite of the freshness of the forest outside, the atmosphere in Werwolf headquarters was always stuffy. At this point Hitler took advice only from people who were as ignorant of the situation at the front as he was himself.[39] The great hour of the yes-men had arrived, embodied in the form of the gnarled and rigid Field Marshal Keitel, who was secretly mocked as 'Lakaitel' – 'Keitel the lackey'.

On 23 July 1942, thirteen months after the start of the Russian campaign, Hitler made another strategic blunder when he ordered in Army Directive 45 that German forces be divided again, this time in the south of the Soviet Union. Army Group A was to advance on the oil-rich city of Baku in Azerbaijan, Army Group B via the Volga city of Stalingrad to the Caspian Sea. A front originally 800 kilometres wide, deep inside enemy territory was thus extended to a barely tenable 4,000 kilometres. The army leadership protested vehemently, and beneath the blazing Ukrainian sun, with temperatures from 45° to 50°C, there were unparalleled expressions of rage. Halder would later say that Hitler's military decisions gave 'full power to wishful thinking'.[40] Speer, the armaments minister, spoke of a 'special kind of derangement with which everyone in

Hitler's immediate entourage regarded the inevitable end'. Military planning had parted company with reality long ago. *Schaulagen* – 'show briefings' – was the name given unofficially to these prettified military meetings: 'Rose-tinted reports from army positions lead us to fear that the critical situation is not being fully acknowledged.'[41]

Hitler's personal physician, Morell
(to the left behind his patient).

When Erich von Manstein, inventor of the 'sickle cut', conqueror of the Crimea and now promoted to the rank of Field Marshal, spoke about the critical situation in the southern part of the Eastern Front, the official Oberkommando log stated: 'As before, no full decisions are being made. It is as if the Führer is not capable of it.'[42] Hitler no longer tolerated generals who argued rationally, who in his opinion only ever wanted to talk everything down. From now on he childishly refused to shake hands with Colonel General Jodl (who was the only member of army command who was not a patient of Morell). Hitler no longer attended communal meals, but retired completely to his log cabin, which he only ever left after dark. When he did fly to the front in mid-August 1942 to get an idea of the military reality, he immediately got terribly sunburnt – 'His whole face burnt dark red, great burns on his forehead, severe pains'[43] – and was extremely glad when he was back in his sheltered hut.

By now, he had more or less given up delivering public speeches. The historian and author Sebastian Haffner describes the retreat of Hitler, formerly a master of publicity: 'He had methodically replaced sobriety with mass intoxication. One might say that he had prescribed himself to the Germans for six years as a drug – which he then suddenly withdrew from them in wartime.'[44] Hitler now missed those ecstasies that his appearances had previously prompted, and which had always amounted to a new injection of the pepped-up feeling that was so important to his self-esteem. In his isolation, all pleasure and energy previously received from the attention of a cheering crowd had to be replaced by chemicals – further cocooning the dictator. 'He was a person who continually needed artificial charging. In a sense Morell's drugs and medicines replaced the old stimulus of mass ovations.'[45]

By now Hitler paid scarcely any attention to affairs of state. He preferred to stay up all night, seldom went to bed before six o'clock, and what he liked best of all was talking to Speer about grandiose architectural projects –

although these were now purely illusory. Even his loyal arms minister and favourite architect, who described his collaboration with Hitler as the 'years of intoxication', and as a real master of repression still raved about the 'heady stimulus that comes with leadership', had to acknowledge that Hitler 'frequently took flight from reality and entered his world of fantasy'.[46]

This remoteness from truth would have serious effects on the course of the war. Hitler often sent his units into battle without any notion of their equipment, fighting power or supplies. But at the same time he was minutely concerned, to the chagrin of the army, with all tactical questions, right down to battalion level, and thought he was indispensable in every respect.* Every word uttered at the military briefings was now being recorded in shorthand so that he could later call generals to heel if they tried to sidestep his increasingly unrealistic orders.

Hitler had been a military dilettante since the order to halt at Dunkirk; now he became a fantasist, while his armies lost themselves in the wastes of Abkhazia and the Kalmuk Steppe, advanced all the way to the Black Sea and erected a vainly fluttering swastika flag on the Elbrus massif in the Caucasus at an altitude of 5,633 metres. In the summer of 1942 Hitler's absorption of injections rose to such a level that Morell had to put in a special order for syringes for the Führer's headquarters at the Engel chemist's shop in Berlin.[47]

---

* Stalin acted quite differently, more or less keeping out of military affairs after the defeat at Kharkov in May 1942 for which he was responsible, and gave a relatively free hand to his supreme command, the Stavka.

ENGEL-APOTHEKE

KÖNIGL. **1739**. PRIVIL.

Pharmacie Internationale

ALLOPATHIE / BIOCHEMIE / HOMÖOPATHIE

Herrn
Prof. M o r e l l

Führerhauptquartier

FERNSPRECHER: 11 07 21
BANK DEUTSCHE BANK
STADTZENTRALE
MAUER STRASSE
POSTSCHECK: 7543

BERLIN W 8
MOHREN STR. 63/64

BETRIFFT:

DEN 29. August 1942

Sehr geehrter Herr Professor !

Auf beifolgendem Rezept bitte ich höflichst noch den
Vermerk " eingetragene Verschreibung" vermerken zu wollen
und mir dann das Rezept zurücksenden zu wollen.

Für die Beschaffungung der bestellten Spritzen bitte ich
um Ausstellung eines Rezeptes oder einer Bescheinigung
woraus hervorgeht, dass die Spritzen für das Führerhauptquartier benötigt werden. Nur auf Grund dieser Bescheinigung ist eine Anfertigung der Spritzen möglich.

Mich Ihnen bestens empfehlend zeichnet mit

Heil Hitler !

Königl. 1739 priv.
Engel-Apotheke
Inh.: ERNST JOST
Berlin W 8, Mohrenstr. 63/64

A letter from the Engel pharmacy to Morell: '. . . For the supply of the ordered syringes I request the issuing of a prescription or a certificate showing that the syringes are needed for the Führer's headquarters. Only on receipt of this certificate can the syringes be prepared. With very best regards, *Heil Hitler!*'

In the autumn of 1942 Rommel, who had switched from Crystal Fox to Desert Fox, was getting into desperate straits in Africa against the British under Montgomery. At the same time Stalingrad was becoming more and more of a psychopathic fixation, given the city's diminishing strategic significance. Hitler was unnecessarily stylizing the progressively dramatic events there into a mythically overcharged fateful battle. His health was going rapidly downhill, while on the Volga the siege was closing in on General Paulus's 6th Army. German soldiers were perishing in their thousands due to hunger, cold and Russian shells. 'Intestinal gases, halitosis, discomfort,'[48] Morell noted of his patient on 9 December 1942, the day when it became apparent that Göring's grandiloquent and unrealistic promise to supply food and fuel for the besieged troops in Stalingrad by means of an air drop had been broken.

A week later Patient A asked his personal physician for advice. Göring had told him he took a medication called Cardiazol when he felt weak and dizzy. Hitler wanted to know 'whether that would also be good for him, the Führer, if he felt a bit funny at important occasions'.[49] But Morell refused: for him, Cardiazol, a circulatory stimulant for which it is difficult to give precise dosages, and which also raises the blood pressure and can easily lead to seizures, was too risky for Hitler, who now had heart problems. But the doctor had understood the message: his boss was asking for stronger remedies to help calm his nerves over the intensifying crisis in Stalingrad. Morell would soon rise to the challenge.

Slaughterhouse Ukraine

You must be healthy, you must stay away from that which poisons your bodies. We need a sober people! In future the German will be judged entirely by the works of his mind and the strength of his health.

Adolf Hitler [50]

Based on the continuing success of his Vitamultin bars, Theo Morell had taken over one of the biggest cooking-oil manufacturers in the former Czechoslovakia, the Heikorn Company in Olmütz (Olomouc) in Moravia, which had been stolen from its Jewish owners. Hitler had organized this special bonus for him in person.*[51] The purchase price was 120,000 Reichsmarks – a ludicrous amount for the lucrative property that the physician converted into the main manufacturing site of his company, Hamma. In his notes he writes: 'It will never again be so cheap to make an acquisition. [. . .] The Aryanized factory goes to me.'[52] Over a thousand employees made such diverse products as poppyseed oil, mustard, scouring powder and the anti-louse powder Russla, which Morell had developed himself and which was largely ineffective but still compulsory for the Wehrmacht. The core business was

---

* In the purchase contract from 29 November 1943 it says: 'The property of the Jew Adolf Heikorn, his wife Wilma (birth name Goldschmied) and their children Friedrich Heikorn and Hedwig Heikorn has been confiscated on the orders of the Secret State Police [Gestapo]. The purchaser expressly declares that he is not a Jew, and that on his side of the legal acquisition no Jews, Jewish business or associations of Jews are involved in any way.'

vitamin and hormone preparations. In order to keep this going the ambitious doctor and mercantile exploiter of Nazi terror needed a constant source of supplies.

Eight kilometres south of Werwolf was the city of Vinnytsia, with its huge and very modern slaughterhouse. The American company Swift had built it shortly before the start of the war to the latest technical specifications and modelled it on the abattoirs of Chicago. All of Ukraine's slaughtering was supposed to be centralized here and everything was fully automated, including the collection of the enormous quantities of blood produced. Morell was impressed: there was nothing like this even in Germany, where 'valuable proteins were still washed away', as he recorded in his notes.[53] The doctor decided to take advantage of this modern facility, and while Hitler barricaded himself away in his hut in the woods from a world that he was currently setting on fire, the self-made pharmacist Morell used the war in the Ukraine to extend his enterprises.

Sensing a huge source of business, he developed a plan that was as simple as it was brazen. He informed Alfred Rosenberg, the Nazi chief ideologist and Reich minister for the occupied eastern zones, that he wanted to found an 'organotherapeutic factory': 'If I am granted the accruals, it will be possible for me to supply the whole of the east with hormones.'[54] By *accruals*, Morell meant thyroid glands, adrenal glands, testicles, prostates, ovaries, Cowper's glands, gall bladders, hearts and lungs – nothing less than all the glands and organs as well as all the bones of all the animals slaughtered in Vinnytsia.

From a business point of view this was a fantastic opportunity to exploit raw materials for the manufacture of doping agents and steroids. Morell was moving restlessly through the occupied country during these weeks to organize his dirty deals. He wanted the right to process all leftovers. He even wanted to recycle the blood of the slaughtered animals for the manufacture of a new nutritional preparation, which was to consist of dried blood and vegetables (mostly carrots).[55] 'I'm often very tired from all the driving,' he wrote to his wife: 'I cover 300 km every other day, sometimes every day. And that on bad Russian cobbled roads.'[56] He planned to drain every last drop of blood from occupied Ukraine to the literal marrow and had taken unscrupulousness to a new level. Increasingly unabashed, he used his consolidated position of power at the court as his own kind of official government department.

The *Gauleiter* Erich Koch, the Reich Commissar of the Ukraine (known as 'Little Stalin' because of his brutality, and also a patient of Morell's), was only too happy to cooperate: wherever animals were slaughtered the doctor would henceforth be authorized to 'collect the waste products required for the manufacture of organotherapeutic medications [. . .] and supply them for the desired application'.[57] Morell expressed his thanks and immediately announced further plans: 'Once I have glands and internal organ matters in order, I will appraise the medical herbs and drugs of the Ukraine. You will see that the organization will be a great success.'[58]

He quickly set up the 'Ukrainian Pharma-Works, Vinnitsia Plant, Manufacturer of Organotherapeutic and Plant Products – Drugs Export'. The firm was immediately set on an expansion course. Morell was not satisfied with western Ukraine but had his eye on the lucrative industrial zone in the Donets Basin. He also set his sights on the steppes by the Black Sea and the Crimea. There he planned to plant 'medical herbs on a large scale, to participate in a strong German economy'.[59]

He was particularly keen on Kharkov, the metropolis in the eastern Ukraine taken by the 6th Army back in October 1941 as a strategically important city, the fourth largest in the Soviet Union. Since its occupation by the Wehrmacht Germany had imposed death and destruction on the city: two thirds of the buildings had been destroyed and the number of inhabitants reduced from 1.5 million to 190,000. Soviet citizens had been thrown from their balconies and hanged in hallways and the doorways of banks and hotels.[60] In the ravine of Drobytsky Yar, SS-Sonderkommando 4a, a unit of Einsatzgruppe C, along with Orp Batallion 314, had carried out a massacre of the Jewish population: 15,000 people were shot; women and children had also been killed in gas wagons. Many inhabitants of Kharkov were transported to Germany as forced labourers, and when an attempt was made by the Red Army to liberate the city in May 1942, some 240,000 Soviet soldiers were imprisoned.

None of that bothered Morell in the slightest. On the contrary, the desperate situation of Kharkov seemed to inspire him: 'It's an unusually interesting task, in a city that has changed possession several times, to take anything that can possibly be taken from it for the war economy,' he wrote to Koch.[61] When he learned that there was an institute of endocrinology in Kharkov that specialized in the treatment of internal secretory glands, Morell turned to Koch again: 'As the institute which belonged to the Russian state is pointless without a supply of glands, and you have been so kind as to allow these bodily organs to me when slaughter takes place, I should like to ask permission to buy this institute and to start the processing of the glands and the manufacture of the materials that are so urgently needed in Germany.'[62]

The answer came the same day by telephone: Morell could have his institute; it was 'transferred' to him. The instruction was now issued to all eighteen abattoirs in the Ukraine: 'According to the decree of the Reich Commissar of the Ukraine organs accruing in the abattoirs [. . .] are to be delivered exclusively and continuously to the Ukrain. Pharma-Works. They should be freed of fat, frozen two hours after slaughter to -15 degrees or brought to the lowest possible temperature.'[63]

Nothing now stood in the way of the new development and mass production of hormone preparations. The doctor wallowed in these prospects, treasuring his own personal exploitation of the Eastern Front: 'We need all that we can get from glands.'[64] Things could never be more favourable: 'I hope that the vacuum drying equipment and the extraction devices will soon arrive. Then the large-scale business can begin.'[65]

But he was running out of time; cheap access to the east wouldn't go on for ever. The front was crumbling, and Morell was unable to take any pleasure from his endocrinology institute. In the spring of 1943 Kharkov was retaken by the Red Army.

'Unfortunately, the events were stronger than we were, and shattered our beautiful hopes and the initial stages of our work,'[66] Morell reported disappointedly, and concentrated on his work in Olmütz in Bohemia–Moravia again.

To transport masses of raw animal materials there, a journey of over 1,000 kilometres, and thus to make as much profit as possible out of the Ukraine, he moved heaven and earth, or rather the whole state apparatus. It was quite natural for the 'Führer's personal physician', as his letterhead had it, to reinforce his own wishes by claiming Hitler's full agreement.

In a phase of the war that was taut to breaking point, when there were only a few hotly disputed communication routes to the east, which were urgently needed for bringing supplies to the troops as well as returning wounded soldiers, Morell blithely used the logistics of the Führer's headquarters to send hundreds of trucks and Reichsbahn wagons countless kilometres across Eastern Europe to shift his plundered tons of pigs' stomachs, pancreatic and pituitary glands, spinal cords and cows', pigs' and sheeps' livers. The strict instruction to everyone at the Führer's headquarters to 'prevent any non-crucial vehicle use' plainly didn't apply to him.[67] He even transported chickens' feet, which were boiled down to make gelatine. The loading list of a typical Morell wagon was: seventy barrels of salted liver, 1,026 pigs' stomachs,60 kilograms of ovaries, 200 kilograms of bulls' testicles. Value: 20,000 Reichsmarks.[68]

A delivery like this came from the Ukraine to his Aryanized factory in occupied Czechoslovakia almost every day. Major Wehrmacht transports remained stranded, because Morell was merciless: if a train with goods for the Ukrainian Pharma-Works didn't get through quickly enough, he picked up the phone and approached the highest authorities 'about the wagon provision'. He would approach the transport commandant's office, then move on to the head of the railways or then to the Reich transport minister, referring to his position and threatening serious trouble if the wagons were not authorized 'to travel with the greatest level of urgency, and made available ideally with a Wehrmacht letter of conveyance'.[69] If his opposite number complied, he was rewarded with the prospect of being presented to Hitler – or at least given a box of silver-wrapped high-class Vitamultin bars.[70] Morell always had his way: his urgent desires were passed on from office to office as factual orders.

This led to even more toxic consequences. To keep his factories operational and as profitable as possible, he did not baulk at the use of forced labour: 'At the moment we are having difficulties getting hold of untrained workers [. . .] so that the loading of wagons with Vitamultin can only be done by girls,' his chief chemist, Dr Kurt Mulli, reported. 'So I will try to import prisoners from time to time. Perhaps it might be possible for you to fetch me a confirmation via Bormann's office that our work deserves top priority.'[71] Mulli knew that his boss could influence even the mighty Martin Bormann, the widely feared *Reichsleiter* of the NSDAP and the Führer's private secretary.

During those months Morell bought such quantities of organs that he exceeded his own capacities. But he insisted on a Ukrainian monopoly and preferred to let the goods rot rather than allow others to help treat them: 'I cannot be expected to pass the raw materials on to my competitors. [. . .] The right to collect and process the glands and organs in the Ukraine belongs exclusively to me.'[72]

Morell focused his attention chiefly on livers. As an organ with an important metabolic function, it breaks down and produces a great variety of substances. Among these are male sexual hormones formed from cholesterol which induce a muscle-building, potency-increasing effect, or corticoids or glucocorticoids, which were seen as miracle remedies because they raise short-term energy levels. Morell was optimistic that these, according to the state of research at the time, would have effects that were both stimulating and generally beneficial. But the liver also contains substances including a great variety of pathogens that provoke immunological reactions – and can set in motion a form of auto-self-destruction if the body is unable to distinguish harmful from harmless materials.

The more chaotic the progress of the war, the more often the frozen livers thawed during transport, because the journey was inevitably stalled for several days. Sometimes it could be three weeks before they reached Olomouc (Olmütz), where the foul-smelling organs were boiled for many hours in large pots with added acetone and methyl alcohol. The poisons were distilled out of them, and what remained was a brown pulp with the consistency of honey. It was diluted with water and put into ampoules: 10,000 per day, labelled 'Hamma Liver'.

But did such a brew ever find its way to the consumer? To the doctor's chagrin, from May 1943 no new medication was allowed to be introduced to the market, due to the regulations of the war economy. But Morell was even able to negotiate that hurdle. Autocratically he turned to the responsible Reich Health Office, run by Reich Health Führer Conti: 'In response to the description of the difficulties that I've been having with my remedies, the Führer has authorized me to do the following: if I bring out and test a remedy and then apply it in the Führer's headquarters, and apply it successfully, then it can be applied everywhere in Germany and no longer needs authorization.'[73]

As sick as it might sound: Morell, formerly a popular doctor from the Kurfürstendamm, now with a pharmaceutical empire that he had built out of nothing, used his patients in the Führer's headquarters – and in all likelihood Hitler himself – as guinea pigs for dubious hormonal preparations and steroids, produced often enough in disastrously unhygienic conditions, then introduced into the bloodstream by injection. The resulting concoction was released into the Reich and to the Wehrmacht: the auto-immunological downfall.

'X' and the Total Loss of Reality

> The Führer's appearance is rather deceptive in regards to his health. If one looks at him only fleetingly, one has the impression that he is in excellent physical condition. But this is not in fact the case.
>
> Joseph Goebbels[74]

With the capitulation of the remains of the 6th Army in Stalingrad, early in February 1943 the Wehrmacht had lost its halo – and, with it, Hitler. His outward reaction was always the same, whether it was to the military disaster on the Volga, Rommel's defeat by the British in Africa, the devastating bombing raids on German cities in the

Ruhr by the Royal Air Force, or the submarine battle in the Atlantic which the Germans were losing. Hitler was consumed by total isolation, accompanied by the unequivocal conviction that only *his* decisions could be correct. He stubbornly insisted on the obvious outcome of a 'final victory', and showed no willingness whatsoever to base his decisions on reason or sobriety. Instead of facing up to the changed situation and seeking new strategies such as a peaceful solution, the system still further ossified – paralleling the condition of Patient A.

Loneliness surrounded Hitler. He visited his Werwolf headquarters for only a few days in the whole of 1943. Otherwise he retreated to the Wolf's Lair again like a wounded animal, where the communal meals and nocturnal tea-drinking sessions were felt to be more and more excruciating. Hitler engaged in lengthy and enervating conversations with himself, spells which lasted until the early morning. These waffling monologues could go on for hours; the Führer's soft baritone addressing no one in particular. Instead his eyes gazed into the distance as if he were talking to a vast and invisible following. He never grew tired of going over his favourite themes yet again: talking about the harmfulness of smoking, preaching against the poisoning of the body and praising his own vegetarian diet, which his personal physician, who received a tax-free allowance of over 100,000 Reichsmarks on 30 January 1943, had recommended on the basis of its vitamin content and restorative properties. To calm his nerves he had the occasion to neglect rules that had once seemed incontrovertible: after dinner Patient A now sometimes drank a beer, or knocked back a slivovitz, which had previously been analysed by the field laboratory, acting on the Führer's orders, for methyl alcohol.[75]

That year, when the fate of the war turned once and for all, a physiological transformation occurred in the rapidly ageing *Gröfaz*. 'Hitler came to me, bent by a heavy burden, with slow, rather weary steps,' wrote one lieutenant general. 'It was as if an inner voice were talking to me: "Look at this old man! He can't carry what he's burdened himself with!" Hitler had declined, and with great emotion I looked into dull, tired eyes. No doubt, those eyes were ill.'[76]

Morell could no longer ignore the physical degradation of the dictator and the demotivating effect that it had on others. But what would cure his patient and turn him back into the leader everyone admired? The cocktail of hormones, steroids and vitamins was clearly no longer enough.

18 July 1943 was a special date. The situation was unusually tense. The Red Army had won the greatest tank battle in military history at Kursk, and thus destroyed all German hopes of a turnaround in Russia. At the same time the Allies had landed in Sicily, and Italy was about to switch sides and abandon its alliance with Germany. Hitler saw all his hopes going up in smoke, and because of the imminent 'betrayal of the Italian army [. . .] he had not slept a wink', as Morell wrote. 'Body tensed hard as a board, full of gases. *Very* pale appearance, extremely nervous. Tomorrow very important discussion with Duce.'[77]

In the middle of the night Morell was dragged from his bed by Heinz Linge, Hitler's valet: the Führer was bent double with pain, and an immediate cure was required. The white cheese he had had for dinner as well as the roulades with spinach and peas had disagreed with him. Morell gave him an injection, but the basic medical treatment didn't work. The doctor wondered feverishly what needed to be done to combat the 'great attack'[78] in this precarious situation. He needed something that worked, something that would numb Hitler's severe pain and keep him functioning. He needed an ace from up his sleeve, and in fact he did have something. But its use was risky.

For the second quarter of 1943, in the bottom right corner of file card 'Pat. A', a substance is listed and underlined several times: Eukodal. A drug manufactured by Merck in Darmstadt, it came on to the market as a painkiller and a cough medicine in 1917, and was so popular in the 1920s that the word 'Eukodalism' was coined. Its extremely potent active ingredient is an opioid called Oxycodon, synthesized from the raw material of opium. The substance was a hot topic among doctors in the Weimar Republic, because many physicians quietly took the narcotic themselves. In specialist circles Eukodal was the queen of remedies: a wonder drug. Almost twice as pain-relieving as morphine, which it replaced in popularity, this archetypal designer opioid was characterized by its potential to create very swiftly a euphoric state significantly higher than that of heroin, its pharmacological cousin. Used properly, Eukodal did not make the patient tired or knock him out – quite the contrary. The author Klaus Mann, who (to the sorrow of his father, Thomas, the famous novelist) was highly experimental in this respect, as in many others, confirms the special status of the substance: 'I don't take pure morphium. What I take is called Eukodal. *Sister Euka*. We find it has a nicer effect.'[79]

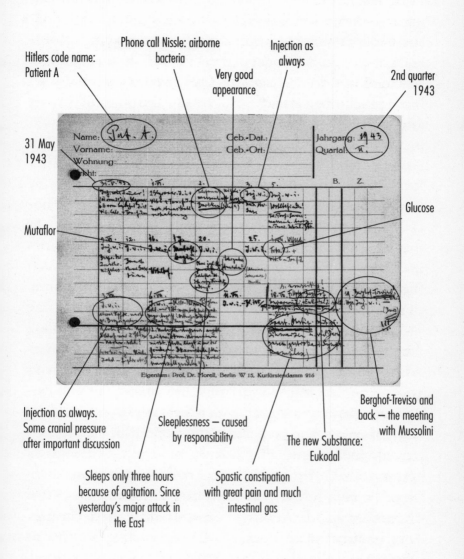

Hitlers code name:
Patient A

Phone call Nissle: airborne
bacteria

Very good
appearance

Injection as
always

2nd quarter
1943

31 May
1943

Mutaflor

Glucose

Injection as always.
Some cranial pressure
after important discussion

Sleeplessness — caused
by responsibility

The new Substance:
Eukodal

Berghof-Treviso and
back — the meeting
with Mussolini

Sleeps only three hours
because of agitation. Since
yesterday's major attack in
the East

Spastic constipation
with great pain and much
intestinal gas

Patient A's file card for the summer of 1943:
first use of the narcotic Eukodal.

Morell debated with himself whether to use this hard drug. The moment of departure for the important meeting with Mussolini was edging closer. Patient A seemed apathetic, was hunched over and talking to no one. Morell knew that Eukodal would pep the Führer up straight away and remove the violent spastic constipation that probably had a psychological cause. But he saw the possibility that after trying it just once, the addiction-prone dictator would be very unwilling to give up this supposed nectar of the gods. After only two to three weeks of regular use, Eukodal can make a person physically dependent on it. On the other hand, world history seemed at stake. The chance that Hitler might not be up to a state meeting of the Axis powers, or that he might even cancel it, was quite unthinkable. Morell decided to take the risk. He injected the new drug subcutaneously – under the skin. It was a momentous decision.

The immediate transformation of Patient A in the minutes and hours after the application was so striking that no one in his entourage could fail to spot it – even if, of course, no one learned the cause for his abrupt change of mood. Everyone sighed with relief at the boss's sudden burst of energy and prepared enthusiastically for the meeting with the Italians. Hitler seemed suddenly in such good spirits that he promptly requested another dose, but Morell initially refused, 'as there were still some important discussions and decisions to be made before the departure at 15.30'. Instead he offered a massage and a spoonful of olive oil, but that didn't suit Hitler, who now claimed to feel dizzy, again jeopardizing his departure. Whether he ordered another injection of the powerful substance or

Morell provided one on his own initiative is not recorded. At any rate the personal physician gave a second injection, intramuscular this time: 'Before leaving for the airfield one Eukodal ampoule i.m.'[80]

A US secret service report written after the war and all eye-witness accounts confirm that Hitler was hyped up at his meeting with Mussolini in the Villa Gaggia near Feltre in the Veneto. The Führer talked for three hours without a break in a dull voice to his beleaguered fellow dictator, who didn't get a single opportunity to speak, but just sat impatiently with his legs crossed on the edge of a chair too big for him, frantically gripping one knee. Mussolini had actually planned to convince Hitler that it would be better for everyone if Italy came out of the war, but all he did was knead his painful back from time to time, dab his forehead with a handkerchief, or sigh deeply. The door kept opening to pass on new reports about the bombing of Rome, which was happening at that very moment. Mussolini couldn't even comment on this, because Hitler was talking non-stop to a room full of painfully embarrassed people about how no one should doubt the imminent victory of the Axis powers. The dejected Duce was effectively talked into the ground by the artificially pepped-up Führer. The result of the meeting: Italy would stick at it for the time being. Morell felt vindicated. He seemed to have manoeuvred high-level politics with his injections, and he noted self-importantly: 'Führer fit and well. No complaints whatsoever on the return flight. Führer declared in the Obersalzberg in the evening that the success of the day was to my credit.'[81]

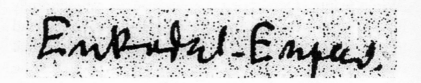

Undecipherable: Morell's handwriting.

A molecule or two away from the pharmacological truth, US investigators after the war suspected that meth-amphetamine was the cause of Hitler's giddy behaviour at his meeting with Mussolini. However, they provided no proof. Why the Americans failed to spot Eukodal, which Morell had recorded in black and white, is clear from the official translations into English of Morell's barely decipherable notes. In these the United States Forces European Military Intelligence Service centre wrongly lists among Hitler's countless medications one called 'Enkadol'.[82] But since no medication of that name appears in the list of narcotics no further importance was placed on it. The idea that it might be *Eukodal* didn't occur to the investigators, particularly since no drug of that name was known in the United States.[83] Morell's scribbled handwriting put the Americans on the wrong track.

Taking Eukodal

Eukodol [sic] is like a combination of junk and C [cocaine]. Trust the Germans to concoct some truly awful shit.

William Burroughs[84]

With the introduction of the new drug, Morell, spitefully described by Göring as the 'Reich Injection Master', had finally made his breakthrough.[85] During the nocturnal tea-drinking session, which was the barometer for telling who was in Hitler's good books, Morell was now the only regular guest. 'He simply had to be there,' wrote Traudl Junge, Hitler's secretary.[86] His relationship with Hitler had become symbiotic.

Financially, too, the doctor's activities had paid off: by now he was seriously wealthy. In 1943, the first Eukodal year, he wondered how he could expand his enterprises still further, and decided to move actively into the opium business. A lucrative pursuit: opium was in short supply because of mounting demand. Since Rommel's defeat in Africa and the landing of British and American troops in Casablanca the German Reich had been cut off from the poppy fields of Morocco. The military situation had also capped the supply routes from Persia and Afghanistan. In the Reich, IG Farben/Hoechst had been looking for a completely synthetic substitute for natural morphine since 1937, and were still in the development phase of a substance that would later become known as Polamidon or methadone. The hunger for an effective painkiller was growing daily, from one overfilled military hospital to the next. Opiates were a precious commodity, particularly during this all-encompassing war with its countless shattered casualties.

Morell wouldn't have been Morell if he hadn't spotted a goldmine here too. He extended his dense network of companies all by himself by phone and mail from his official room in the Führer's headquarters. In Riga he bought the firm Farmacija for the sole reason that it had an opium laboratory and an interesting storeroom: 'The warehouse, with a value of 400,000 RM, contains a supply of raw morphine and opium to a value of about 200,000 RM.'[87] This would also discreetly secure supplies for Patient A. For a long time Hitler's drugs had been bought through the Engel chemist's shop in Berlin, but recently the pharmacist there, Herr Jost, had repeatedly demanded 'prescriptions in line with the regulations of the narcotic drugs act so that they can be entered in the narcotics list'.[88]

Thus, Hitler's personal physician became an opium producer, and in the second half of 1943 – when the Wehrmacht was forced to retreat along the whole of the Eastern Front – the game continued. Outwardly acting the part of the abstainer who works tirelessly for the fate of Germany,[89] Hitler allowed himself the luxury of Eukodal in the spartan, windowless concrete hole of his headquarters. We can only surmise how often he took the drug. Twenty-four applications are recorded by the end of 1944. But was that all? One is struck by a lapidary 'x' that occurs frequently in Morell's entries. Also the remark 'injection as always' gives the reader pause because the phrase is meaningless when applied to the case of a multi-drug-user who consumed many dozens of different substances every week.

If it is true that a dictatorship is defined as a secret that as few people as possible know, but which affects as many people as possible,[90] then Morell's treatment was truly totalitarian. As long as no one knew of the clandestine activities within Hitler's own body, he remained unimpeachable. For Morell there were only two possibilities:

either limit the use of Eukodal or encrypt his record of it, to protect himself and his patient against outside attacks. If Hitler demanded the substance in greater quantities – explicitly or by subtle means – the doctor applied the cipher. That may have been why the dictator was so determined that his physician should never leave his side, but should always remain available – to give him that 'x': the biochemical buffer between him and the world. At one point there is a marginal note explaining the placeholder, claiming that 'x' means nothing more or less than glucose. However, glucose is often abbreviated to 'Trbz.' (*Traubenzucker*), so the statement loses credibility.

We may assume that 'x' at times referred to Eukodal, which Hitler used to make himself look outwardly convincing, and to artificially conjure up the old magic that he had previously radiated quite naturally. The dictator's notorious suggestive powers, particularly in difficult situations, are well known. In his diary entry for 10 September 1943, for example, Goebbels raves about Hitler's surprisingly fresh physical appearance, even though 'the exertions of the last day and the last night have of course been huge. [. . .] Contrary to expectation his appearance is extraordinarily good [. . .] He has had hardly two hours' sleep, and now looks as if he had just come back from a holiday.'[91] Reich Commissar Koch spoke with similar enthusiasm about the contagious effect: 'I myself have been charged with new energy, and left my discussion with the Führer freshly inspired.'[92] On 7 October 1943 all the *Reichs-* and *Gauleiter* (Reich and district leaders) came to the Wolf's Lair for a meeting to lament the increasing unimpeded air raids on German cities. A pharmacologically bolstered Hitler delivered a fiery speech in which he expressed his unshakeable conviction about an imminent victory so winningly that his guests returned optimistically to their bombed-out communities, firmly believing that the Reich must have some special innovation that would finally deliver victory. '11 o'clock: injection as always. Right forearm very swollen. Appearance very good,' Morell noted for this day.[93] And when Hitler flew shortly afterwards to Breslau (Wrocław) to boost the morale of several thousand junior officers from all parts of the Wehrmacht, Morell was at the ready with his syringe: 'Injection as always.'[94] The result: loud chants of '*Sieg Heil!*' from the young officers, who returned to battle freshly motivated.

Hitler's closest colleagues, like the members of his High Command, who were not *au fait* with these drug fixes often reacted with incomprehension and disbelief to their Führer's unrealistic optimism. Did Hitler know something they didn't? Did he have some kind of miracle weapon up his sleeve that could turn the war around? In fact it was the immediate high of the injections that allowed Hitler to feel like a world ruler and gave him a sense of the strength and unshakeable confidence that he needed to make everyone else keep the faith in spite of all the desperate reports coming from every front. A typical Morell entry from this period: '12.30 p.m.: because of talk to the General Staff (*c.* 105 generals) injection as before.'[95]

For Christmas 1943 – with the Red Army just beginning the Dnieper–Carpathian operation in continuation of its summer offensive – Morell was sent a centenary edition of Goethe's *Faust* by the Bavarian Ministry of the Interior, to 'remind you not only of your friends in Munich, but also of your student days when you, as you tell us, were known as Mephisto'. This short inscription contains nothing less than the core of this German drama about Hitler and his personal physician. 'But then, as today, you were certainly not the evil spirit, but the good one,' the state secretary added and, being unaware of the actual circumstances, probably thought nothing more about it.[96] Morell wrote a letter of thanks for the special edition by return of post. We may doubt whether he had much time to immerse himself in the book. Treating Patient A kept him busy around the clock.

The increasing biochemical entrenchment of the Führer had one other consequence: anyone who wanted a talk with him was soon also grateful for a pharmacological booster to help survive the meeting unscathed. Communicating in a state of dejection, exhaustion or even just sobriety with a doped-up commander on whom your life depended, one who could forgive no one, even himself, the slightest sign of despondency, became too precarious for many. Hitler couldn't bear failure or weakness: anyone who looked ill, slack or even uninspired was quickly out of the picture. He had often explained the dismissal of a prominent figure as being on grounds simply of ill-health.[97] Morell took advantage once again: as there was no sick room in Restricted Area 1, the doctor with his field pharmacy in the 'drone barracks' was the man with the emergency supply on site. Hitler's valet, Linge, for example, was immediately given the hardcore drug Eukodal even for a case of flu, so that he could stay fit for duty and good-humoured. The fat doctor always kept a supply of different remedies for officers, adjutants or orderlies and thus inveigled himself into the good books of the aides who were so important for life in the bunker. The doctor also liked to help generals who wanted to put themselves in a calm, confident state before meeting their supreme commander.[98]

Pervitin was considered the most effective substance for surviving a briefing. Morell knew about the dangers of the upper and wrote to a patient who asked for a prescription from him: 'This isn't a power food. It isn't oats for the horse, it's the whip!'[99] And yet he unhesitatingly handed out the Temmler preparation, and word of the use of methamphetamines in the Wolf's Lair made waves as far as Berlin.[100] Conti, Pervitin's old enemy, got wind of the way the drug was being doled out so generously and wrote to Bormann requesting that all district leaders and prominent Party members be informed about the dangers of so-called 'stimulants'. He assumed that there were high levels of abuse even at senior levels. Bormann's reaction to the letter is unknown.

What we do know is that if Hitler's visitors needed exponentially harder drugs to withstand the pressure in that meeting room, this further reinforced an atmosphere of augmented reality in the inner circles of the Nazi leadership. The long-term consumption by Patient A, which no one was allowed to know about, was contagious. Hitler's multi-addictive presence replaced any relationship with reality among all the people in his immediate entourage.

One Reich, One Dealer

The extent of systematic drug abuse in the Nazi state is apparent from documents that refer to dubious connections between the army's main medical depot and the German military secret service. In 1943 the Wehrmacht's central pharmacy delivered 568 kilograms of pure cocaine and 60 kilograms of pure heroin to the Foreign/Counter-Intelligence Office.[101] These are huge quantities that exceed the annual medical requirements of the entire German Reich many times over. Spies, however, had no authorization from the opium section of the Reich Health Office to receive these 'special deliveries'. The lion's share went to a Department Z, which took care of the organization and administration of the secret service, as well as Department ZF, which was responsible for finances. The latter department on its own received half a ton of cocaine hydrochloride, a quantity worth millions. Might this have been a way of getting hold of foreign currency by exporting pure substances? Perhaps it was also used to bribe important contacts abroad, whom the Nazis wanted to keep onside in difficult times.

In December 1943 the Army Medical Inspector wrote an urgent letter to put a stop to these clandestine deals. He prohibited the distribution for any reason other than 'healing purposes in the usual doses'.[102] This demand didn't impress the head of counter-intelligence, Admiral Canaris. In April 1944, 2 kilograms of cocaine hydrochloride, 1.5 kilograms of morphine hydrochloride and 200 grams of heroin were delivered to SS-Sonderkommando Wimmer in North Africa, which was carrying out the sabotage operations against the Allies in the Sahara, and possibly doing a thriving drugs trade at the same time. The deliveries to the secret service were made on the express wishes of the recipients. They wanted Merck's cocaine in its original packaging: that internationally popular product from Darmstadt.[103] What was done with it has not as yet been discovered. One Reich, one dealer.

Patient B

Either you give up smoking or you give up me.
Adolf Hitler to Eva Braun[104]

When General Field Marshal von Manstein demanded at the briefing session on 4 January 1944 that the front on the Dnieper river bend be drawn back to avoid a further military disaster, Hitler became so worked up that, 'because of spasms', he called for Morell, who gave him a restorative Eukodal injection that calmed him down.[105] On the same day the Red Army crossed the 1939 eastern Polish border and marched relentlessly towards the German Reich. Five days later Hitler once again demanded the strong opioid, 'for flatulence (excitement)', as Morell recorded[106] – and when the dictator had to speak to his people shortly afterwards in a radio address, the doctor noted: 'Afternoon, 5.40 p.m.: before big speech (radio for tomorrow) injection as always.'[107]

At the end of February 1944 the Wehrmacht was on the point of having to retreat from the whole of Ukraine and Hitler was holed up in the snowy Berghof, his frozen cloud-cuckoo-land of a home in Obersalzberg, where his lover, Eva, nineteen years his junior, was staying. A place where he could watch ravens and perform his wearying impersonations of the sounds made by different machine guns used in the Second World War – whether he did so high or not, we cannot tell. And at teatime there was always steaming hot streusel cake made from a family recipe by Morell's wife, Hanni: 'the best *Streuselkuchen* in the world'.[108]

Dense snow was falling outside the enormous panoramic window of the big drawing room. Opposite was the mystical Untersberg, which lay covered in white, glittering in the winter light. Legend had it that the Emperor Barbarossa slept there until his resurrection and the reinstatement of a glorious Reich. Since the defeat in Stalingrad Hitler had an almost physical dread of snow, and called it the shroud of the mountains. The Führer barely stepped outside the door.

In any case the situation offered little comfort to the Germans. The Russians, clearly resistant to the cold, were preparing to retake the Crimea, and the coolly rational British were bombing Berlin and other cities in the frozen Reich. Germany's former allies, Bulgaria, Romania and Hungary, threatened to break away from Hitler and defeats accumulated everywhere. In Italy the Allies were marching northwards slowly but inexorably. Successful field marshals like von Manstein[109] and von Kleist*[110]

---

* When arresting him, the Americans found the 63-year-old general and tank commander with his hands trembling. The drawers in his lodgings were filled with opiates and syringes.

were dismissed because they persisted in expressing views of their own.

Hitler's personal physician certainly wasn't fired – quite the contrary. On 24 February 1944 his patient awarded him the Knight's Cross of the War Merit Cross. While bestowing him with this high honour, Hitler described him as a gifted doctor, the saviour of his life and a pioneering but misunderstood researcher in the field of vitamins and hormones.[111] By way of thanks, a short time later the freshly decorated physician gave his patient 'Vitamultin injections for the first time (for fatigue and freshness). Before the injection very tired and exhausted, without sleep. After that very lively. Two hours' discussion with Reich foreign minister. In the evening over dinner very fresh compared with midday, very lively discussion. Führer extremely pleased!'[112]

Morell also treated Eva Braun more often now: Patient B made the work easy for him, as she demanded the same medication as Patient A in order to be on the same wavelength as her lover. In his hormone dispensation, however, Morell made an exception from this synchronization. Hitler received testosterone for his libido, while Braun was given medication to suppress menstruation so that quite literally speaking their chemistry was right, and they could at least enjoy some sexual success in the momentary breaks between increasingly lengthy military briefings. At any rate that was what Hitler strived for, despite rumours to the contrary. He even on occasion claimed that relationships outside marriage were in many respects superior, since they were rooted in natural sexual attraction. He seemed convinced of the beneficial effect of physical love: without sex, he claimed, there was no art, no painting and no music. No civilized nation, Catholic Italy included, could manage without extra-marital intercourse. Morell in turn provided indirect information about the kind of copulation performed at the Berghof, when he stated after the war that Hitler had sometimes cancelled medical investigations to conceal wounds on his body from Eva Braun's aggressive sexual behaviour.[113]

Outwardly the image of a healthy 'Führer world' was widespread even in the spring of 1944, in spite of the disastrous military situation. The Berghof, whose walls were hung with the works of old masters, played an important part in the dissemination of propaganda, and contributed considerably to the continuing media imple-mentation of the Führer cult. When the man and his faithful German shepherd, Blondi, stood at the edge of the forest in early spring, gazing into the distance, Braun (personally trained by the official Reich photographer, Heinrich Hoffmann) was always there, having chosen his ties beforehand. Issuing instructions on how Hitler should pose, she put her Agfa Movex into action. Even today clips shot by Braun still circulate on the internet. Anyone who sees these pictures might think that Hitler was the most ascetic, conscientious, modest person in the world. No hard drugs are injected; instead fawns come into view or, failing that, children are stroked and Easter eggs hid-den, while the self-justifying Speer paces back and forth on the terrace in his light-grey pinstripe. The personal doctor can also be seen munching cake and putting a brave face on things.

Eva Braun stands in for Leni Riefenstahl in capturing Hitler on film.

But when Eva Braun turned the camera off, the masks fell straight away, and she again started digging her fingernails into her forearm and biting her lips until they bled – while Hitler's hand shook so much when he was drinking apple tea that the cup rattled on the saucer, embarrassing everyone. As for Morell, he was so run down by now that he could hardly climb a flight of stairs. Admittedly the personal physician found no rest, because everyone needed him. Going to see the fat doctor was part of *bon ton*. Meanwhile his patients had come to include all the top-ranking officials of the Reich and their allies: he treated Mussolini, who was given the code name

'Patient D'; industrialists like Alfried Krupp or August Thyssen (fee for treatment 20,000 Reichsmarks[114]); many *Gauleiter* and Wehrmacht generals; Leni Riefenstahl, who was given morphine enemas; the SS chief, Himmler; the foreign minister, von Ribbentrop ('Patient X', or 'Rippenshit', as American Intelligence later nicknamed him); the Minister of Armaments, Albert Speer; the Japanese ambassador, General Hiroshi Oshima; and the wife of Reich Marshal Göring, who had injections on alternate days of 'Vitamultin forte' – whatever was hidden behind that label.

More and more influential National Socialists made the pilgrimage to Morell – even if it was only a way of announcing their closeness to Hitler and confirming their own position. Above all, of course, Hitler claimed the time of his personal physician, and Morell, who was himself in poor health by now, complained to the wife of the economics minister, Funk, another patient: 'At all times of day and night I have to follow the instructions that I get from above. At the moment I drive up to the Führer at noon to possibly give him treatment, and come back to the hotel at almost two o'clock in the afternoon, to lie in bed all day so that I'm able to accompany the Führer again the following day.' By now Morell was hooked on the needle himself, and his assistant, Dr Weber, had to travel from Berlin to the remote Berghof, as he 'is the best at giving injections, and the only one guaranteed to find my veins'.[115] What Morell was treating himself with is not recorded.

Illnesses, medicines and mass murder define everyday life at the Berghof in the first half of 1944. The bowling alley, still an attraction in the 1930s, was hardly used now. Camouflage nets hung over the famous panoramic window because of the constant fear of air raids; everyone vegetated in an eternal twilight, sitting around, either by a stove on the bench or in expensive armchairs, staring at the dust-gathering Gobelins: vampire-like figures who had a fear of natural light. Even when the sun shone outside, the electric lamps were burning inside. The thick carpets gave off a musty smell.

The supreme commander of the Navy came for the Führer's fifty-fifth birthday: Grand Admiral Dönitz reported on the establishment of a special unit with miracle weapons, brought models of new mini-submarines as a present and asked his commander-in-chief to do everything to keep the Baltic ports open in return. Hitler, as mad for boats as a child for toys, blindly promised Dönitz that he would. On his birthday Patient A's personal physician injected him with a cocktail of 'x', Vitamultin forte, camphor and the plant-based coronary prophylactic Strophanthin,[116] followed the next morning by an injection of Prostrophanta, a concoction for heart conditions made by Morell's company, Hamma. There were also intravenous injections of glucose, more Vitamultin and, as the cherry on the cake, a home-made preparation of parasite-liver, whose intramuscular injection would immediately brand a medical practitioner today as a quack, and possibly put him behind bars.[117] Patient A sincerely thanked his physician as the only one who could help him.

The birthday party was disturbed only by an air raid warning: the sirens wailed, the big artificial fog device was turned on and the Berghof, that refuge from reality, sank into artificial whiteness like a nightmare version of mystic Avalon, cut off from the world by an opaque veil. For fear of damage to his heart and 'ever greater breathlessness [from] discharged gas' Morell briefly fled to the valley.[118]

Everything was back to normal at dinner-time. Hitler had once again demonstrated his moral superiority by describing his guests' beef bouillon as 'corpse brew', ate some Harz mountain cheese, with spinach pudding, stuffed gherkins, barley gruel, kohlrabi balls and six Vitamultin bars, as well as Euflat and anti-gas pills for his flatulence, and pig's heart muscle extract in phosphoric acid as a general tonic. After dinner the supposed vegetarian dozed off briefly while gripping his knife, his hands folded over his belly. His magical doctor's terrible table manners are still the stuff of legend: having downed his obligatory glass of port, Morell also leaned back in his armchair and closed his eyes behind his thick spectacle lenses – as always, he closed them from bottom to top, a feared, gruesome-looking oddity of Morell's. Both men had weak hearts, and both were gradually growing old.

Eva Braun had lit the fire and put on an American jazz record. She wanted to watch *Gone with the Wind* for the thousandth time because of her affinity for Clark Gable, her favourite actor. With stolen gold from Jewish fillings lining his mouth, *Reichsleiter* Bormann brushed the idea aside with a cynical smile: 'The Führer doesn't need the relaxation of a movie . . . what he needs is a powerful shot.'[119] Morell gave a start, thought someone was talking to him, was ashamed of his sleepiness and quickly told everyone a story from the old days, from his time as a ship's doctor in Africa, which they all knew anyway. Then apple cake was served. After eating, Hitler's stomach cramps were eased with Eukodal in his private quarters: 'When I put this into your vein, please start slowly counting. Once you have reached fifteen, you won't feel any more pain.'[120]

In the weeks after his birthday, while the Red Army prepared 'Operation Bagration', which would free their way to East Prussia from the end of June 1944, Hitler's health deteriorated further. Eva, usually accompanied by her Scotch terriers, Stasi and Negus, was more and more appalled by the worsening appearance and increasingly frail constitution of her long-term lover. When she criticized him for walking with a stoop he tried to play down his unstoppable decline by joking that he was carrying heavy keys in his pocket. His knees were now obviously trembling when he stood on the balcony for more than a few moments, the two of them looking out on a clear day at the reddening sky above far-off, burning Munich, and Eva wondering fearfully whether her smart little house, which Hitler had bought for her in the elegant district of Bogenhausen, was still standing. Hitler was nearly finished off, and Goebbels had probably seldom lied more shamelessly than when he wrote in his diary entry for 6 June 1944, the day of the Allied Normandy landings: 'Professor Morell is helping me a little to improve the slightly weakened state of my health. He has also been a strong support to the Führer's health recently. At my meeting with the Führer I can confirm that he looks dazzling, and that he is in good spirits.'[121]

In fact Hitler's mood on D-Day – another nail in the

coffin for the Nazi state – was subject to severe fluctuations. At nine in the morning he is said to have bellowed across the breakfast room: 'Is this the invasion or isn't it?'* When Morell hurried over and gave him an injection of 'x', he calmed down, suddenly appeared affable and light-hearted, enjoyed the day and the fine weather, and clapped everyone he met jovially on the shoulder.[122] At the midday briefing, in spite of the looming military disaster, to everyone's astonishment he revealed a beaming face, and at the lunch that followed – semolina dumpling soup, mushrooms in a ring of rice, apfelstrudel – he fell into one of his endless, distracted monologues. This time it was about elephants, which were the strongest animals in existence, and which, like him, abhorred meat. Next Hitler described in detail the horrors of a slaughterhouse he had visited in occupied Poland. Girls in rubber boots had waded in blood up to their ankles. Meanwhile, Morell was preparing his next injection, made from the glands of slaughtered animals.

On the evening of 6 June Hitler still didn't believe that the invasion on the Atlantic north coast was actually happening, but was satisfied with the idea that this was just a mock assault, a decoy manoeuvre designed to provoke him into over-hasty reactions. This was not the case. In fact the Allies had established themselves along substantial stretches of coast by the end of the day and taken the Germans by surprise. The Western Front opened up. In military terms the German Reich now had no chance at

---

* According to other accounts, Hitler had merely slept in that morning, since in spite of the important events no one had dared to wake him.

all. But there was something that cheered Hitler up that day: Goebbels had at last given up smoking.

On 14 July 1944 the Führer left his Berghof, for ever. During the flight to the Wolf's Lair the curtains remained closed. Patient A had: 'flu and conjunctivitis in both eyes. Head-water [hydrocephalus] has flowed into his left eye.'[123] He was given an adrenalin solution as well as reports on the advances of the Allies through France, the approach of the Red Army towards the border of the Reich and the latest bombing raids on German cities. He struggled to put on his reading glasses to be able to decipher all the bad news. He didn't look down from the plane window.

Operation Valkyrie and its Pharmacological Consequences

The park around the Wolf's Lair was resplendent with lush green, the summer was hot, the forest shimmered, and Theo Morell fastened a facial mosquito net over the visor of his fantastical uniform cap. The wooden barracks of the Führer's headquarters had been given a splinter shield of strong reinforcing walls, Goebbels was smoking again, and on 20 July 1944: 'Patient A 11:14 injection as always.'[124] On the file card the procedure is recorded as 'x'.

Pharmacologically pepped up, Hitler ran to the ground floor building in which the military briefing was being held on this fateful day. Some officers were already waiting outside the door. The dictator drew his strong eyebrows together so that the ridge above them became more defined, and shook hands with everyone around him. He then stepped into the interior of the barrack, whose windows were open against the oppressive heat. While the remaining twenty-four participants were grouped around a long oak table, he alone sat down on a stool and began to play with a magnifying glass. Lieutenant General Heusinger, who stood on his right, morbidly described the desolate situation on the Eastern Front. Claus Schenk Graf von Stauffenberg, who had arrived a little late, shook hands with Hitler, shoved his brown brief-case under the table, as close to his target as possible. A little later he left the room again, inconspicuously. At 12.41 an admiral walked to one of the windows to get fresh air. Hitler bent low over the table so that he could get a better view of the map, resting his chin on his hand, his elbow on the tabletop. It was 12.42. The general was explaining: 'If the army group doesn't come back from Lake Peipus at last, there will be a catastrophe –' There was a terrible explosion.

'I saw a bright, clear, jetting infernal flame, and thought to myself that it could only be an English explosive. German explosives do not have such an intense bright-yellow flame.'[125] Hitler's own description of events sounds strangely detached, as if spoken from behind a veil. The blast sent him flying from the middle of the room to the door. Wired on 'x', the dictator may have experienced the explosion as if wrapped up in cotton wool, and felt as invulnerable as Wagner's Siegfried – while all around him the seriously wounded officers fought for their lives, their hair in flames. As if he were just a bystander, he reported that a moment later 'I couldn't see anything clearly through the thick smoke. I saw only a few figures lying in the haze and moving. I was lying in the barrack, near the left door post; on top of me a few slats and beams. But I was able to get up and go on my own. I was just a little dizzy and slightly dazed.'[126]

Morell heard the explosion from his workspace and immediately assumed it must be a bomb. Moments later Hitler's valet, Heinz Linge, came rushing in: the professor had to come quickly to the Führer. The physician hastily picked up his black case and lumbered heavily out into the sultry summer air. A general lay on the floor with one leg torn off and one eye lost. Morell wanted to stop and tend to him, but Linge dragged him on: the Führer was more important.

It didn't take them long to reach Hitler, who presented a grotesque picture, smiling blithely and sitting on his bed even though his forehead was bloody, his hair was burnt off at the back of his scalp, and there was a saucer-sized burn on his calf: 'Keitel and Warlimont led me to my bunker,' the dictator reported with a lively, almost cheerful expression: 'On the way I saw that my trousers were badly torn, and that bare flesh was visible everywhere. Then I washed, because my face looked like a Moor's – and then changed my clothes.'[127]

When Hitler pointed out that Mussolini was coming for an important state visit in two hours, Morell took out his tools and injected 'x' again. That it was just glucose and not an effective painkiller seems hardly likely. Patient A had dozens of splinters in his body, and these now had to be removed individually – a painful procedure. But Hitler wasn't bothered. His two burst eardrums were bleeding, but even that didn't trouble him, and he impressed everyone with his apparent courage.

On the medical file for Patient A, Morell recorded that Hitler hadn't been agitated in the slightest. His pulse was normal, as always. None the less the physician recommended that he stay in bed. But Hitler, full of beans from his injection, was already standing in freshly polished boots and announced that it was ridiculous for a healthy man to receive guests in bed. Wrapped in a bulging black cloak, he went to the Wolf's Lair railway station and waited impatiently for Mussolini, who said, dumbfounded by Hitler's apparent physical integrity: 'That was a sign from heaven!'[128]

In reality Hitler had been more severely affected than it at first appeared. He had lost his hearing almost entirely and he began to have severe pains in his arms and legs as the effects of 'x' abated in the evening. Blood was still flowing uninterruptedly from both ears. Psychologically the attack had devastating consequences. In the traditional day-on/day-off rhythm, Patient A now received his 'x' against the pain and the shock to his nerves. In this critical phase after the attempted coup he couldn't afford to miss a dose. However, the presentation of Hitler as an invincible, even invulnerable hero didn't always work. When he welcomed a group of army officers a week later, their excited cries of *'Heil Hitler!'* died away when they laid eyes on him as he entered the room. All of a sudden the gap between the fiction of the Führer and the real-life Hitler was all too apparent.

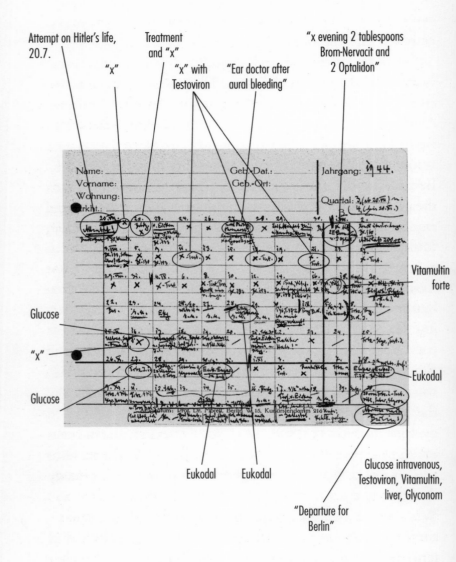

Attempt on Hitler's life, 20.7.

"x"

Treatment and "x"

"x" with Testoviron

"Ear doctor after aural bleeding"

"x evening 2 tablespoons Brom-Nervacit and 2 Optalidon"

Vitamultin forte

Glucose

"x"

Glucose

Eukodal

Eukodal

Eukodal

"Departure for Berlin"

Glucose intravenous, Testoviron, Vitamultin, liver, Glyconom

From the attempt on Hitler's life to the move from the Wolf's Lair: Patient A's increasing drug abuse.

At Last, Cocaine!

O night! I took some cocaine
and blood dispersion is under way,
hair turns grey, the years flee,
I must, I must in ardour
blossom once again before I decay.

Gottfried Benn[129]

Because of the injury to both eardrums, word was sent to the nearby reserve field hospital to bring Dr Erwin Giesing, an ear, nose and throat specialist, to the Wolf's Lair. He, too, quickly realized what was happening in the senior echelons. Although he had been told, before their first meeting, that Hitler was a kind of 'powerful, mystical Superman', it was a bent, halting figure that he met, wearing a dark-blue striped dressing gown and slippers on his bare feet.[130] Giesing describes his impressions precisely: 'The face was pale, slightly swollen, and there were large bags under both bloodshot eyes. The eyes did not make the fascinating impression so often ascribed to them in the press. I was particularly struck by the wrinkles from either side of the nose to the outer corner of the mouth, and by the dry, slightly cracked lips. His hair was already clearly mixed with grey and rather unkempt. The face was well shaven, but with somewhat withered skin, which I attributed to fatigue. The speech was unnaturally loud and tended towards a shout, and later became somewhat hoarse. [. . .] An aged, almost depleted and exhausted man, who had to make do with what was left of his strength.'[131]

In a neurological respect, the specialist diagnosed the patient as normal: no hallucinations, no incontinence, functioning memory, and sense of time and space. 'Emotionally unstable, however – either love or hate. Constant flux of thoughts, his statements always relevant. [. . .] the Führer's psychological condition is very complex.'[132]

Examining Hitler's burst eardrums, Giesing found a marked sickle-shaped tear in the right ear, and a smaller injury in the left. When treating the sensitive tissue with acid, he admired Hitler's extraordinary impassivity. He felt no pain any more, Patient A boasted. And, in any case, pain only existed to make people harder. Giesing couldn't have guessed that perhaps he didn't feel the pain because he had been given drugs by his personal physician shortly beforehand. There were no discussions between the two doctors. And while Giesing learned nothing from Morell about what he had administered, Morell had no idea what the new doctor was prescribing to the patient: 'I was not briefed by ear specialist Dr Giesing,' Morell noted sourly.[133] The two doctors disliked each other from the first moment. When Morell approached Giesing, on his arrival, with the words 'Who are you? Who called you? Why didn't you report to me?', Giesing fired back: 'As an officer I only have to report to my military superiors, not to you, a civilian.'[134] After that the top dog refused to even look at the newly recruited specialist.

Giesing described the personal physician on another occasion with little sympathy and an acid pen: 'Morell comes in, distinctly short of breath and panting. He shakes only Hitler's hand and asks agitatedly whether anything in particular happened during the night. Hitler says no.

He slept well, and even digested the previous night's salad without any difficulty. Then, with the help of Linge, he takes off his coat, sits back down in his armchair and pulls up his left sleeve. Morell gives Hitler the injections. He pulls the needle out again and wipes the puncture site with a handkerchief. Then he leaves the room and goes into the office, holding in his right hand the used syringe and in the left empty ampoules, one large and two small. He goes with the ampoules and a syringe into the adjacent orderlies' bathroom, rinses the syringe out himself and destroys the empty ampoules by throwing them into the toilet. Then he washes his hands, comes back into the office and says goodbye to everyone present.'[135]

But Giesing didn't come to his Führer empty-handed either. His favourite remedy for treating pains in the ear, nose and throat area was cocaine, the very substance the Nazis abhorred as a 'Jewish degeneration drug'. This choice is not as unusual as it might seem as not many alternatives for local anaesthesia were available at the time,[136] and cocaine was stocked as a medicine in every chemist's shop. If we can believe Giesing, the only source in this case, between 22 July and 7 October 1944, on seventy-five days, he administered the substance over fifty times in the form of nose and throat dabs, a highly effective surface application. This was pure, first-class stuff, the famous Merck cocaine, delivered from Berlin by courier train as an extremely psychoactive 10 per cent 'cocaine solution' in a sealed bottle, responsibly signed for by the SS pharmacist in line with the regulations of the Reich Security Main Office. In the Wolf's Lair Hitler's valet kept it locked up under his personal care.

Again, this obvious application of drugs is barely noticed by Hitler's biographers, even though it is worth mentioning because of its strong euphorigenic potential for the critical phase after the assassination attempt.[137] The procedure went like this: in the morning Assistant Surgeon Brandt brought his colleague Giesing to a tent behind the guest bunker, where they went through the strict security measures in place since 20 July. Giesing's bags were emptied, every instrument was examined; even the lightbulbs of the otoscope were taken out and screwed back in again. Giesing had to hand over his uniform cap and his dagger, empty out the contents of his trouser and jacket pockets on to the table, and turn out his pockets. He got only his handkerchief and keys back, and his fountain pen and pencil were returned afterwards. He was frisked from top to bottom. Cocaine was left out of these rigid controls; it was already inside. Now Linge, the valet, went into action, taking the bottle out of the drugs cabinet in the orderly room and inviting Giesing to make his examination.[138]

Patient A expressed his gratitude for this variation in the menu. According to Giesing's report he claimed that 'on cocaine he felt considerably lighter and carefree, and that he could also think more clearly'. The doctor explained to him that the psychotropic wave was the 'medicinal effect on the swollen nasal mucous membrane, and that it was now easier to breathe through the nose. The effect usually lasted between four and six hours. He might have a slight cocaine sniff afterwards, but it would stop after a short time.' Hitler supposedly asked whether this swabbed application could not be made once or twice a day – even when the aural passages requiring treatment were healed again after 10 September. Giesing, who saw his star in the ascendant, agreed, but claims to have pointed out to the patient that all cocaine was absorbed by the nasal mucous membrane and passed into the blood supply, so he had to warn against too high a dose. But Hitler went on requesting this application, and during the next few days, in spite of profuse perspiration, he confirmed the success: 'It's a good thing you're here, doctor. This cocaine is wonderful, and I'm glad that you've found the right remedy. Free me from these headaches again for a while.'[139]

Those headaches had probably also been caused by the constant crashing and screeching that had been putting the nerves of the residents of the innermost restricted zone of the Wolf's Lair on edge for the last few days: the construction unit's jackhammers and heavy machinery were hastily erecting a new, even more strongly reinforced *Führerbunker*. Patient A could only bear the noise while on cocaine, and the restorative drug made him feel as if he wasn't ill at all: 'Now my mind is freed again, and I feel very well.' But one concern preyed on his mind: 'Please don't turn me into a cocaine addict,' he said to his new favourite doctor, to which Giesing replied, reassuringly: 'A real cocaine addict snorts dry cocaine.' Hitler was heartened: 'I don't intend to become a cocaine addict.'[140]

So the Führer had his nose swabbed and went to the military briefing full of artificial confidence. The matter was clear as far as he was concerned: the war against the Russians would somehow be won. When he received another dose from Giesing on 16 September 1944, he had a very special brainstorm: one of those feared, pseudo-genius Führer's ideas. He told his baffled entourage that despite their vast inferiority in terms of men and materials, he wanted to go back on the offensive on the Western Front. Immediately, he formulated an order demanding 'fanatical determination from all soldiers fit for duty'.[141] Though everyone advised him against the hopeless enter-prise of a second Ardennes offensive, the dictator refused to be deterred: victory would be his!

In consequence Giesing started to feel unsettled by Hitler's affinity for cocaine – which erases all feelings of self-doubt and encourages megalomania – and he wanted to stop administering the potent swabs. But Hitler wouldn't let him: 'No, doctor, continue as before. This morning I have a terrible throbbing head that probably comes from the sniffing; concern for the future and the continued existence of Germany are consuming me more and more with each passing day.'[142] Still, Giesing's medical scruples outweighed his duty to obey, and he refused Hitler the drug. Defiantly, the supreme commander didn't appear at the military briefing that day, 26 September 1944, but announced huffily that he was no longer interested in the situation in the east, where the whole front threatened to collapse. Intimidated, Giesing came round and promised cocaine, but in return he demanded a full check-up of Hitler. Patient A, who had previously always forbidden such an examination, consented, and on 1 October 1944 he even appeared naked, as he had otherwise generally refused to do, solely to wheedle for himself some of that coveted blow: 'Look in my nose again and put that cocaine thing in to get rid of the pressure in my head. I have important things to do today.'[143]

Giesing obeyed and administered the drug, this time in such a dose that Hitler is believed to have lost consciousness and for a short time there is supposed to have been a danger of respiratory paralysis. If the account given by Giesing is accurate, then the self-described abstainer almost died of an overdose.

Speedball

Hitler responded to just about every drug, with the exception of alcohol. He wasn't dependent on one particular substance, but on substances generally that gave him access to pleasant, artificial realities. Within a very short time he had become the most passionate consumer of cocaine, but from mid-October 1944 he was also able to abandon the drug and to rely instead on other stimulants. In retrospect Hitler – like cocaine-users tend to do – shifted this phase of his existence into a doughty pose: 'The weeks since 20 July have been the hardest of my life. I have fought with a kind of heroism that no German could have dreamed of. In spite of serious pain, hours of dizziness and nausea, I have remained on my feet and fought against all of this with iron energy. I have often survived the danger of collapse, but through my will I have always taken control of the situation.'[144]

The words 'iron energy' and 'will' need only be replaced by 'Eukodal' and 'cocaine' and we already come a little closer to the truth. The Luftwaffe adjutant Nicolaus von

Below also used these incorrect terms when describing his Führer in the weeks after the assassination attempt: 'He was sustained only by a strong will and his heightened sense of mission.'[145] In fact, it was his strong cocaine and his heightened quantity of Eukodal. Because Eukodal was now being administered in the grand style – the dosage had doubled in comparison with the previous year to 0.02 grams, almost four times the typical medical application.[146]

During those weeks, cocaine and Eukodal – the Führer's mixture, the cocktail in his blood – mutated into the classic speedball: the sedating effect of the opioid balancing the stimulating effect of the cocaine. Enormous euphoria and highs that are felt in every last fibre of the body result from this pharmacological pincer movement, in which two potent molecules with opposite biochemical effects fight for dominance in the body. This produces both a strong circulatory overload and insomnia, and the liver desperately fights against such an onslaught of poisons.

During that last autumn of the war, and of his life, the dictator drew on a wealth of artificial paradises. When Patient A stepped on to his pharmacologically created Mount Olympus, setting his heels down first, as always, bending his knees, clicking his tongue and flapping his wrists, imagining that his thoughts were crystal clear and that he could rearrange the world to his own liking, it was impossible for his generals, more than sobered by the oppressive situation at the front, to get through to him. The medication kept the supreme commander stable in his delusion, built up an unassailable rampart, an impregnable defence that nothing could penetrate. Any doubts were swept away by his chemically induced confidence.[147] The world could sink into rubble and ashes around him, and his actions cost millions of people their lives – but the Führer felt more than justified when his artificial euphoria set in.

Hitler had read Goethe's *Faust* as a young man. In the autumn of 1944, by enjoying the fruits of the labours of Sertürner, who discovered morphine as a young medical researcher in the days of Weimar classicism, and is seen as the father of Eukodal and all other opioids, Patient A entered into a pact with Mephisto once and for all. The narcotic not only rid him of his severe intestinal spasms – that was the publicly acceptable outcome – but also sweetened the moment. It is not possible to prove clinical dependence, but Morell's almost undecipherable diary for September 1944 gives us an idea of how often this hardcore drug was really administered. But beyond these records it is by no means impossible that Eukodal made its way into Hitler's bloodstream also as 'x', 'injection as always' or simply unrecorded. Whoever starts taking Eukodal, and has ready access to it, will in most cases never give it up again.

On 23, 24/25 and 28/29 September 1944 – just to examine a typical week – Patient A was given the potent narcotic four times, always with a day's pause in between. This is the typical rhythm of an addict, and contradicts the idea of a purely medical application. One striking feature is the combination with the anticonvulsive eupaverin, a synthetic analogue of the plant-based agent papaverine from the opium poppy, which calms the muscles and is a comparatively harmless medication, because it does not cause dependency. This double pack – deliberately or not – disguised what Hitler was actually consuming. For a long time even the Führer confused the similar-sounding medications and demanded eupaverin when he actually meant Eukodal. In Morell's words: 'The Führer was very happy about it, and gratefully pressed my hand and said: what a stroke of luck that we have eupaverin.'[148]

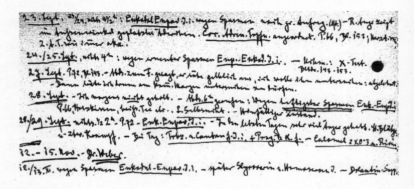

Eukodal every other day: the typical rhythm of an addict.

We can only surmise how the dictator felt after an intravenous injection of 0.02 grams of the highly potent substance when, moments after the injection, its effects were felt by the oral mucous membranes and he got the 'taste', or drip, as addicts call it. The energy always came suddenly, within a few seconds, and from all directions: a felicitous, enormously calming force, and when Hitler said: 'Doctor, I'm so glad when you arrive in the morning'[149] he was being unusually honest. In the morning he got a jab that created a heightened feeling that corresponded so perfectly to his own image of greatness – and which reality no longer supplied.

The Doctors' War

You have all agreed that you want to turn me into a sick man.

Adolf Hitler[150]

The power of the personal physician was approaching a high point during that autumn of 1944. Since the attempt on his life Patient A needed him more than ever, and with each new injection Morell gained further influence. The dictator was closer to him than he was to anyone else; there was no one he liked to talk to as much, no one he trusted more. At major meetings with the generals an armed SS man stood behind every chair to prevent any further attacks. Anyone who wanted to see Hitler had to hand over his briefcase. This regulation did not apply to Morell's doctor's bag.

Many people envied the self-styled 'sole personal physician' his privileged position. Suspicion about him was growing. Morell still stubbornly refused to talk to anyone else about his methods of treatment. Right until the end he maintained the discretion with which he had initially approached the post. But in the stuffy atmosphere of the haunted realm of the bunker system, where the poisonous plants of paranoia sent their creepers over the thick concrete walls, this was not without its dangers. Morell even left the assistant doctors Brandt and Hasselbach, with whom he could have discussed the treatment of Hitler, consistently in the dark. He had mutated from outsider to diva. He told no one anything, wrapping himself in an aura of mystery and uniqueness. Even the Führer's all-powerful secretary, Bormann, who made it clear that he would have preferred a different kind of treatment for Hitler, one based more on biology, was banging his head against a wall when it came to the fat doctor.

Patient A and his personal physician: 'My dear doctor, I'm so glad when you arrive in the morning.'

As the war was being lost, guilty parties were sought. The forces hostile to Morell were assembling. For a long time Himmler had been collecting information about the physician, to accuse him of having a morphine addiction and thus of being vulnerable to blackmail. Again and again the suspicion was voiced on the quiet: might he not be a foreign spy who was secretly poisoning the Führer?

As early as 1943 the foreign minister, von Ribbentrop, had invited Morell to lunch at his castle, Fuschl, near

Salzburg, and launched an attack: while the conversation with von Ribbentrop's wife initially revolved around trivial questions such as temporary marriages, state bonuses for children born out of wedlock, queuing for food and the concomitant waste of time, after the meal the minister stonily invited him 'upstairs, to discuss something'.

Von Ribbentrop, arrogant, difficult and blasé as always, tapped the ash off his Egyptian cigarette with long, aristocratic fingers, looked grimly around the room, then fired off a cannonade of questions at the miracle doctor: was it good for the Führer to get so many injections? Was he given anything apart from glucose? Was it, generally speaking, not far too much? The doctor gave curt replies: he only injected 'what was necessary'. But von Ribbentrop insisted that the Führer required 'a complete transformation of his whole body, so that he became more resilient'. That was water off a duck's back for Morell, and he left the castle rather unimpressed. 'Laymen are often so blithe and simple in their medical judgements,' he wrote, concluding his record of the conversation.[151]

But this was not the last assault Morell would bear. The first structured attack came from Bormann, who tried to guide Hitler's treatment onto regular, or at least manageable lines. A letter reached the doctor: 'Secret Reich business!' In eight points 'measures for the Führer's security in terms of his medical treatment' were laid out, a sample examination of the medicines in the SS laboratories was scheduled and, most importantly, Morell was ordered henceforth always 'to inform the medical supply officer which and how many medications he plans to use monthly for the named purpose'.[152]

Der Chef der Sicherheitspolizei   Berlin, den 9. Juni 1944
und des SD

IV A 5 b (IV C 4 alt) - 33/44 g.Rs.-

An den

Reichsführer -SS

Feldkommandostelle

Maßnahmen für die Sicherheit des Führers hinsichtlich der
medikamentösen Versorgung.
- -

1.) Die von Herrn Professor M o r e l l für den Führer
benötigten Arzneimittel - siehe auch Ziffer 3.) Absatz 2 - bezieht
der Sanitätszeugmeister SS - u. Pol. gegen Barzahlung

a) von den Fabriken des Herrn Prof. M o r e l l,
b) soweit erforderlich, von der Großindustrie.

2.) Die unter 1.) genannten Medikamente werden stichproben-
mäßig in den Laboratorien des Reichsarztes SS u.Pol. auf Verun-
reinigung überprüft, ohne dass in den genannten Laboratorien
die mit der Prüfung Beauftragten wissen, für welchen Zweck die
betreffenden Medikamente vorgesehen sind.

3.) Herr Professor M o r e l l soll baldmöglichst gebeten
werden, dem Sanitätszeugmeister Angaben darüber zu machen, welche
und wieviel Medikamente für den genannten Zweck er monatlich zu
verbrauchen gedenkt.

Um die Sicherheit noch weiter zu vergrössern und im
Interesse der vereinfachten Handhabung für Herrn Professor Morell
sowie, um für alle vorkommenden Möglichkeiten die Sendung reich-
haltiger ausgestalten zu können, wird vorgeschlagen, daß Herr
Professor M o r e l l dem Sanitätszeugmeister hierbei nicht nur

Bormann's unsuccessful attempt to control Morell's actions:
the memo describes the SS wanting to obtain and test
samples of all Morell's medications for Hitler and insists
that in future Morell give a full account of what he intends
to give to his patient.

In fact this remained a rather helpless approach from Bormann, who was not usually helpless. On the one hand his intervention turned Hitler's medication into an official procedure, but on the other he wanted as little correspondence as possible on the subject, since it was important to maintain the healthful aura of the leader of the master race. *Heil Hitler* literally means 'Health to Hitler', after all. For that reason the drugs, as detailed in Bormann's letter, were to be paid for in cash to leave no paper trail. Bormann added that the 'monthly packets' should be stored ready for delivery at any time in an armoured cupboard, and made 'as identifiable as possible down to the ampoule by consecutive numbering (for example, for the first consignment: 1/44), while at the same time the external wrapping of the package should bear an inscription to be precisely established with the personal signature of the medical supply officer'.[153]

Morell's reaction to this bureaucratic attempt to make his activities transparent was as simple as it was startling. He ignored the instructions of the mighty security apparatus and simply didn't comply, instead continuing as before. In the eye of the hurricane he felt invulnerable, banking on the assumption that Patient A would always protect him.

In late September 1944, in the pale light of the bunker, the ear doctor, Giesing, noted an unusual coloration in Hitler's face and suspected jaundice. The same day, on the dinner table there was a plate holding 'apple compote with glucose and green grapes'[154] and a box of 'Dr Koester's anti-gas pills', a rather obscure product. Giesing was perplexed when he discovered that its pharmacological components included atropine, derived from belladonna or other nightshade plants, and strychnine, a highly toxic alkaloid of *nux vomica*, which paralyses the neurones of the spinal column and is also used as rat poison. Giesing indeed smelled a rat. The side-effects of these anti-gas pills at too high a dose seemed to correspond to Hitler's symptoms. Atropine initially has a stimulating effect on the central nervous system, then a paralysing one, and a state of cheerfulness arises, with a lively flow of ideas, loquacity, and visual and auditory hallucinations, as well as delirium, which can mutate into violence and raving. Strychnine in turn is held responsible for increased light-sensitivity and even fear of light, as well as for states of flaccidity.[155] For Giesing the case seemed clear: 'Hitler constantly demonstrated a state of euphoria that could not be explained by anything, and I am certain his heightened mood when making decisions after major political or military defeats can be largely explained in this way.'[156]

In the anti-gas pills Giesing thought he had discovered the causes of both Hitler's megalomania and his physical decline. He decided to treat himself as a guinea pig: for a few days Giesing took the little round pills himself, promptly identified that he had the same symptoms and decided to go on the offensive. His intention was to disempower Morell by accusing him of deliberately poisoning the Führer, so that Giesing could assume the position of personal physician himself. While the Allied troops were penetrating the borders of the Reich from all sides, the pharmacological lunacy in the claustrophobic Wolf's Lair was becoming a doctors' war.

As his ally in his plot, Giesing chose Hitler's surgeon, who had been an adversary of Morell's for a long time. Karl Brandt was in Berlin at the time, but when Giesing called he took the next plane to East Prussia without hesitation, and immediately summoned the accused man. While the personal physician must have worried that he was being collared for Eukodal, he was practically relieved when his opponents tried to snare him with the anti-gas pills, which were available without prescription. Morell was also able to demonstrate that he had not even prescribed them, but that Hitler had organized the acquisition of the pills through his valet, Linge. Brandt, who had little knowledge of biochemistry and focused his attention on the side-effects of strychnine, was not satisfied with this defence. He threatened Morell: 'Do you think anyone would believe you if you claimed that you didn't issue this prescription? Do you think Himmler might treat you differently from anyone else? So many people are being executed at present that the matter would be dealt with quite coldly.'[157] Just a week later Brandt added: 'I have proof that this is a simple case of strychnine poisoning. I can tell you quite openly that over the last five days I have only stayed here because of the Führer's illness.'[158]

But what sort of illness was that exactly? Was it really icterus – jaundice? Or might it be a typical kind of junkie hepatitis because Morell wasn't using properly sterile needles? Hitler, whose syringes were only ever disinfected with alcohol, wasn't looking well.[159] His liver, under heavy attack from those many toxic substances over the past few months, was releasing the bile pigment bilirubin: a warning signal that turns skin and eyes yellow. Morell was being accused of poisoning his patient. There was an air of threat when Brandt addressed Hitler. Meanwhile on the night of 5 October 1944 Morell suffered a brain oedema from the agitation. Hitler was unsettled beyond measure by the accusations: *Treachery? Poison?* Might he have been mistaken for all those years? Was he being double-crossed by his personally chosen doctor, Morell, the truest of the true, the best of all his friends? Wouldn't dropping his personal physician, who had just given him a beneficial injection of Eukodal, amount to a kind of self-abandonment? Wouldn't it leave him high and dry, vulnerable? This was an attack that might prove fatal, as his power was based on charisma. After all, it was the drugs which helped him artificially maintain his previously natural aura, on which everything depended.

Since the start of the Führer's rapid physical decline these internecine struggles between the doctors turned into a proxy war for succession at the top of the Nazi state. The situation was becoming worse: Himmler told Brandt he could easily imagine that Morell had tried to kill Hitler. The *Reichsführer-SS* called the physician to his office and coldly informed him that he had himself sent so many people to the gallows that he no longer cared about one more. At the same time, in Berlin, the head of the Gestapo, Ernst Kaltenbrunner, summoned Morell's locum, Dr Weber, from the Kurfürstendamm to a hearing at the Reich Security Main Office on Prinz-Albrecht-Strasse. Weber tried to exonerate his boss, and voiced his opinion that a plot was utterly out of the question. He claimed Morell was far too fearful for such a thing.

Finally the chemical analysis of the disputed medication was made available. The result: its atropine and strychnine content was far too small to poison anyone, even in the massive quantities that Hitler had been given. It was a comprehensive victory for Morell. 'I would like the matter involving the anti-gas pills to be forgotten once and for all,' Hitler stated, ending the affair. 'You can say what you like against Morell – he is and remains my only personal physician, and I trust him completely.'[160] Giesing received a reprimand, and Hitler dismissed him with the words that all Germans were freely able to choose their doctors, including himself, the Führer. Furthermore, it was well known that it was the patient's faith in his doctor's methods that contributed to his cure. Hitler would stay with the doctor he was familiar with, and brushed aside all references to Morell's lax treatment of the syringe: 'I know that Morell's new method is not yet internationally recognized, and that Morell is still in the research stage with certain matters, without having reached a firm conclusion about them. But that has been the case with all medical innovations. I have no worries that Morell will not make his own way, and I will immediately give him financial support for his work if he needs it.'[161]

Himmler, a dedicated sycophant, immediately changed tack: 'Yes, gentlemen,' he explained to Hasselbach and Giesing: 'You are not diplomats. You know that the Führer has implicit trust in Morell, and that should not be shaken.' When Hasselbach protested that any medical or even civil court could at least accuse Morell of negligent bodily harm, Himmler turned abrasive: 'Professor, you are forgetting that as interior minister I am also head of the supreme health authority. And I don't want Morell to be brought to trial.'[162] The head of the SS dismissed Giesing's objection that Hitler was the only head of state in the world who took between 120 and 150 tablets and received between eight and ten injections every week.

The tide had turned once and for all against Giesing, who was given a cheque from Bormann for 10,000 Reichsmarks in compensation for his work. Both Hasselbach and the influential Brandt were out of luck as well, also damaging the latter's confidant Speer, who had his eye on Hitler's succession. The three doctors had to leave headquarters. Morell was the only one who stayed behind. On 8 October 1944 he rejoiced in the happy news: 'The Führer told me that Brandt had only to meet his obligations in Berlin.'[163] Patient A stood firmly by his supplier. Just as every addict adores his dealer, Hitler was unable to leave the generous doctor who provided him with everything he needed.

The dictator told his physician: 'These idiots didn't even think about what they were doing to me! I would suddenly have been standing there without a doctor, and these people should have known that during the eight years you have been with me you have saved my life several times. And how I was before! All doctors who were dragged in failed. I'm not an ungrateful person, my dear doctor. If we are both lucky enough to make it through the war, then you'll see how well I will reward you!'[164]

Morell's confident reply can also be read as an attempt to justify himself to posterity, because the physician put it baldly on record: 'My Führer, if a normal doctor had treated you during that time, then you would have been taken away from your work for so long that the Reich would have perished.' According to Morell's own account, Hitler peered at him with a long, grateful gaze and shook his hand: 'My dear doctor, I am glad and happy that I have you.'[165]

The war between the doctors was thus shelved. Patient A had put a stop to a premature dismissal. The price he paid was the continued destruction of his health by a personal physician who had been confirmed in his post. To calm his nerves the head of state received: 'Eukodal, eupaverin. Glucose i.v. plus Homoseran i.m.'[166]

Self-obliteration

Life in headquarters is now such that one can write little about it, as the conditions are more or less all internal in nature. I look forward to being able to tell you that the Führer is fit and well, and concerned day and night with how he can improve and master the fate of Germany. I am still very close to the front in the east.

From a letter from Theo Morell[167]

Just like the potent substances in Hitler's blood supply, his existence itself, which had seemed solid for so long, dissolved gradually into Nirvana. This is a development worth following if we are both to understand how the formerly energetic Führer was transformed into a human ruin, and to gauge how this process interacted with historical events.

In the last quarter of 1944, while the fronts closed in on all sides, the vice tightened, intestinal cramps intensified, and Hitler managed to survive his little remaining time by taking strong narcotics and erecting a pharmacological barricade around himself. The deluded totalitarian system that he himself had created did not allow for a sober Führer. Since he was convinced that he alone could realize all the ambitious goals of National Socialism during his own lifetime, and did not trust any potential successor to establish the German World Reich, he could under no circumstances give up. With Morell's drugs, he could keep going and maintain his tunnel vision. Under no circumstances did Hitler want to come down from his megalomaniac Führer-trip, in spite of the disastrous military situation. He refused to come to his senses: if so, he would be obliged to notice the vanity, the madness, of the whole enterprise. In complete denial, he couldn't allow himself to doubt his battle, waged against the whole world, or even lose his taste for the war, which he himself had unleashed and already lost long ago. Remorselessly the needle penetrated his skin, the plunger was pulled back, the stuff shot into the veins and he escaped again into self-delusion.

The fact was that between the autumn of 1941, when he started being given hormone and steroid injections, and the second half of 1944, when first the cocaine and then above all the Eukodal kicked in, Hitler hardly enjoyed a sober day. This helped him to never break out of his own closed system, never to awaken from the nightmare, until the very end. The chasm was definitive and irreparable: as soon as any psychological bridge to reality was tentatively rebuilt, it was immediately blown up by a further pharmacological explosion.

Drugs were fuel and a stand-in for a lack of commitment: by now he found that his illusions could be bolstered only by narcotics. He travelled from headquarters to headquarters, from bunker to bunker, from disinhibition to disinhibition – unbounded, homeless, always on his way to the next futile military action, the next fix that would let him repress all consequences, while ignoring all possible side-effects. He moved in a permanent fog: a doped-up performance athlete unable to stop – until the inevitable collapse.

The Superbunker

My dear old friend, I hope I can still call you that, even though you're now an international celebrity. But I know your character. The German people are very grateful to you for your beneficial work, as we would be lost if the strong hand was missing. And that this hand has remained strong until today is your inextinguishable merit.

From a letter to Theo Morell[168]

To better protect himself against future attempts on his life, infections or any other kind of attack, on the afternoon of 8 November 1944 Patient A moved into a brand new refuge within the Führer's Restricted Area at the Wolf's Lair. Instead of the usual two-metre-thick concrete ceilings, this one had a seven-metre-thick concrete gravel casing. The windowless block didn't have any direct ventilation and looked like an ancient Egyptian tomb. The quantities of material exceeded many times over the usable space that they surrounded. Hitler worked, slept and vegetated there, in total isolation, locked in his delusion and living off his own substance. He himself could see only positive sides to the new habitation, which seemed to have fallen into the forest like a monstrous foreign body from the sky. The dictator happily stated he now had more room to walk about inside. Morell calculated the Führer's sleeping and working area was 23 cubic metres larger than in the old bunker. Of course, the doctor always had access to the otherwise isolated sarcophagus-like building, to inject him 'intravenously with Eukodal for excessive stress' to celebrate the move.[169]

Morell had known for a long time the state of his patient and how quickly Hitler was going downhill, or turning in on himself, and how much people were talking about it. Letters that the doctor wrote to his wife, various *Gauleiter* and old acquaintances during the late autumn of 1944 express the desperate desire to depict reality other than it was. This also included mailing the daily menus from the Wolf's Lair. These were supposed to provide proof to outsiders of Hitler's 'simple and reasonable way of life'.[170] Whereas he had never previously mentioned his patient's health to third parties, he now communicated an ostentatiously good mood to all and sundry. A collection of his lines: 'My high-up patient is very well. [. . .] My most important patient is always very well. [. . .] An improvement is fully in place. [. . .] I am glad that my patient's health is in a good state. [. . .] My patient's health is very good, and I hope I will be able to keep him in his old, fresh state for the German people for a long time to come. Apart from the Duce I have in fact been able to heal several other heads of state and can actually be very contented with the success of my medical efficacy.'[171]

But Patient A was not at all well. In fact Morell could only simulate, stage-manage, inject back into shape, a healthy Hitler for increasingly shorter intervals. Often Hitler lay pale and haggard on a simple field bed in his new concrete residence, in his white nightshirt under a military blanket. An adjustable lamp was suspended over his head; a bedside table and a low rack were packed to the brim with sheets of paper, situation maps, open books and urgent reports. In the midst of this chaos was a telephone that never rang. The light-grey walls gave off the bleak smell of unset concrete. The bed was scattered with broken pencils. Lost somewhere among the mess were nickel-framed glasses he was ashamed of because he could no longer put them on by himself due to the extreme tremors in his hands. None the less, Morell wrote: 'I can report that the F. is full of beans. [. . .] It is my greatest joy, reassurance and satisfaction that my patient is very well, and that with his vigour and freshness he is a match for any task, and could master any crisis. [. . .] It may be of some comfort to you if I can assure you that our Führer is in a good state of health.'[172]

But as soon as the effect of the Eukodal waned, the trembling began, and in the last few weeks of 1944 only

From teetotaller to junkie.

grew in intensity. Soon it came to dominate all discussions of the state of Hitler's health. Aware of this, the ashen Führer tried with all his strength to suppress the shaking, which only made it worse. The saluting arm held stiffly and tirelessly aloft was now a thing of the past. Nervous, violent vibrations of all his extremities had taken over. 'Left hand very strong tremor,' wrote Morell. Then: 'Increased tremor in the right hand.' Or: 'The left leg is not trembling now, but the left arm and the left hand are.'[173] Hitler buried his fingers in his coat pockets to conceal the fact. By now it could hardly have been described as trembling, as it had graduated to shaking. His entourage was seriously alarmed. Panzer General Guderian, now head of the Army General Staff, reported that Hitler had to put his right hand on his left and his right leg over his left leg to make the shaking less visible when he was sitting down. Hitler's hand vibrated, oscillated and manoeuvred of its own free will so much that many people thought it was intentional. If he folded his arms in front of his chest, his whole torso was set in motion. Morell recommended baths and rest. Hitler asked 'if he couldn't be given injections for it'.[174]

But injections wouldn't alleviate the problem. Quite the contrary. In search of the cause for his trembling limbs and stooped posture, medical historians have diagnosed the dictator as suffering from arteriosclerotic Parkinson's disease, a shaking palsy probably provoked by an auto-immune disorder. With Parkinson's, the body's neurones are mistaken for foreign bodies by the immune system and attacked – the possible result of his having consumed outrageous preparations made of animal hormones. The consequences are that dopamine-producing nerve cells wither and there is a lack of nourishment to the essential nuclei of the cerebral cortex, which is responsible for learning and control processes. In his notes Morell also expressed a suspicion of Parkinson's, although not until April 1945.[175] There is no way of telling whether the diagnosis is accurate. Another, perhaps supplementary, explanation is that Hitler's notorious shaking was the direct effect of his unchecked drug consumption.

At any rate Morell was not allowed to leave his patient alone during this phase. On the one hand the physician was now leading his leader, but on the other he had become his prisoner. No one could imagine the grief this position caused him, he complained. For years he hadn't been able to move far from Hitler, he hadn't been his own master for a long time, and he was forced to neglect everything in his own life: his beloved wife, his practice on the Kurfürstendamm, the factories and research laboratories in Olmütz and Hamburg. Even when his brother died, Morell was not given permission to go to the funeral, as he had become indispensable. Hitler swiftly countered each of his suggestions: 'After I informed him of the death of my brother, the F. was very concerned about my trip, as the west was in severe danger. I suggested a plane (this was out of the question, as there were always large numbers of hostile fighter planes in the skies), car (I wouldn't be able to bear such a long journey, in spite of my reassurances to the contrary), railways (can only be used conditionally, due to air raids).'[176]

Hitler flatly refused the locum suggested by Morell

for the brief period of his absence: he suspected that the SS doctor Stumpfegger 'might not give such good injections'. Or might the reason have been that Stumpfegger didn't know the secret of 'x'? Morell insisted on retaining one last scrap of his own private family life. Despite all attempts to keep him in the Wolf's Lair, he did travel to his brother's funeral and on the way back called in briefly on his wife in Berlin. Hitler gave him a bodyguard from the Reich Security Service and became more indignant than ever after the return of his doctor: '3.30 p.m. with the Führer: patient unfriendly, no questions. [. . .] Major rebuff.'[177] Morell quickly got his needles out, took a deep breath, wiped the pearls of sweat from his forehead and stuck the point of the platinum needle into his patient's forearm: 'Glucose i.v. plus Vitamultin forte, Glyconorm, Tonophosphan.' Hitler put his left hand on his belt buckle and breathed out noisily, hunched his shoulders and pursed his thin, pinched lips, which made his mouth look even smaller. Then his face relaxed, and Morell skilfully massaged the swallowed air up from Hitler's belly. They were already back on the same wavelength.

Track Marks

While the Red Army was taking more and more towns in East Prussia in November 1944, Hitler's veins were so wrecked that even the expert shot-giver Morell could hardly penetrate them. The skin of the veins, perforated too many times, was inflamed, scarred and a peculiar shade of brown. Morell had to take a break: 'I cancelled injections today, to give the previous puncture holes a chance to heal. Left inside elbow good, right still has red dots (but not pustules), where injections were given. F. says this wasn't the case before.'[178]

It actually made a crunching noise every time Morell gave him a shot. Each jab created a new wound that joined the previous one, and it produced an elongated, growing crust, what junkies call 'track marks', when one jab is followed by the next to form an unlovely line. Even Hitler was gradually becoming nervous, and worrying about what the huge number of injections was doing to him: 'When I gave him the intravenous injection the Führer thought I wasn't rubbing the area long enough with alcohol so that he often developed small red pustules at the needle holes.' But Morell had another explanation for the condition: 'Blood low in oxygen, from months sitting in the bunker with no daylight or fresh air, and venous, as becomes apparent when applying a tourniquet, and consequently not sufficiently coagulable, and the needle hole staying red.' Hitler remained suspicious: 'Führer still attributes this to bacteria, and thinks bacteria might be entering his body with the injections.'[179]

Out of necessity, Morell wanted to stop the orgy of shots for a while. But in the end Hitler swept all qualms aside and his auto-aggressive qualities came to the fore. In spite of the unpleasantness that the countless injections caused him, he didn't stop demanding them, and when receiving his doctor the first thing he said was that he didn't need treatment, but that he did need an injection: 'Six o'clock in the morning: I am to go to the patient immediately. [. . .] There in twenty minutes. Führer had worked through the night and had a very momentous decision to make, which had left him deeply irritable. The anxiety had become increasingly powerful until at last, quite suddenly, as always when he became very agitated, a convulsion had set in. He didn't want an examination, as that only intensified the pain. I quickly prepared a combined injection of Eupaverin and eukodal and administered it intravenously, which was very difficult given the many recent inoculations; but in the process I observed that we must spare the veins for a while. As I had to pause before giving him the injection, relaxation took place during the injection and the pain was gone. The F. was very happy about it and gratefully shook my hand.'[180]

Twenty minutes between phone call and application: most addicts can only dream of having such a dealer. Hitler valued his doctor's constant availability, and on 31 October 1944 he praised him, saying that the 'rapid intervention yesterday morning had led to a complete recovery'. Morell replied reassuringly: 'If such a state should recur, he was to call straight away, even if it was the middle of the night. [. . .] It would give me the greatest pleasure to be able to help him.'[181]

Often during those last weeks in the Wolf's Lair Patient A made use of his twenty-four-hour room service for even the hardest substances, and called Morell out even after midnight, shamelessly citing all kinds of tiny aches and pains or nervous strains. While an orderly brought the doctor's bag back to the 'drone barracks', the doctor waited by his patient until the effects took hold. On 8

November 1944, when the high wasn't strong enough, Morell generously added a little extra. 'Wednesday 00.30. Suddenly awoken. All of a sudden the Führer has severe gas distension in his body. As he told me, at the moment he has to make the biggest decisions of his life, and this is putting an ever greater strain on his nerves. Intravenous Eukodal–eupaverin initially eases the pain and the convulsions only partially. In response to his request for another half-injection, I have the bag brought back and see that I have injected only 0.01 Eukodal intravenously instead of 0.02. After another injection of 0.01 Eukodal intravenously the pains and the spasm immediately start to ease. The Führer thanked me effusively for this immediate assistance and was then completely happy.'[182]

An addict notices immediately when he hasn't been given the full batch. An addict knows nothing but the longing for the next, completely satisfying shot; every other aspect of existence disappears into the background, regardless of whether it is daytime or the middle of the night. In this period after the attempt on his life, when Hitler's drug consumption reached record levels, the dictator finally lost his biochemical balance – and his health. Stauffenberg hadn't killed him, but he had indirectly turned him into a drug addict. Hitler was degenerating. His face turned ochre, his eyelids sagged, the shaking of his limbs was getting worse and worse, and his concentration was clearly declining. Under Allied questioning after the war Hitler's second surgeon, Hanskarl von Hasselbach, who referred disparagingly to Morell's treatments as 'witchcraft',[183] sketched the medical development as follows: until 1940 Hitler looked much younger than he really was, but after that he had aged rapidly. Until 1943 his outward appearance matched his age, but later his rapid physical decay became obvious.

The fact is, Eukodal was first used in 1943 but was injected so often between September and December 1944 that one must consider the possibility of a physical dependency. The happy fix came at a cost of unpleasant side-effects: insomnia, tremors and constipation. Hitler suffered from all of them. As soon as the high began to ebb, his digestive tract reacted with 'spastic obstipation' (severe constipation) and he had 'no evacuation, painful wind'.[184] At night he lay in bed with his eyes open: 'Then I can't go to sleep, [. . .] in the dark I keep seeing the General Staff maps in front of me, and my brain goes on working, and it takes hours before I can break free.'[185] He claimed the only reason he couldn't get to sleep was the British bombers flying over the Reich territory, but it was probably the drugs that were keeping him awake. To give him the rest he needed, Morell had to administer barbiturate-based narcotics like Luminal or Quadro-Nox. The cycle continued.

Probably as a consequence of the frequent Eukodal shots, Hitler's digestion barely worked now, and as far as his intestinal complaints were concerned, he had reached the spot where Morell had started treating him with Mutaflor in 1936. Because of Patient A's chronic constipation, he had to take camomile suppositories, which provoked him 'to the toilet. I had to stay outside (he even locked the door)', but it did no good: 'The fluid didn't stay inside; he immediately had to push it out again (unfortunately!) [. . .] Führer is supposed to try to sleep (without medication!).'[186] The simplest bodily functions grew into strenuous physiological operations which were recorded as conscientiously as if they were events at the front, as described in the Wehrmacht Oberkommando's war diary: 'From four until six four evacuations, two of which were weaker and two very strong. At the second, after the passing of an obstruction, explosive water evacuation. The third and fourth were very foul-smelling, and particularly the fourth (probably a decomposing agglomeration that had previously been left behind, and had become a cause of gases and the formation of toxic substances). Relatively improved condition and change of facial expression. He only called me to impart to me the happy news of the effect.'

The Question of Guilt

On 21 November 1944 lunch was rice gruel and fried celery slices with mashed potato, after which the Wolf's Lair closed. Hitler had been in his new superbunker for less than a fortnight, but the Russians were too close and headquarters had to be evacuated. With windows tinted to hide the landscape of bomb damage and too much reality, a carriage rattled off towards the Reich capital. It was the Führer's special train *Brandenburg* and the stations it passed had been cleared of people. As Hitler saw no chance of prevailing against Stalin's Red Army, he had given up on the east. As an alternative he was planning his second Ardennes offensive – dreamed up in September on cocaine – perhaps trying to repeat the *Blitzkrieg* miracle of the spring of 1940, or at least to change tack in the west so as to obtain a negotiated peace there at the last minute.

The arrival in Berlin-Grunewald was at 5.20 in the morning, under conditions of strictest secrecy. The shorthand secretary recorded: 'Confidential, Keep Silent!' Hitler, who was concerned about losing his voice because of a nodule on his vocal cords, spoke only in a whisper anyhow. His eyes were no longer focused on his surroundings, and stared instead at imaginary points. Again and again he greedily sucked oxygen from a little portable army oxygen device which Morell had acquired for the journey. Seldom had Hitler's mood been darker or grimmer. Everyone knew: the plan to repel the huge forces of the Americans and the British was illusionary, but the supreme commander continued as if he were certain of victory. In truth he was so badly affected 'by the great agitation [. . .] caused by his distended stomach and seizures' that only Eukodal could help.[187] A day later he also received 0.01 grams of morphine. Two days later, on 24 November 1944, Morell recorded: 'I didn't think injection was necessary. But Führer wants to have some for faster recovery.'[188] Again, three days later, 'the Führer wants to have injections because of imminent hard work'.[189]

But what effect was this uncontrolled consumption of multiple drugs having on Hitler's intellect, on his mind? Was the dictator still compos mentis? The philosopher Walter Benjamin, who had experimented mainly with hashish but also with Eukodal a decade previously (orally, which considerably diminishes its addictive potential), describes the psychological effect of being permanently intoxicated: 'It is perhaps no self-deception if I say that in this state you develop an aversion to the open air, the (so to speak) Uranian atmosphere, and that the thought of the outside becomes almost a torture. It is [. . .] a dense spider's web in which the events of the world are scattered around, suspended there like the bodies of dead insects sucked dry. You have no wish to leave this cave. Here, furthermore, the rudiments of an unfriendly attitude towards everyone present begin to take shape, as well as the fear that they might disturb you, drag you out into the open.'[190]

The chemist and author Hermann Römpp writes that long-term abuse of opiates causes 'damage to the character and the will. [. . .] Intellectual creativity is impaired, although there is no actual loss of earlier intellectual possession. Even the most upstanding characters will not baulk at swindling and deceit.' Paranoia and a morbid mistrust of one's immediate surroundings also arise.[191]

In fact, Hitler's bunker mentality had discovered in Eukodal the ideal end-time drug for the hapless final battle. His numbness, his rigid view of the world, his tendency towards the fantastical and the unscrupulous transgression of all boundaries – all of this was ominously supported by the opioid that he used so frequently in the last quarter of 1944. During this time, when the Allies were entering the Reich from both east and west, the powerful narcotic erased any doubts about victory, any empathy for civilian victims, and made Hitler even more unfeeling about both himself and the outside world.

On this tranquillizing painkiller the Führer was fully in command of himself: this was the true Hitler, and that was how he had always been. The overestimation of his own significance and misjudgement of his opponents were both captured in his blueprint, *Mein Kampf*, published in 1925. His opioid addiction only cemented an already existing rigidification, a tendency to delegate violence, and contributed to the fact that in the last phase of the war and in the genocide of the Jews he never once thought of relenting.

So the goals and motives, the ideological fantasy world, were not the result of drugs, but established much earlier. Hitler did not murder because he was living in a haze – quite the contrary: he remained sane until the end. His drug use did not impinge on his freedom to make decisions. Hitler was always the master of his senses and he knew exactly what he was doing. He acted always in an alert and cold-blooded way. Within his system, based from the beginning on intoxication and a flight from reality, he acted systematically and with terrible consistency to the end. He was anything but insane. A classic case of *actio libera in causa*: he could go on taking as many drugs as he liked to keep himself in a state in which he could commit his crimes. It does not diminish his monstrous guilt.

4

The Wonder Drug (1944–1945)

The evil wound, how to heal it?
Richard Wagner, *Tristan und Isolde*[1]

In the second half of 1944 Hitler's soldiers lost on all fronts. Paris fell to the Allies at the end of August. On 23 August the Wehrmacht had to move out of Greece and was in retreat across the whole of Southern Europe. On 11 September American troops reached the German border near Trier. Wherever you looked, the blood-drained, exhausted, overpowered Wehrmacht was fighting a losing battle. Now only Pervitin helped soldiers either to keep going or to flee the enemy. One tank commander reported laconically: 'We are driving without stopping until we're out of Russia. We swap over every 100 kilometres, gulp down Pervitin and stop to fill up.'[2]

Studies show that two thirds of those who take crystal meth excessively suffer from psychosis after three years.[3] Since Pervitin and crystal meth have the same active ingredient, and countless soldiers had been taking it more or less regularly since the invasion of Poland, the *Blitzkrieg* on France or the attack on the Soviet Union, we must assume psychotic side-effects, as well as the need to keep increasing the dosage to achieve a noticeable effect.[4]

It is no wonder that Pervitin fever should have flourished in 1944 as well. A letter from the Temmler Works to the General Commissar of Health and Medicine shows that even a few months before the end of the war the company requested distribution of the raw materials ephedrine, chloroform and hydrochloric acid for the production of Pervitin. Four million tablets were to be pressed from these 'for armament and war'.[5] Because of the British bombings, the laboratories had been transferred to the little half-timbered town of Meisenheim in south-west Germany, to a brewery, in fact, where the two favourite drugs of the wartime Germans were now being manufactured under a single roof: beer and meth.[6]

The Luftwaffe didn't stop using performance-enhancing drugs either; an official scientific and medical conference in July 1944 was devoted to that very subject.[7] The army medical service also used Pervitin, namely for transporting the wounded. In November 1944 the senior doctors of the medical trains of Army Group A set up experiments in which they compared the effect of morphine with the effect of a cocktail of morphine and Pervitin.[8] It turned out that even severely wounded patients could be kept in a 'good state of mind' if they were given two Pervitin pills as well as an opiate injection.[9] Their spirits improved as their desire to get better was intensified – which made their redeployment all the more likely.

But many soldiers didn't want to be redeployed. They

were exhausted, run down, and they needed longer and longer periods of recovery. For many the propaganda slogans about fighting to the last cartridge rang hollow. No more talk of eagerness, the mood was downcast.[10] But there was no letting up. A typical daily order from Field Marshal Gerd von Rundstedt ended with him saying that the hour decreed that they must recklessly advance. One instruction from Supreme Command reads: 'Stress and losses are possible. Medical considerations cannot be taken into account. The situation requires all it takes', and this of course included chemicals.[11]

Ideology had long lost its hold, and the leadership could think of nothing to motivate their soldiers apart from the increasingly shallow-sounding formula of a 'final victory'. So the Wehrmacht decided to develop new preparations which linked so powerfully with receptors in the central nervous system that even soldiers who were as good as dead would pull themselves together trying to mutate into victors on the battlefield. As fanciful as it seems, in parallel with the laborious effects to develop a miracle weapon, amid the heavy losses of this final phase, the search for a miracle drug which would turn the tables by chemical means was now operating at full blast.

On-site Visit: Medical Academy of the Bundeswehr, Munich

The Bundeswehr, the current German army, bases its Medical Academy – the contemporary equivalent of the MA, where Ranke had undertaken his Pervitin experiments

– in a former SS barracks. Instead of the questionable meth pusher of the Wehrmacht, I find myself talking to a friendly Dr Volker Hartmann, who is the Captain of the Navy Medical Corps. He leads me across the enormous military compound, past a tank emblazoned with Red Cross insignia and a grounded medical helicopter. 'Threat Level Alpha', a sign announces. Hartmann is reassuring: this means 'everything's ok'. In line with this, Hartmann sets out his very personal vision of a future German army, arguing in favour of entirely humanitarian deployments, without weapons. 'The Germans can't fight properly any more anyhow – and perhaps they shouldn't. Our strengths lie elsewhere.' Hartmann, at any rate, has served almost everywhere: as a ship's doctor on the training barque *Gorch Fock*, on a frigate off the coast of Lebanon, on a supply ship at the Horn of Africa, in Banda Aceh in Indonesia as part of the Bundeswehr's tsunami relief, in Kosovo and in Afghanistan. In Mazar-e-Sharif he was commander of the medical task force for the German medical service. When the head of a company requested the upper modafinil for operations against the Taliban, Hartmann refused to issue the prescription. Modafinil is a psychostimulant, and its precise mechanism of action still unknown. In sport the substance is forbidden as a doping agent; school pupils and students sometimes use it as a smart drug to increase concentration and performance. 'I didn't want to be responsible for possibly addicted soldiers, quite apart from the ethical and political significance,' he says, explaining his decision, 'I confiscated it all.'

The military and drugs is a field Hartmann has been

working in for many years. Among other things, he revealed the extraordinary story of the German navy's attempts to develop a miracle drug during the final phase of the Second World War. He tells me about it when we meet for the second time, at Odeonsplatz in Munich, where on 9 November 1923, after a drink-sodden night in the Bürgerbräukeller, the Nazis failed in their attempted putsch. Now it is late September, a mild evening. The offshoots of the Oktoberfest are raging around us: a lot of people in traditional costume, a lot of beery good humour swills about in the air.

'When Hitler's putsch happened the Bavarian police stood over there and fired,' Hartmann says, pointing at the spot. 'One of the first Nazis to be fatally wounded had linked arms with Hitler and pulled him to the ground. At the same time Hitler's bodyguard was peppered with bullets and fell on top of him. More than a dozen were shot dead on the spot, as were four policemen and a bystander. The onlookers charged in all directions. It was total chaos. Hitler picked himself up and fled, barely hurt. Sometimes history is determined by chance.'

We sit down in the nearby Pfälzer Residenz Weinstube, a wine bar, whose façade bears a plaque to the four dead Bavarian policemen – the first victims of the Nazis. Inside we order a white wine spritzer – which during Oktoberfest, where beer reigns, almost seems heretical. Hartmann gets into his stride. It's a dirty story about the navy, which likes to present a clean, proper appearance, trying hard to be a model of moral integrity.

The Quest for the Miracle Drug

The real war will never get in the books.

Walt Whitman[12]

In the German navy there was a senior officer called Hellmuth Heye. In the 1950s he stood for parliament on behalf of the conservative CDU, but on 16 March 1944 he still wanted to win the Second World War, and was sitting with two colleagues in a meeting room in the coastal city of Kiel. Heye was a commanding admiral of the so-called small battle units, the *K-Verbände*, and directly answerable to the naval supreme commander, Karl Dönitz, who, for a few days, would become Hitler's successor in early May 1945. The situation at sea wasn't promising for the 'Imperial Navy', as it chose to call itself in contrast with the 'National Socialist Luftwaffe'. The battle in the Atlantic was lost. The British had cracked the radio code that the Germans assumed was unbreakable. Because of Allied air superiority and the resulting heavy losses, not to mention bad planning in the armaments industry, the U-boat war had to be suspended. Since then the Allies had been bringing in supplies from America to Britain, and preparing for the invasion of Normandy. That was precisely what Heye wanted to prevent with his new units in the spring of 1944.

Hitler hailed the small battle units as a real chance to stop the Allied landings: 'If I've got them I can resist the invasion.'[13] Even during an arms conference in early January 1944 at the Wolf's Lair, in the presence of the arms minister, Speer, and the head of the SS, Himmler, as well as several field marshals, Hitler had demanded the accelerated production of the supposed miracle weapons in which he put so much hope. These were new kinds of two-man U-boats, midget submarines and one-man torpedoes. The huge enemy superiority was to be nullified by the tactic of launching numerous small attacks. It was David versus Goliath, albeit less biblical: the *K-Verbände* were seen as the new celebrity units of the navy. Their special operations would be based on surprise effects – on their not being discovered or located. The supposed aim was to creep up to the big enemy ships, ready the torpedo, and *attack*. Therefore they would have to spend several days and nights un-interruptedly under water – distinctly longer than the forty-eight hours that a high dose of Pervitin would have kept them awake for. No special naval training was planned for these life-threatening operations; instead there would be special drugs that far surpassed everything that had gone before.

If there was ever a time in this war when perseverance was necessary, this was it. In the spring of 1944 Heye frantically tried to find a 'quickly available medication that will keep soldiers who are on solo operations for longer than usual and for those who are not in a position to sleep awake and ready for deployment'. The drug was also supposed to 'boost the soldier's confidence and mobilize his reserves of strength'.[14] But who could develop such a substance?

Admiral Heye swore by 'D IX', a combination of cocaine, Pervitin and Eukodal.

In civilian life Prof. Dr Gerhard Orzechowski, naval staff surgeon and head pharmacologist of the Naval Supreme Command on the Baltic, was a professor of pharmacology at Kiel University. During the German occupation of France he worked in the Naval Medical Research Institute for U-boat Medicine in Carnac in Brittany, where he had studied performance-enhancing substances.[15] The bespectacled scientist seemed like the right man for the experiment of squeezing the last residues out of the battle-weary troops, pepping up the mini-sub fighters and forcing through the final victory by means of pharmacology. Orzechowki's explicit goal was to use chemicals to 'make man a beast of prey'.[16]

Such an approach suited Heye, since he wanted to deploy the one-man fighting boat known as a *Neger* ('Negro' – a play on the name of its inventor, Richard Mohr, i.e. Moor). It was shaped like two torpedoes, one on top of the other, the lower one being the weapon itself. In the upper part were the control seat and the pilot's cockpit, protected by a watertight Plexiglas dome: a ride on the bomb. Through a simple iron-sights visor the combination of carrier torpedo and live torpedo could be aimed at a target; with good vision the pilot launched the weapon by foot pedal. Then he had to speed back to the safety of the harbour – an uncertain endeavour given the US fighter bombers target-shooting at those Plexiglas domes poking out of the water.

For these kamikaze commandos Orzechowski suggested ten different preparations under the abbreviations D I to D X: Drug 1 to Drug 10. They consisted of different quantities of Eukodal, cocaine, Pervitin and Dicodid, a

The drug designer Orzechowski: 'Making man a beast of prey'.

semi-synthetic morphine derivative similar to codeine but considerably more potent. Those were the strongest known substances in the world, thrown together at random – a sign of how lax the navy had become in its treatment of drugs, and of how desperate the situation was.

On 17 March 1944 the pharmacy of the navy hospital in Kiel produced five tablets of each of the ten creations; a day later fifty soldiers from the Blaukoppel training camp ingested them. Everything had to be done quickly, and serious tests of the complex interactions of the individual ingredients didn't occur for reasons of time. D IX was the front runner: a mixture of 5 milligrams of Eukodal, 5 milligrams of cocaine and 3 milligrams of methamphetamine. A brutal combination that might even have been to Hitler's taste. The medical head of the Navy, Admiral

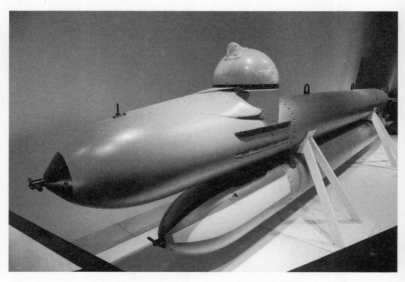

Use only while on strong drugs: the one-man combat vessel *Neger*.

Staff Surgeon Dr Greul, had to rubber stamp D IX, as cocaine in its powder form was banned from prescription. Heye also gave the project a green light. The medical service quickly prepared 500 tablets for the *Biber* (Beaver), a mini-U-boat with two torpedoes, as well as for the *Neger*.

In spite of extreme secrecy, the search for the wonderdrug was being talked about – especially among the SS. They too were increasingly reliant on special commandos, and interested in new discoveries. A collaboration was on its way, one which the navy later wanted to forget. The notoriously unscrupulous Obersturmbannführer Otto Skorzeny, head of SS secret operations and known to the Western services (who overestimated his actual abilities) as 'the most dangerous man in Europe', came to Heye's headquarters on 30 March 1944. Since his involvement in the abduction of the arrested Mussolini in September 1943, both Hitler and Himmler supported him in all his undercover operations. Officially the man with the striking scar on his face only wanted to see the small battle units' new weapons, but Skorzeny, who had never made a secret of his hard-drug use, had come chiefly because of Orzechowski's promising D IX. He immediately took charge of a thousand tablets to test them 'on a special operation'.[17]

So what were the effects of D IX? 'In all subjects unpleasant disturbances occured after taking one to two tablets,' says one of the few surviving reports. 'Subjects who were previously fresh and rested displayed shaky hands during a brief euphoria, and those who were already tired complained of weak knees and tautness in the muscles. A general paralysis of the central nervous system set in, the desirable euphoria immediately subsided, decision-making power and intellect were inhibited, energies impaired, the critical faculties diminished, profuse perspiration followed a feeling of hangover, a high degree of fatigue and dejection.'[18]

This sounds anything but promising. And yet D IX was administered – and led to a fiasco for the navy. Two thirds of *Biber* pilots did not survive their daredevil operation. The supposed miracle drug, because of its strong side-effects, made combat deployment more difficult rather than easier. It was dropped as swiftly as it had been developed.

In the meantime the German military situation had drastically deteriorated. The Allies had landed on the European continent, and huge forces were advancing towards the western border of the Reich. From autumn 1944 German hopes rested on a new small battle device, again supposedly revolutionary because of its outstanding diving capability, the *Seehund* (Seal). Heye's plan was to direct these mini-subs to the Thames estuary and the beaches of Normandy in order to blow up Allied ships. The *Seehund*'s navigation represented an extraordinary challenge, however. Conditions were extremely cramped. Meals were warmed up in a heatable pot, and the crew were obliged to answer the call of nature in empty food tins.[19] 'Bearing up for four days in this combat vessel will be difficult and not always possible without stimulants,' wrote the navy Medical Officer, Dr Hans-Joachim Richert, who was now responsible for treating the *K-Verbände*. He seems to have had qualms about using chemical intoxicants to overcome these natural difficulties, when he writes

Datum	Ort	Eintragungen
Zu: 11.10.44.	Timmendorfer Strand	Dr. Orzechowski über ein wachhaltendes und
		leistungssteigerndes Mittel für Seehund. In
		diesem Kampfmittel müssen 2 Mann etwa 4 Tage
		Einsätze fahren. Die Bedingungen sind ähnliche
		wie im Hecht. Die Soldaten sitzen in gepolsterten
		Stühlen hinter einander. Die Rückenlehne des
		vorderen Sitzes kann umgelegt werden, sodaß ein
		Mann zeitweise liegen kann. Antrieb über Wasser
		durch Diesel-, unter Wasser mit E-Motor, Luft=
		erneuerung mit Injektorverfahren. Verpflegung
		durch Konserven, die mittels eines elektrischen
		Topfes gewärmt werden. Der vordere Mann ist
		Kommandant und navigiert, der achtere ist L.I.
		und bedient die Maschinenanlage. Der Letztere hat
		in dem ihm zur Verfügung stehenden Raum sehr wenig
		Bewegungsfreiheit. Die Bedingungen in dieser Hin=
		sicht für den vorderen Mann sind besser, zumal er
		im Turm sitzen bzw. stehen kann. Das Aushalten
		für 4 Tage in diesem Kampfmittel wird schwierig
		und ohne Reizmittel nicht immer möglich sein.
		Die militärische Führung steht auf dem Standpunkt,
		daß in diesem Krieg, wenn es erforderlich ist,
		auch Schädigungen durch stark wirkende Medikamente
		in Kauf genommen werden müssen, sofern sie die
		Durchführung von Einsätzen ermöglichen. Zur Aus=
		wahl stehen neben Bohnenkaffee die Mittel Cardiazol- Pervitin Coffein und Cocain. Mit Prof. Dr. Orzechowski
		werden die notwendigen Versuche besprochen.
15.10.44.	- " -	Aufstellung der K - Flottille 212 (Linsen).
16.10.44.	- " -	Stabsarzt d.Lw. Dozent Dr. Malorny zur Ver=
		fügung Kom.Adm. U.-Boote abkommandiert. Zusammen=

From a naval doctor's war diary:

'Dr Orzechowski about a stimulating and performance-enhancing substance for *Seehund*. Bearing up for four days in this combat vessel will be difficult and not always possible without stimulants. The military leadership takes the view that in this war, if required, damage as a result of powerful medications must be taken into account in so far as they make it possible to carry out operations. The substances available apart from coffee are Cardiazol-caffeine, Pervitin and cocaine. The necessary experiments will be discussed with Prof. Orzechowski.'

in a rather detached manner in his war diary: 'The military leadership takes the view that in this war, if required, damage as a result of powerful medications must be taken into account . . .' On 11 October 1944 Richert met the drug designer Orzechowski near Lübeck to talk about 'a substance that would keep *Seehund* crews awake and boost their performance'.[20]

Since preparations combining several hard drugs were largely rejected because of severe side-effects, the two men discussed whether high doses of pure cocaine or pure methamphetamine could keep a person awake and efficient for more than two days and two nights. Time was pressing. Nine days later, on 20 October 1944, Grand Admiral Dönitz visited the small battle flotilla, aware that Hitler was breathing down his neck with his belief in this new miracle weapon. Richert informed him that the 'conditions for the submarine *Seehund* with a deployment duration of 4 x 24 hours are difficult and call for the development and testing of new kinds of medication'. To avoid a further disaster like the one that had occurred with D IX, the decision was made to carry out experiments beforehand, to 'establish the tolerability and effectiveness of high doses of cocainum hydrochloricum in pill form, high doses of Pervitin in chewing gum and smaller doses of cocainum hydrochloricum and basicum in chewing gum'.[21]

But where and on whom should such tests, which were plainly far from hazard-free, be carried out? Connections to the SS, which had been made through Otto Skorzeny, were remembered. Might these open certain strongly secured doors to the navy? Dönitz gave his ok. Heye also agreed. The clean-cut navy men in their neat uniforms again got into contact with the SS, and a secret collaboration began, one which up until today has not been fully studied. In late November 1944 a gate indeed was opened to the naval doctor Richert, who was to run the experiments. It led to a huge facility, and the steel lettering over the entrance spelled out the words: '*ARBEIT MACHT FREI*', meaning 'WORK WILL SET YOU FREE'.[22]

Business Trip to the Concentration Camp

Cold wind blasted over the open space, surrounded by a circular wall three metres high, which had flowerpots of evergreen plants arranged symmetrically on top. The perimeter was secured with an electric fence and in front of that were rolls of barbed wire, and a raked gravel strip: 'NEUTRAL ZONE. Live ammunition will be fired without warning'.

Sachsenhausen concentration camp, thirty-five kilometres north of Berlin on the edge of the small town of Oranienburg, was opened in 1936, the year of the Olympic Games. As an equilateral triangle, its architectural concept was based on the principle of total surveillance. From the balustrade of main tower A, painted pastel green and partly timbered, a single guard could see the barracks arranged in four arches around the semi-circular parade ground. A single machine gun could keep all the prisoners covered. Altogether over 200,000 people from around forty nations would be confined here until just before the end of the war: political opponents, Jews, Sinti and Roma, homosexuals, Jehovah's Witnesses, the citizens of occupied European countries, 'anti-social elements', alcoholics, drug addicts. Tens of thousands of detainees perished from hunger, illness, forced labour, mistreatment and medical experiments. In the autumn of 1941 an estimated 13,000–18,000 Soviet prisoners of war were executed with a shot to the back of the neck in a special facility that was designed to standardize the killing process.

One other perfidious speciality of the camp was the so-called 'shoe-walking unit'. Prisoners had to test the resilience of soles for the German shoe industry on uninterrupted forced marches. Companies such as Salamander, Bata and Leiser sent their latest models to the camp: they were seeking a substitute for leather, which was rationed during the war. The shoe-testing ground, parts of which can still be seen today, was a track 700 metres long, consisting of 58 per cent concrete road, 10 per cent cinder path, 12 per cent loose sand, 8 per cent mud that was kept constantly under water, 4 per cent chippings, 4 per cent coarsely gravelled paths and 4 per cent cobbles. This was designed to provide a cross-section of all the roads in Europe that German soldiers walked upon during their campaigns.

The shoe-walking unit was a punishment unit. Anyone who was found guilty of refusing to work, or caught playing cards, bartering or stealing food from the mess or the kennels, ended up here. 'Laziness', refusal to obey orders or even the suspicion of homosexual acts could also lead to referral. To start with, the unit consisted of 120 prisoners. A master cobbler from Sensburg in East Prussia, Dr Ernst Brennscheidt, a career civil servant who never joined the SS or the NSDAP but who was known for his cruelty, expanded this to 170 prisoners. He increased the daily walking quota to over forty kilometres by speeding up the pace. For this marathon he also made the prisoners carry around rucksacks weighing 25 pounds, so that greater stress would be put on the soles. Often he made inmates wear shoes that were too small or ordered different sizes for left and right feet, supposedly to collect additional data.

The foreman in charge of the march had a series of numbered cardboard markers at the ready, and as soon as the shoe walkers had performed one round, he put one of these markers in a lead-lined wooden box attached to a pole, so that they could be more or less accurately counted. Every ten kilometres shoes were examined to see how worn they were. Prisoners were ordered to lie down, perform knee bends, crawl or jump on the spot. Often enough one of the emaciated 'shoe walkers' would collapse. In these instances, Brennscheidt would unleash one of his Alsatians. In step, breaking step or goose-stepping, they marched even in bad weather to avoid financial losses. The German economics ministry paid for the maintenance costs of the shoe-walking track. The Reich economics office controlled the material tests centrally, and only allowed leather substitute materials to go into production once they had been successfully tested in Sachsenhausen. It paid the camp six Reichsmarks per day, per prisoner. In the case of rubber soles, after several improvements they could withstand 3,000 kilometres, or a seventy-five-day march. Still, most materials were unusable long before that. Leather fabrics barely survived a thousand kilometres, but a sole made of Igelit, a form of soft PVC, survived for over 2,000 kilometres.[23] All of this was painstakingly noted down. According to estimates, up to twenty people died on the track every day.[24] The SS called this 'extermination through labour'.

Pill Patrol

From 17 until 20 November 1944, the navy hired the shoe-walking unit for a 'Secret Command'. On the first evening, at half past eight on the dot, the prisoners were given high doses of drugs by the naval doctor Richert: the enormous quantity of 50–100 milligrams of pure cocaine in pill form, 20 milligrams in chewing gum or 20 milligrams of Pervitin, also as chewing gum (about seven times the dosage of the traditional Temmler pill). Thirty minutes later the effect set in, and the march on the testing track began – a walk that literally lasted to the end of the night.

Between four and five o'clock in the morning (seven or eight hours of tramping in the dark later), most of

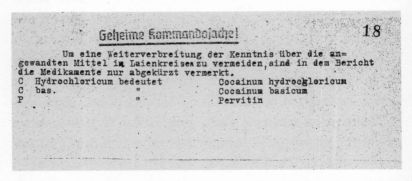

'Secret Command Matter!': Substance names were abbreviated in reports to avoid the retransmission of knowledge about medications used.

them gave up 'because they were footsore'.[25] The camp inmate Odd Nansen, later co-founder of UNICEF, described the experiments: 'Just now a singular patrol is marching round and round the parade ground interminably. All are kitted up and sing and whistle as they walk. That's the "pill patrol". They're being used to test out a new energy pill. How long can they keep going full steam on it? After the first forty-eight hours it's said that most of them had given up and collapsed, although the theory is that after taking this pill one can perform the impossible. No doubt the Germans could use a pill like that now.'[26]

Richert's notes do not mention the abuse that the inmates were subjected to during this torture. 'Experimental subject No. 3', the twenty-year-old Günther Lehmann, was the only one still walking the next morning. He had taken 75 milligrams of cocaine, and went on performing his lonely rounds, a total of ninety-six kilometres, 'without fatigue', as the experimental records cynically put it.[27] At one o'clock he was sent to the barracks to join the others. All the pumped-up inmates waited there until the evening, unable to sleep. At 8 p.m. the drug experiment was repeated. Another sleepless night for the prisoners: totally blitzed on strong cocaine, on strong crystal meth, in the concentration camp.

The next day at eight in the evening there was 'fresh distribution of medication. The group remained in their room under the same conditions.' The men played cards, talked, read. Some of them lay down, dozed off momentarily, then woke up again. The following day Richert described their appearance: 'Nos. 1, 10 and 11 look sleepy in the morning,

No. 9 well rested; the others do not seem affected. They continue about their business as before. 7.30: medication administered once more.' On the fourth day at four in the afternoon the experiment was ended, and the forced participants staggered back to their barracks.

Meanwhile a second group had to begin their march carrying heavy bags, forming a new pill patrol. These prisoners had been given Lehmann's performance as a standard. The threat was that if they gave up sooner than he did they might face death. Consequently almost all of them covered the ninety-six kilometres required. The naval staff doctor noted with satisfaction: 'On this medication, state of mind and will are largely eliminated. [. . .] The experimental subjects have clearly been forced into a state contradicting their predispositions.' In spite of their exhaustion and their weak constitutions the camp inmates were mutating into marching machines. Such results pleased Admiral Heye, as he could not assume that his soldiers would by natural means drum up the necessary strength and motivation for the futile final battle.

But which doses had proved to be best? Richert once again: 'The goal of keeping people awake and efficient for days and nights without, or with only minimal, sleep lies within the realm of possibility with the application of substances A–D. Substances B and C take priority.' 'B' and 'C' were cocaine salt and cocaine base, each 20 milligrams in chewing gum. Consequently Richert's decision was that the young marines should plough their way through the final waves of the war while chewing cocaine gum – for four sleepless days and nights per mission.

- 1 -
Geheime Kommandosache!

Arzneimittelversuch zur Hebung der Leistungsfähigkeit

und achhaltung vom 17. - 20.11.44.

<u>Zweck des Versuches:</u> Grobe Prüfung über Verträglichkeit und
Wirkung von:

Medikament	A	= C.hydrochl. in verschiedener Dosis, (in Pillen
- " -	B	= C. " 20 mg in Kaugummi form)
- " -	C	= C.bas. 20 mg in Kaugummi
- " -	D	= P. 20 mg in Kaugummi

<u>I. G r u p p e .</u>

Lfd. Nr.	N a m e	Alter	Gewicht	Größe	1-malige Arzneimittel- gabe innerhalb 24 Stun- den.
1.	F.B.	18	80 Kg.	1,79	100 mg von A
2.	P.	24	80 "	1,89	100 mg " A
3.	G.L.	20	52 "	1,71	75 mg " A
4.	F.Schw.	21	70 "	1,75	50 mg " A
5.	H.T.	22	71 "	1,72	50 mg " A
6.	A.F.	23	53 "	1,66	B
7.	E.F.	24	68 "	1,75	B
8.	Z.M.	23	70 "	1,73	C
9.	M.P.	23	66 "	1,67	C
10.	R.Schm.	20	72 "	1,73	D
11.	W.Schm.	25	66 "	1,66	D

Wie aus der Aufstellung ersichtlich ist, handelt es sich
um junge Männer zwischen 18 und 24 Jahren, die ausreichend er-
nährt und in gutem Kräftezustand sind.

<u>17.11.</u> Tagsüber nur leichte Arbeit.

20.30 Uhr Einnahme der Arzneimittel.
21.00 " Beginn des Gepäckmarsches mit 25 Pfund schwerem Tornister.
Nach 2 1/2-Stunden Marsch jeweils 20 Minuten Pause.

<u>18.11.</u> Zwischen 4 und 5.Uhr scheiden die meisten Teilnehmer in-
folge wundgelaufener Füße aus; abgesehen von lfd.Nr. 2. und 3.
sind alle im Marschieren untrainiert und haben Schuhwerk, das
nicht von ihnen eingelaufen wurde.

<u>Marschleistungen:</u>

Lfd. Nr.	1.	43 Klm.
	2.	38 "
	3.	96 " marschierte am 18.11. bis 11.00 Uhr.
	4.	28 "
	5.	40 "
	6.	41 "
	7.	51 "
	8.	41 "
	9.	41 "
	10.	58 "
	11.	41 "

Nr. 3. als trainierter Marschierer geht bis 11.00 Uhr ohne Er-
müdung weiter und tritt um 13.00 Uhr wieder zum Marschieren an,

<u>gibt</u>

'Secret Command matter!': Naval drug tests at Sachsenhausen
concentration camp.

As pointless and inhuman as these experiments were, the navy doctor seemed to have enjoyed his business trip. He even planned further tests. These were to examine 'how the capacity for concentration in the course of such sleepless days and nights reacts under the effects of medication'. Due to time constraints, or perhaps because the Allies were advancing steadily further, these follow-up experiments were never carried out.

There were no members of the navy medical service among the accused at the doctors' trials in Nuremberg. Even after the war they always claimed never to have had anything to do with the SS. But that is not the case. The quest for so-called performance-enhancing drugs, which had begun at the Military Medical Academy with Ranke, had perverted into enacting experiments on human beings at concentration camps authorized by the German navy.

Going Under

On 7 December 1944 Dönitz stood in Dresden in front of 5,000 members of the Hitler Youth. Most in the crowd were only teenagers, fifteen or sixteen, and there were even ten- to twelve-year-olds. On the podium, beside the microphone, a mini-U-boat had been positioned, looking like a large-scale urn, decorated with garlands of flowers. The Grand Admiral was hailing it as Germany's only hope of a final victory: the intention of his speech was to recruit volunteers. Countless members of the Hitler Youth signed up and over the next few days were driven in trucks with blacked-out numberplates to the ports where they were to be deployed. Only there were they given uniforms for these top-secret missions.[28] Obviously these young men didn't know what awaited them when they pulled on their caps, each with a little gold sawfish[29] stitched on to it, and clambered aboard the hastily riveted-together torpedo vehicles and received their just as hastily pressed pills or cocaine-spiked chewing gum. Soon most of them would drown wretchedly, like kittens in a sack.

Senior Midshipman Heinz Mantey describes a training voyage on the *Seehund*, in which he and his leading engineer were given a pep pill whose contents they could only guess at: 'We felt somehow elated and almost weightless, everything appeared in improbable colours.'[30] Soon aural hallucinations set in, and Mantey and his fellow pilot

Suicide mission with cocaine chewing gum.

thought they were hearing otherworldly music. The fittings in the boat began to glow and changed shape and size in front of their eyes. But there was more to the experience than just pleasant visions. The effect grew stronger and stronger, until it became frightening. Confused, they rose to the surface and meandered around for hours. They were completely unable to remember their course later on.

This zonked odyssey was not a one-off case. One midshipman reported that 'the pep pills were doled out very generously'.[31] He himself never ran out. Another *Seehund* pilot confirmed that at the start of the mission he had been given five small red pastilles, with the instruction to take them one at a time in the event of fatigue. Knowing nothing about the effects and possible side-effects, he took all the doses prophylactically within two hours. As a result, he stayed awake for four consecutive days and nights.

Another pilot described his mission in detail: in January 1945 it was his task to establish whether the Thames Estuary was suitable as an area of operations for missions lasting five days and four nights. Everything in his diving boat was crammed in so tightly that he could barely squeeze himself through the gap. And then there was the high dosage. 'It was frightening.'[32] His seat was adjusted, he was strapped in, surrounded by defective technology and hastily cobbled-together apparatus, cut off from contact with the outside world, inexperienced in navigation, alone on the high seas with a lot of drugs in his blood, in a metal box full of explosives: it is not a surprise that he didn't ever arrive at the Thames Estuary.

Others completely lost control of the situation. The drug took hold of one midshipman, and the constant rocking immediately affected his bowels. Meanwhile the unchanging rhythm kept pumping from the engines like a heartbeat. When he had to take a pee he did it sitting down, right into the bilge, where his turkey breast snack lay spoiling in the oily water. 'I'd never been seasick, but now I threw my guts up, and kept on spewing. It wasn't seasickness, it was sickness, and the temptation just to let everything go became stronger and stronger. We had now spent two days without proper sleep. I was sweating in spite of the cold. All that sitting was gruelling. Rocking, stench, noise, damp.'[33]

The navy's doped-up small battle units stood in for the last remains of a once-feared army that wanted to conquer the world. As late as April 1945 *Seehunde* were still setting off. One commander stated that he had taken several tablets even before the launch. On the high sea he saw houses and streets appearing in front of him. 'Suddenly I had the feeling that a crow was trying to hack away at the back of my neck. I jerked my head around and looked into the grinning engines of a Lockheed Lightning that was speeding towards us. At the same moment two black dots came away from the body of the plane.' He and his engineer somehow escaped unharmed. From the fifth until the seventh day of their mission they each took between fifteen and twenty tablets per day, a sorry record. When their mini-U-boat reached the base at IJmuiden, where the partially destroyed cranes of the docks stood out against the low sky, the men tied a white towel to the periscope and sat down with their arms round each other on the edge of the turret. They surrendered, regardless of whom they were surrendering to, regardless of what happened to them. 'Seven days without sleep were over at last.'[34]

The Reich didn't only collapse in the dense claustrophobia of the Führer's bunker in Berlin. It also went into terminal decline in the freezing waves of the North Atlantic while its navy was chemically pumped up on cocaine chewing gum tested on concentration camp inmates. There the mini-submarines bobbed, dived and drifted, and jammed inside them were the young torpedo fodder of the Navy, on the hardest drugs that soldiers have ever taken. Hellmuth Heye, the admiral responsible, commented on the missions on 3 April 1945 in a radio address delivered at 14.48: 'Situation reports show that fighting group did and risked everything in full deployment to fulfil the mission task. In spite of an uncertain situation at the front and unverifiable rumours, the troop marched onwards against the returning tide. Again it has been proven that there is still a way if the Führer and the troops are cast from the same mould. If immediate success eluded us, there still remains the achievement of which we may be proud.'[35]

Perhaps the Führer and the troops were cast from the same mould – they were, at least, taking similarly powerful substances. Heye's assertion that the pilots climbed enthusiastically into their doomed vehicles was pure cynicism. These involuntarily spaced-out men certainly didn't want to belong to a 'fighting elite' any more. What happened here was that their last reserves had just been chemically unlocked.

Hellmuth Heye survived the war. Throughout his life

he remained associated with the German armed forces, and in 1961 he became ombudsman to the military within the CDU-led Federal government under Chancellor Adenauer. His soldiers, embroidered gold sawfishes on their caps, still lie in their steel coffins at the bottom of the sea.

Brainwashing

After his arrest by the Americans, SS-Hauptsturmführer Dr Kurt Plötner of Leipzig University was described as having 'a strong physique, a round head shape, mid-blond hair, blue eyes'. He had 'horn-rimmed glasses, was short-sighted, with full cheeks, beardless. Sword scar on the left temple – phlegmatic type.'[36] In Dachau concentration camp[37] as department head of the Institute of Practical Military Research he had tested 'chemical methods for the abrogation of the will'. They were based on experiments undertaken in Auschwitz extermination camp by Dr Bruno Weber, the director of the Hygienic Bacteriological Research Centre in Auschwitz, with barbiturates, morphine derivatives and mescaline. These experiments were inspired by the Gestapo, where there was frustration at their limited success in gaining information from imprisoned Polish resistance fighters.* Unlike Sachsenhausen, which was chiefly concerned with

---

* Previously Georg Elser, who attempted to take Hitler's life, was given high doses of Pervitin after his arrest to make him speak and reveal possible backers, without success.

endurance tests, Auschwitz was focused on brainwashing and consciousness control.

Plötner continued this barbaric series of tests in Dachau, and gave unwitting prisoners mescaline, a psychoactive alkaloid that occurs naturally in the Mexican peyote cactus. The substance, which has been used for thousands of years in rituals by America's indigenous cultures to commune with ancestors and gods, can cause powerful hallucinations. In the 1920s mescaline was popular among thinkers, artists and psychologists, as it supposedly expands consciousness. Aldous Huxley would describe the effect in his book *The Doors of Perception*. But the development of the effect of a drug is always dependent on the circumstances under which it is taken. Plötner did not intend to liberate his guinea pigs' thoughts with mescaline, quite the contrary. Like his predecessor Dr Weber in Auschwitz he wanted to find out whether better results could be achieved through brainwashing in interrogations.[38]

'All questioning is a forcible intrusion. When used as an instrument of power it is like a knife cutting into the flesh of the victim,' Elias Canetti wrote in *Crowds and Power*.[39] If a person's freedom relies largely on the protection of personal secrets, Plötner attempted to develop a particularly sharp blade to penetrate deep into the hidden heart of the individual. For a test group of thirty people the perverted SS shaman secretly dissolved mescaline in coffee or alcohol and began an innocuous conversation with the unsuspecting test subjects. After thirty to sixty minutes a change took place. The alkaloid had passed into the bloodstream via the mucous membrane of the stomach. The experimental subjects who were 'opened up' by the drug were now informed that in this special zone where the interrogation was taking place Plötner had direct access to their soul. He suggested they should tell him everything of their own free will or something terrible would happen. The perfidious strategy worked: 'When the mescaline took effect, the investigating person could extract even the most intimate secrets from the prisoner if the questions were asked skilfully. They even reported voluntarily on erotic and sexual matters. [. . .] Mental reservations ceased to exist. Emotions of hatred and revenge could always be brought to light. Tricky questions were not seen through, so that an assumption of guilt could easily be produced from the answer.'[40]

Plötner could not finish his series of tests. The Americans liberated the camp and confiscated his documents. It was a treasure trove for the US secret services. Under the leadership of Charles Savage and the Harvard medic Henry K. Beecher, the experiments were continued under the code name Project Chatter and other rubrics at the Naval Medical Research Institute in Washington DC. These were used as a matrix for extensive series of investigations that spanned the whole of the 1950s, involved thousands of human guinea pigs, and whose results would be used by the Americans to try to unmask Soviet spies in the Korean War. Like the Germans, they were concerned with 'becoming precisely acquainted with the way in which these drugs took effect, as a practical instrument for their possible use on (civilian and military) prisoners'.[41] Just as the victorious USA appropriated the Third Reich's discoveries in rocket science and the exploration of outer space, the Nazi drug experiments were imported to explore inner worlds.[42] The secret US programme MKUltra based on Plötner's initial work took 'Mind Kontrol' as its goal – the spelling with a 'K' could be read as a nod to its German origins.

Plötner himself was never punished for his crimes, but lived in hiding in north Germany as 'Herr Schmitt' until 1952. In the soccer World Cup year of 1954 the medical faculty of Freiburg University appointed him as an extraordinary professor.

Twilight of the Drugs

The higher a man rises the more he has to be able to abstain [. . .] If a street-sweeper is unwilling to sacrifice his tobacco or his beer, then I think, 'Very well, my good man, that's precisely why you're a street-sweeper and not one of the ruling personalities of the State!'

Adolf Hitler[43]

The first American convoy entered the conquered port of Antwerp on 28 November 1944. Allied supply routes were in this way secured. In December US troops advanced on a broad front from the west towards the border of the Reich. Morell wrote on 9 December 1944 about his visit to Hitler: 'Wanted to do without injection, but then on request, because of imminent major efforts, 10 ccm glucose plus homoseran 10 ccm intramuscular.' On the following night Eukodal was also injected into the vein.[44]

During that winter those 'major efforts' were multiplying to an alarming extent. Hitler, self-stylizing himself as a kind of fleshly seismograph for the coming defeat, experienced the 'most intense levels of stress of his whole life [. . .] and the very greatest nervous tensions caused by imminent events and the constant terror attacks on Germany cities'.[45] He repeatedly professed he needed an injection to be able to endure it all. On 10 December 1944 he was travelling towards yet another of the Führer Headquarters, this time called Adlerhorst ('Eagle's Eyrie'), near Bad Nauheim. From here he planned his illusionary blow against the west, the second Ardennes offensive. His personal physician noted: 'Called 4.30 this morning. Führer having convulsions again. Eukodal eupaverin i.v. Most exciting day of whole life. A great victory must be won! 11.30 in the morning: Führer still having convulsions and has had no sleep, although big discussions are constantly necessary. Departure dependent on a few important pieces of news that are awaited. Larger injections in the train not possible because of inevitable cold when stepping outside, but in his view one more big intravenous injection necessary.'[46]

On 11 December the desolate luxury train arrived at the new headquarters in the Taunus mountin range near Frankfurt at the crack of dawn. Hitler summoned the commanders of the Western Front, who had for security reasons been divided into two separate groups. Everyone's guns and bags were confiscated, and then the baffled generals were driven back and forth through the bare winter forest to make them lose their bearings. At last they stopped in front of a bunker. The generals walked between rows of black-clad SS men towards a 'bent figure with a pale, sunken face, collapsed on his chair, with trembling hands, hiding his left, violently twitching arm to the best of his ability', as General von Manteuffel described him.[47] The frightening, drooling wreck's name was Adolf Hitler. He had just slurped down two rice gruel soups to give him some strength and acted as if he had the situation under control. He set out a kind of attack plan to the toadying officers but had to admit that this was a gamble, and was 'disproportionate to our available forces'.[48] In Morell's notes the ghostly meeting is whitewashed thus: 'Führer had discussion lasting several hours with about forty to fifty generals. Führer supposed to have been very fresh and lively, inspiring and impulsive. Excellent health.'[49]

This second Ardennes offensive proceeded quite differently from the first, in the spring of 1940. This time it relied on tricks and the hope of bad weather, so that the Allied pilots couldn't bomb the remaining German outposts too easily. SS-Obersturmbannführer Skorzeny was operating with a thousand men in stolen American uniforms with D IX in their combat packs behind enemy lines to cause confusion. This spread a rumour that they were planning to assassinate the American commander, Dwight D. Eisenhower, and, for a short time, some US units were actually quite preoccupied by the extra security measures they had to put in place.

But the superficiality of the German action soon became apparent. Both the Wehrmacht and Waffen-SS were knocked back amid great losses. On 19 December 1944 Hitler ate spinach soup and then ordered 'liver and

Pervitin, requested because of current excess of work'.[50] So he was now taking methamphetamine as well – Morell doesn't say whether it was injected or taken orally. The former seems likely, since he mentions it in a single breath with the liver preparation that he always injected. After the war Ernst Günther Schenk, formerly Himmler's nutrition adviser, claimed that Patient A also took the stimulant orally on a regular basis, as a clandestine mixture with the Nobel-Vitamultin: he reportedly examined one of the gold-wrapped bars in the Institute for Defence Pharmacy at the Military Medical Academy, and presumably discovered that it contained both Pervitin and caffeine.

The Führer also spent New Year's Eve of 1944/5 in a state of intoxication: first, in combination with glucose, he took a hormone-rich animal liver injection, then a holiday gift of Eukodal was taken intravenously. Although the dosage level went unrecorded, Morell did record the effect: 'Führer is almost calm. The trembling in his left arm or rather his hand only very slight.'[51]

As usual the state of the dictator's health was lauded to the outside world. In the edition of the weekly magazine *Das Reich* published on the last day of 1944, Goebbels wrote: 'The man whose goal it was to save his people, and furthermore to shape the face of the continent, is entirely averted from the everyday joys and bourgeois comforts of life. More than that: in fact, they don't even exist for him. [. . .] You need only linger in his presence to feel physically how much power he exudes, how strong he is.' The propaganda minister also had an explanation for the obviously poor posture of the head of state: 'When he holds his head slightly bowed, it comes from studying so many maps. [. . .] He is modesty personified. If the lunch and dinner tables of our whole nation were laid like that of the Führer, we would not need to be worried about German food supplies.'[52]

The last large-scale attack by the Luftwaffe ended fatally on the morning of 1 January 1945. Almost a thousand planes launched for one final gasp. But in spite of strict secrecy the Allied fighters and anti-aircraft defences reacted very effectively, and several dozen Luftwaffe pilots turned out to have had their last ever rations of Pervitin. It was on the return flight of the ones who had escaped the enemy that the true disaster happened. The German planes came under heavy fire from their own anti-aircraft gunners, who had not been informed about the mission. In this macabre way the Luftwaffe destroyed itself against its own cloudy sky. After that there were no more missions worthy of the name.

On 2 January 1945, the first work day of the New Year, which was the last year for National Socialism, Hitler felt 'well, apart from the tension of the current offensive. He asked about getting rid of the tremor in his left hand; tranquillizers needed but cannot be given because they would inhibit his powers of reason, on which the demands are constant and intense and of the greatest importance.'[53]

This entry represents a turning point, because afterwards Eukodal was not administered again. Had Morell recognized at last how lost Hitler was in unreal domains? Or did he want to reduce the quantity of drugs for a quite different reason, because he had a new concern: their increasing scarcity? The British were repeatedly bombing the pharmaceutical factories of the Reich and causing severe damage to German manufacturing capacities. Two weeks before Christmas the manufacturer of Eukodal and cocaine, the Darmstadt-based Merck Company, was hit. Seventy per cent of its facilities were in ruins. One employee reported: 'During this time the bulk of the workforce – 2,292 Germans and about 700 foreigners – were busy trying to bring order to the chaos of destruction. [. . .] Productivity was, taken overall, extraordinarily low, as almost two thirds of working time was lost to air raids.'[54] Could it be that Morell's supplies had run out and there were no more on the way?

On 16 January 1945 the Eagle's Eyrie was evacuated; the second Ardennes offensive had failed pitifully. Dispirited, patient and doctor took the train to the capital, retreated along with the Führer's inner circle into the bunker beneath the Reich Chancellery and thus reached the final stage in their denial of reality. Once Morell had complained in a letter that he had only been in Berlin for a few days over the past few years, and hadn't seen his wife for six months. Now he was back on the Havel and the Spree – but buried away under the ground like a mole. On 17 January 1945, a day after their arrival, Warsaw was seized by the Red Army. Stalin's troops were advancing inexorably.

On 30 January 1945, exactly twelve years after the National Socialists first seized power, the Red Army created a bridgehead west of the Oder and directly threatened Berlin. At the briefing session on the same day, which was followed by his final radio address, Hitler appeared in euphoric mood once again.

On 3 February 1945, 2,264 tonnes of bombs fell on the Reich capital. Thousands of people died. The U-Bahn was hit in fifty places at once; a packed overground train was struck just as it was leaving Belle-Alliance-Platz (now Hallesches Tor). The sky had a blood-red glow; the survivors hurried through dense palls of smoke. At Schlesisches Tor, another underground station, a big banner hung for a few hours: 'We want peace one way or the other!'[55] The Military Medical Academy on Invalidenstasse, where Ranke had once researched, now stood with charred roof-beams, empty window frames and bomb craters on the sports ground. The remains of the walls still smoked. The sirens wailed constantly, the anti-aircraft guns fired, the hellish dance constantly renewed itself, and people lay in slit trenches.[56] Eleven days later the centre of Dresden, where hundreds of thousands of refugees were huddled, was flattened from the air.

Meanwhile the drugs depot in the Führer's bunker was emptying. At least this could be a possible explanation of why Morell's notes cease to mention the formerly beloved substances. On 18 February he wrote: 'F. wants to try and get by without tranquillizers.'[57] Apart from a few ampoules of his home-brewed parasite liver preparation, there now seemed to be hardly anything left.[58] The symptoms that Hitler showed during those weeks indicate withdrawal: the tremors were getting worse and his body was going into rapid decline. At his final speech to the district leaders on 24 February 1945 he had finally lost his power of suggestion. He made a pitiful impression on his visitors, stood bowed, drooling. His announcements about the navy's new miracle weapon, Heye's small battle units, which would bring about the great miracle of a turn in the war's fortunes, now fell on deaf ears. The same day Morell wrote to the Reich Ministry of the Interior with a request for the release of new steroids made to his own recipe: two adrenal gland and pituitary gland preparations.[59] This wildly unreal request did not receive a reply. One possible reason for Morell's urging was that since there were hardly any pharmaceuticals left in the whole of Berlin, he was finding it increasingly difficult to honour prescriptions for Patient A. His assistants scoured the rubble-strewn city: 'It could only be processed and filled in the 6th pharmacy (1st at Zoo), where it was prepared for collection tomorrow. [. . .] Medication is very hard to get hold of even for the main medical depot of the SS main office. Most are discontinuing supplies because the factories have been bombed out.'[60]

The worst thing that could happen to a dealer happened to Morell. His source had run dry. It is the cardinal sin of the provider, to suddenly be out of the product. 'For four to five days the patient has been extremely pensive and has a weary, exhausted appearance. He wants to try and manage without tranquillizers,' said Morell, commenting on the shortage, and added with a note of concern: 'The

Führer is acting rather strangely towards me, short and in an irritable mood.'[61] None of this is proof, yet it is a set of clues which suggest that in the last quarter of 1944 Hitler had become addicted to Eukodal – and now yearned for the narcotic. It was unlikely he voiced such a wish aloud or explicitly in those final weeks in the bunker at the Reich Chancellery. But the signs indicate that he was gradually understanding what he had allowed to happen to him, and what a pharmacological blind alley he had ended up in.

The end of the final battle was approaching, and Hitler had lost his high, his Führer's rush, once and for all. He dragged himself painfully along the low passageways of the catacombs, thrust his torso forwards, pulled his legs after him, tipped to the right, supported himself on the bare wall and shuffled back from sitting room to conference room. All his energy for self-stylization had gone: whatever the reason for his abstinence from Eukodal, without the drug all that was left behind was a shell of a man whose uniform was spattered with rice gruel. Without the substances to which his body had become accustomed, his system ceased producing endorphins. His dopamine and serotonin balance suffered, along with his sympathetic nervous system. There was no feeling of well-being now, no protection against the menacing outside world. All that remained was over-sensitivity. The concrete walls might still have been standing, but the chemical bunker had been dissolved.

Now the Führer had irrevocably entered the reality of his lost war. Everything weighed upon him all of a sudden, and as an infinitely heavier burden than before – naked as he was without the hormones of happiness. Eukodal could have helped him now. In a second he would move from total pain to total paradise, and experience the most powerful emotions. Euphoria would flood through him, he could regain his faith and motivate everyone else to emerge victorious from the war. But Eukodal no longer existed for him, and without intoxication the last briefing sessions in March and April 1945 were so depressing as to be terrible. The generals seemed to be trying to hoodwink him all the time. The thing that could never have happened was happening, history was repeating itself, the military had stopped obeying their supreme commander and he constantly thought he was being sabotaged. Hitler started shouting, waving his arms around, raging, raving, his face so distorted that it was barely recognizable. It was only through aggression that he could defend himself against the traitors he sensed everywhere.

Goebbels, who now barely left his boss's side, openly addressed this decay and certified that Hitler was not in the condition that he should have been in. Meanwhile the propaganda minister was highly critical of Morell's methods of treatment: Hitler's body was shaking and had been doped repeatedly with all manner of pills and narcotics. On several occasions, he noted, he had wondered whether the prophylactic injections, which should have been trying to prevent every illness as soon as the first symptoms appeared, were not in fact making too big a demand on Hitler's health, and his life.

At six o'clock in the morning, after the military briefing, during which he had fumbled ceaselessly with his empty pill-box, Patient A lay completely exhausted and apathetic on a small sofa, filled only with the single thought that the best meal of the day was on its way: a mug of hot chocolate and cakes, three plates full of them. Sugar was the final drug: one more minute release of dopamine, one more small reward for the soul. Those bright blue eyes, once so hypnotic, were now dull. Crumbs stuck to his purple lips: a sweet-eating human ruin wrapped in slack skin. His body felt numb, as if he were no longer present in it. His temperature was always high. Every so often he'd go into the oxygen tent.

The sight of Hitler now only caused revulsion or at best pity. Everyone circled around him, trying in vain to make him feel good. Still his condition kept deteriorating. In the past all his loyal followers had been nervous at the first cough or sniffle; now his tooth enamel was decaying, his gums were drying up and his ruinous teeth were falling out. His brain, irreversibly damaged by neurotoxins, was no longer receiving stimulation: all the receptors that the transmitters could have filled were switched off. Everything had stopped working, the old delusory loops were just repeating themselves in his head: the paranoia, the panic about the red pustules, about the Jews, the Bolsheviks, the whisky drinker Churchill. Terrible headaches set in. He started digging into his yellow skin with a pair of golden tweezers, with aggressive, nervous movements, to get rid of the bacteria which had presumably passed through his body's boundaries and entered his system, and were now destroying him from within. Morell wanted to try bloodletting to bring the patient some kind of relief, but because of the fatty, hormone-saturated pig's liver injections his blood had become as thick as jelly and clotted immediately, so the measure failed. Hitler, with one last trace of gallows humour, suggested that they might at least be able to make 'Führer-blood sausage' out of it.[62]

Patient A wheezed pitifully as he endured his withdrawal. He trembled with anxiety from head to toe, he chewed the air, he lost weight, his kidneys were failing, and so too was his circulation. He could barely concentrate now. He was tormented by a painful yearning: an unquenchable thirst from each cell of his body. His left upper eyelid was so swollen that he couldn't see out of it and he kept pressing and rubbing at it. But 'the Führer does not want to wear an eye-patch'.[63] He only left the bunker for a short time, venturing into the garden of the Reich Chancellery, where he stumbled over rubble and the dusty wind circled him like the cloak of defeat. He dragged himself back inside. There was *Streuselkuchen*, each piece specially crumbled for him. Without a functioning set of teeth he slurped up the sweets, too much air entering his gut as he did so. Everyone in his entourage threw something into the Führer-machine that they themselves had bred, that they themselves had developed. The broken robot rattled once more, issued a pointless military order, avenged himself on someone, or passed death sentences on close colleagues like Karl Brandt, his former surgeon who had fallen into disfavour in the war between the doctors.

The historian Sebastian Haffner is mistaken when he describes the reports of Hitler's physical decay in the bunker beneath the Reich Chancellery as 'hopelessly overdrawn'.[64] In fact they are not precise or far-reaching enough, because they do not take sufficiently into account the possible moment of withdrawal. It is difficult to produce a diagnosis at this distance in time given the incomplete nature of the material. It is as if Hitler were less concerned with the loss of the world war than with the physical torments that he himself was going through, and which would not stop until his suicide.

At this point the potentate still stood by his personal physician. When on 3 March 1945 he undertook one last journey to the front at the Oder river, fifty kilometres east of Berlin, he forbade Morell to come with him for safety reasons. The physician noted, not without some pride: 'Because we might have suffered serious injuries through accidents and low-flying planes. If something happened to me, he would not have a doctor. [. . .] It was far more important to him while he was travelling that he would always find me at home waiting for him.'[65]

But how long would that *home* still exist? On 7 March the Americans crossed the bridge at Remagen and thus the Rhine. In the east Danzig fell to the Russians, likewise Vienna to the south. At this point Morell was treating Hitler more or less at random, administering vitamins and galvanic treatments against general nerve damage. The Führer – who had, characteristically, never gone near any of Berlin's great specialist clinics like the Charité hospital – now presented an utterly squalid image, which helps to explain his last great destructive experiment. On 19 March 1945 he issued the so-called Nero decree, which took his nihilism to the limit. Hitler ordered nothing less than the complete destruction of Germany: 'All military transport and communication facilities, industrial establishments and supply depots, as well as anything else of value within Reich territory [. . .] are to be destroyed.'[66] All locks, weirs, dams, canal bridges and harbour facilities were to be blown up, all electric cables pulled up, all banks and any remaining cultural monuments were to be levelled. Because of a lack of resources this final product of his hatred was never fully realized. The German Reich's destructive powers were finally spent, and the supplies in Hitler's medicine cabinet were similarly exhausted.

On 8 April, Morell informed his patient that there were no more Vitamultin bars left. The supplies that still existed were now injected: obscure substances such as strophantose I and II, Benerva forte, Betabion forte, Omnadin – hastily requisitioned remnants. Substances hardly anyone had heard of were suddenly injected every two days. In the late phase of the war, these drugs were thrown on to the chemical front, in the same way as the fourteen-year-olds who had just been sitting at their school desks were now manning the Flak.

On 16 April 1945 the direct assault on Berlin began. Four days later Patient A celebrated his last birthday. Morell's hands were shaking and he had a blackout when he was trying to give Hitler his birthday injection. Attending Physician Stumpfegger was summoned and applied everything the drugs cabinet still had to offer: 'Strophantose, Betabion forte i.v. plus Harmin', the latter an alkaloid made from Syrian rue.[67] Together with this, Morell added rather desperately: 'I replaced the heart capsules with liver, which is intended to achieve a highly stimulating effect.'[68]

The Dismissal

> I will leave all the men of history behind me. I want to
> be the greatest, even if the whole German people perishes
> in the process!
>
> Adolf Hitler to Theo Morell[69]

The next day, while the Russians shelled the city centre
with their 'Stalin organs', Hitler's personal physician was
sacked. What was the point of a dealer who was out of
stuff, and in such poor shape that he couldn't even give
an injection? 'Do you think me a fool?' Hitler yelled at
the dumbfounded Morell, who was paying him a visit
carrying a tray with a caffeine injection that he'd managed
to drum up from somewhere. 'You probably want to give
me morphine,' Hitler raged. When Morell protested, his
patient grabbed him by the collar and spat: 'Go home,
take off your uniform and act as if you've never seen me!'[70]

Crazy advice, because Morell's villa at the Havel river
had been bombed out, the windows of his practice on
the Kurfürstendamm were nailed up with cardboard, the
partition wall in the waiting room had collapsed. With
almost comical haste the plump doctor, after briefly collapsing at Hitler's feet when Hitler threatened to have him
shot, left the bunker and climbed the thirty-seven steps
to ground level. Panting and clutching his heart, he threw
himself into the last available official vehicle and wept
like a child. A Condor plane took off at two o'clock in the
afternoon, with the distraught doctor inside. Flying low
over Russian lines and burning villages, the pilot braved

searchlights and anti-aircraft fire to cross the American line at Partenkirchen, and after a considerable amount of searching about landed on a still usable runway at Neubiberg military airport south of Munich.

Morell's destination was the little town of Bayrisch Gmain near Berchtesgaden, to which he had evacuated his research laboratory. For a few days there he acted as if all was somehow well, frantically immersed himself in his correspondence, attended to his collapsing pharmaceutical business, tried to operate his half-assembled electron microscope, a present from Hitler, and spoke with his last remaining employee. Probably already in a state of quasi-insanity, he asked the revenue office for a deadline extension on his profit, corporation and business tax declaration, 'since due to staff difficulties we are unable to deliver our final version any sooner'.[71]

The Final Poison

I'm not doing politics any more. It repels me so much.

Adolf Hitler [72]

Göring, too, in a ridiculous camouflage uniform bursting at the seams, had fled to southern Germany. If he had to fall into anyone's hands he wanted it to be the Americans, not the Soviets. Referring to Hitler's inability to act, he sent a telegram from Bavaria to the bunker, emphasizing his ambitions to become Hitler's successor. Hitler raged about his deputy, accusing him of weakness and betrayal.

He had known for a long time, he said, that Göring was a morphine addict* – and stripped him of all positions and offices.

On 27 April, Hitler gave his followers potassium cyanide, regretting in a broken voice that he could not offer them anything better. Goebbels' wife, Magda, gave six of the capsules to her children. Patient A had his dog, Blondi, poisoned, as a test. He didn't yet lay a hand upon himself. In his political testament, which he could barely sign because his hands were shaking so much, while dying of his own toxins he raged one last time against the Jews. He tried to blame them for everything, and described them as 'the poisoners of the world'.

Meanwhile methamphetamine was being handed out to kid-soldiers in front of the Olympic Stadium, to keep them from going haywire at the sight of the advancing tanks and heavy artillery of the Red Army. As his morning gift, Grand Admiral Dönitz had sent a declaration of loyalty to his Führer along with a Berlin-bound cargo of fresh recruits – destined for an early death, as they had never even been trained for urban fighting. In the centre of the city, the bunker became the focus of the battles that were closing in on every side. There were explosions or implosions on every corner. Walls shook under the impacts. In the garden of the Reich Chancellery, where Hitler no longer ventured for a breath of fresh air, the soil was hurled incessantly into the air. Everywhere

* When arrested by the Allies, Göring was carrying a suitcase that held 24,000 opioid tablets (mostly Eukodal), and taking twenty times the usual dose. In the Palace Hotel in Gondorf, Luxembourg, where he was interned, that amount was gradually reduced by the American guards and doctors.

around, buildings burned and collapsed, while a fire storm sucked flames and smoke and oxygen upwards.

The place where this downfall occurred was far from silent. It was an inferno, the end of a terrible journey, a phase of madness which had lasted for twelve years, in which men had been afraid of reality, had tried to flee it more and more and in the process had brought the most terrible nightmares to fruition. During those final hours Hitler was devoured by his imaginary bacilli. Throughout the whole of his life he had tried to eliminate them, but it hadn't worked. Now he planned a double suicide. He had engaged in intense discussions about the problem with his closest circle: what if his hand shook too much when he pulled the trigger? The man who had brought about so many terrible things would now escape responsibility, and because there was no Eukodal left for a 'golden shot', he opted for the bullet. Only the pistol is stronger than the needle. He hastily married Eva Braun, who had travelled 'to the besieged city', as Hitler dramatically described it in his personal testament.[73] After the ghostly wedding ceremony spaghetti was served, with tomato sauce on the side, hydrogen cyanide for dessert and a bullet in the brain from a 6.35 mm Walther.

On 30 April 1945, at about 3.30 p.m., Patient A perished from his own system of repressed reality, overdosing on his own poisonous mixture. His bid to make the world rise up in a state of total intoxication was condemned to failure from the outset. Germany, land of drugs, of escapism and worldweariness, had been looking for a super-junkie. And it had found him, in its darkest hour, in Adolf Hitler.

Morell's Implosion

When Hitler's suicide became public, obedient compatriots followed his example all over the Reich. Honour demanded it – or the fear of consequences. In the city of Neubrandenburg, for example, there were over 600 spontaneous suicides, in the little town of Neustrelitz 681 – over 100,000 in Germany as a whole. Thirty-five army generals, six Luftwaffe generals, eight navy admirals, thirteen Waffen-SS generals, five police generals, eleven of the forty-three *Gauleiter*, leading heads of the Gestapo and of the Reich Security Main Office, some senior SS and police leaders: they all fled reality, following their Führer one last time. On 8 May 1945 the Wehrmacht surrendered. Some of the drugged-up underwater combatants from Heye's *K-verbände* weren't aware of this and, high as kites, went on fighting for another four days and nights until the twelfth of May, in a war that had ceased to exist.[74]

In mid-May 1945 Theo Morell was tracked down by a *New York Times* reporter, Tania Long, to his hiding-place in Bavaria. Her article appeared a few days later under the headline 'Doctor describes Hitler injections'. Shortly afterwards the former personal physician was taken prisoner by the Americans in Bad Reichenhall, and remained there for almost two years. In his many interrogation sessions Morell spoke incoherently, frequently contradicting himself, and sank into long silences and deep depression. Everything he had built up, his one-man pharmaceutical empire, was destroyed; unlike many others, Morell did not make the transition into a new age.

His questioners learned little about Hitler; they couldn't even bring accusations of war crimes against the completely feeble doctor, who sat apathetically in his cell and experienced episodes of paranoia, in which he thought Himmler was after him as he had been during the doctors' war. At any rate, he was no use as a witness for the Nuremberg trials. Apart from 'I wish I wasn't me', barely a single coherent sentence issued from his mouth.[75] So the Americans dismissed the bulky doctor with the dicky heart in the early summer of 1947, and dropped him off outside the central station in Munich. Morell cowered there, the once powerful man with the gold rods of Asclepius on his collar, now in a worn-out coat, shoeless on the bare cobbles, until a half-Jewish Red Cross nurse took pity on him and put him in a hospital in Tegernsee, where he died on 26 May 1948.

Acknowledgements

These learned gentlemen [. . .] will not neglect to find my
ideas entirely ludicrous; or indeed, they will do better than
that, they will elegantly ignore them completely. Do you
know why? Because they say I'm not an expert.

Johann Wolfgang von Goethe[1]

Mutating from novelist to author of a non-fiction history
book was a surprising and by no means a natural process,
but always a happy one. Some allies, friends and confidants
were closely involved in this transformation. It all began
with the Berlin DJ Alexander Krämer, who told me the
Nazis took loads of drugs – and wondered whether that
might be developed as an idea for a film. We pursued this
idea, and after Janina Findeisen suggested looking into
the archives to find out the actual facts, it got exciting. I
would like to give my warmest thanks to all the archivists
who helped me in Berlin, Sachsenhausen, Koblenz,
Marbach, Munich, Freiburg, Dachau and Washington DC.
I received early inspiration from the historian Peter
Steinkamp. Another expert whom I should particularly
like to thank is Volker Hartmann of the Bundeswehr
Medical Academy, and also Gorch Pieken, Scientific
Director of the Bundeswehr's Military History Museum
in Dresden. My gratitude goes to Sylvie Lake and Douglas

Gordon for their incomparable contributions, and also to Michael Stipe for helping me find the right English title – and to my very special agents, Tanja Howarth and Matthias Landwehr, my editors Lutz Dursthoff, Simon Winder, and Ben Hyman, and to Helge Malchow, my German publisher, who had the initial idea of setting this material out in a non-fiction book. Above all I am grateful to Hans Mommsen, the great late modern historian, who has given me a great deal of support. In any case, one thing has become apparent: a non-fiction book is a collective process. So I should like to thank everyone who helped me – whether they are mentioned here or not.

Norman Ohler

Bibliography

The most important sources for this book are unpublished documents. Archives opened specially for this research, unpublished material and countless reports and files from German and American state archives have been complemented by interviews with contemporary witnesses and military historians. In this context I should point out that because of retention periods certain aspects of the Third Reich still cannot be consulted in London archives. And in Moscow access by researchers to the secret archives of the former Soviet Union is still severely restricted.

A. Unpublished Sources

'Ärztliches Kriegstagebuch des Kommandos der K-Verbände', 1 September 1944–30 November 1944, Dr Richert, BArch-Freiburg RM 103–10/6

'Ärztliches Kriegstagebuch des Kommandos der K-Verbände', Arnim Wandel, BArch-Freiburg N906

'Ärtzliches Kriegstagebuch des Kreuzers *Prinz Eugen*' 1 January 1942– 31 January 1943, vol. 2, 'Geheime Kommandosache: ärztlicher Erfahrungsbericht über den Durchbruch des Kreuzers *Prinz Eugen* durch den Kanal in die Deutsche Bucht am 11 February 1942 bis 13 February 1942', BArch-Freiburg RM 92–5221/Bl. 58–60

'Ärtzliches Kriegstagebuch Waldau, Chef des Luftwaffenführungsstabes: März 1939 bis 10.4.1942', BArch-Freiburg ZA 3/163

'Bericht über die Kommandierung zur Gruppe Kleist, 12.7.1940', BArch-Freiburg RH 12–23/1931

'Bericht über Gesundheitslage des Kdo.d.K. und Hygiene des Einzelkämpfers: geheime Kommandosache', BArch-Freiburg N906

'Conditions in Berlin, March 1945', in SIR 1581–1582, RG No. 165, Stack Area 390, Row 35, Box 664, p. 1, National Archives at College Park, Md

Germany (Postwar) 1945–1949, Bureau of Narcotics and Dangerous Drugs: Subject Files, 1916–1970, Record Group 170; National Archives at College Park, Md

Giesing, Erwin, 'Bericht über meine Behandlung bei Hitler', Wiesbaden, 12 June 1945, Headquarters United States Forces European Theater Military Intelligence Service Center: OI – Consolidated Interrogation Report (CIR), National Archives at College Park, Md

'Hitler, Adolf: A composite picture', Entry ZZ-6, in IRR-Personal Name Files, RG No. 319, Stack Area 230, Box 8, National Archives at College Park, Md

'Hitler as seen by his doctors', No. 2, October 15, 1945 (Theodor Morell) and No. 4, November 29, 1945 (Erwin Giesing), National Archives at College Park, Md

Hitlers Testament, BArch-Koblenz N1128, Nachlass Adolf Hitler

Institut für allgemeine und Wehrphysiologie, BArch-Freiburg, RH 12–23, especially RH 12–23/1882 and RH 12–23/1623

Interrogation report on one German naval POW, in Entry 179, Folder 1, N10–16, RG No. 165, Stack Area 390, Box 648, National Archives at College Park, Md

Landesarchiv Berlin, A Rep. 250-02-09 Temmler

'Life History of Professor Dr. Med. Theo Morell', in IRR-Personal Name Files, RG NO. 319, Stack Area 230, Row 86, Box 8 [XE051008], National Archives at College Park, Md

Nachlass Joseph Goebbels, BArch-Koblenz N1118
Nachlass Theodor Morell:
  BArch-Koblenz N1348
  Institut für Zeitgeschichte Munich: IfZArch, MA 617
  National Archives, College Park, Md, Microfilm Publication T253,
    Rolls 34–45
Suchenwirth, Richard, 'Hermann Göring', BArch-Freiburg ZA
  3/801
————, 'Ernst Udet: Generalluftzeugmeister der deutschen
  Luftwaffe', BArch-Freiburg ZA 3/805
Unveröffentliches Kriegstagebuch des Heeres-Sanitätsinspekteurs,
  Sanitätsakademie der Bundeswehr
Waldmann, Anton, Unveröffentlichtes Tagebuch, Wehrgeschichtliche
  Lehrsammlung des Sanitätsdienstes der Bundeswehr

B. Published Sources, Documents

Bekämpfung der Alkohol- und Tabakgefahren: Bericht der 2. Reichstagung
  Volksgesundheit und Genußgifte, Hauptamt für Volksgesundheit der
  NSDAP und Reichsstelle gegen den Alkohol- und Tabakmißbrauch,
  Berlin-Dahlem, Reichsstelle gegen den Alkoholmißbrauch, 1939
Deutsche Reich und der Zweite Weltkrieg, Das, vol. 4: *Der Angriff auf die*
  Sowjetunion, Stuttgart, Militärgeschichtliches Forschungsamt, 1983;
  and vol. 8: *Die Ostfront 1943/44. Der Krieg im Osten und an den*
  Nebenfronten, Stuttgart, Militärgeschichtliches Forschungsamt,
  2007
Heeresverordnungsblatt 1942, part B, no. 424, p. 276: 'Bekämpfung des
  Mißbrauchs von Betäubungsmitteln', BArch-Freiburg RH
  12–23/1384.
Kriegstagebuch des Oberkommandos der Wehrmacht, ed. Percy Ernst
  Schramm, 8 vols. Frankfurt am Main, 1982 [1961]

Prozess gegen die Hauptkriegsverbrecher vor dem Internationalen Militärgerichtshof Nürnberg, 14. November 1945–1. Oktober 1946, Der, vol. 41, Munich, 1984

Reichsgesetzblatt I, 12 June 1941, p. 328: '6. Verordnung über Unterstellung weiterer Stoffe unter die Bestimmungen des Opiumgesetzes'

C. Quoted Literature

Aldgate, Anthony and Jeffrey Richards, *Britain Can Take It: The British Cinema in the Second World War* (2nd edn), London, 2007

Ballhausen, Hanno (ed.), *Chronik des Zweiten Weltkrieges*, Munich, 2004

Bekker, Cajus, *Einzelkämpfer auf See: die deutschen Torpedoreiter, Froschmänner und Sprengbootpiloten im Zweiten Weltkrieg*, Oldenburg/ Hamburg, 1968

Below, Nicolaus von, *Als Hitlers Adjutant 1937–45*, Mainz, 1980

Benjamin, Walter, *Einbahnstraße*, Frankfurt am Main, 1955

———, *Gesammelte Schriften*, Frankfurt am Main, 1986

Benn, Gottfried, *Sämtliche Werke*, vol. I: *Gedichte 1*, Stuttgart, 1986

———, 'Provoziertes Leben: ein Essay', in Gottfried Benn, *Sämtliche Werke*, vol. IV: *Prosa 2*, Stuttgart, 1989

Bezymenskii, Lev, *Die letzten Notizen von Martin Bormann: ein Dokument und sein Verfasser*, Munich, 1974

Binion, Rudolph, . . . *dass Ihr mich gefunden habt*, Stuttgart, 1978

Bloch, Marc, *Strange Defeat*, trans. Gerard Manley Hopkins, Oxford, 1949

Böll, Heinrich, *Briefe aus dem Krieg 1939–45*, Cologne, 2001

Bonhoeffer, Karl, 'Psychopathologische Erfahrungen und Lehren des Weltriegs', *Münchener medizinische Wochenschrift*, vol. 81 (1934)

Bradley, Dermot, *Walther Wenck, General der Panzertruppe*, Osnabrück, 1982

Burroughs, William, *Naked Lunch*, Paris, 1959

Canetti, Elias, *Masse und Macht,* Hamburg, 1960 [*Crowds and Power,* trans. Carol Stewart, London, 1960]

Churchill, Winston, *Zweiter Weltkrieg,* vols. I and II, Stuttgart, 1948/49 [*The Second World War,* vol. 1: *The Gathering Storm,* London, 1948; vol. 2: *Their Finest Hour,* London, 1949]

Conti, Leonardo, 'Vortrag des Reichsgesundheitsführers Dr. Conti vor dem NSD-Ärztebund, Gau Berlin, am 19. März 1940, im Berliner Rathaus', *Deutsches Ärzteblatt,* vol. 70 (1940), no. 13

Dansauer, Friedrich and Adolf Rieth, *Über Morphinismus bei Kriegsbeschädigten,* Berlin, 1931

Eckermann, Johann Peter, *Gespräche mit Goethe,* Frankfurt am Main, 1987

Falck, Wolfgang, *Falkenjahre: Erinnerungen 1903–2003,* Moosburg, 2003

Fest, Joachim C., *Hitler: eine Biographie,* Berlin, 1973

Fischer, Hubert, *Die Militärärztliche Akademie 1934–1945,* Osnabrück, 1985 [Munich, 1975]

Fischer, Wolfgang, *Ohne die Gnade der späten Geburt,* Munich, 1990

Fleischhacker, Wilhelm, 'Fluch und Segen des Cocain', *Österreichische Apotheker-Zeitung,* no. 26 (2006)

Flügel, F. E., 'Medikamentöse Beeinflussung psychischer Hemmungszustände', *Klinische Wochenschrift,* vol. 17 (1938), no. 2

Fraeb, Walter Martin, *Untergang der bürgerlich-rechtlichen Persönlichkeit im Rauschgiftmißbrauch,* Berlin, 1937

Fränkel, Fritz and Dora Benjamin, 'Die Bedeutung der Rauschgifte für die Juden und die Bekämpfung der Suchten durch die Fürsorge', *Jüdische Wohlfahrtspflege und Sozialpolitik* (1932)

Freienstein, Waldemar, 'Die gesetzlichen Grundlagen der Rauschgiftbekämpfung', *Der öffentliche Gesundheitsdienst,* Series A (1936–7)

Friedlander, Henry, *Der Weg zum NS-Genozid: von der Euthanasie zur Endlösung,* Berlin, 1997

Frieser, Karl Heinz, *Die Blitzkrieg-Legende: der Westfeldzug 1940*, ed. Militärgeschichtliches Forschungsamt, Munich, 2012

Gabriel, Ernst, 'Rauschgiftfrage und Rassenhygiene', *Der Öffentliche Gesundheitsdienst*, Series B, vol. 4 (1938–9)

Gathmann, Peter and Martina Paul, *Narziss Goebbels: eine Biografie*, Vienna, 2009

Geiger, Ludwig, *Die Morphin- und Kokainwelle nach dem Ersten Weltkrieg in Deutschland und ihre Vergleichbarkeit mit der heutigen Drogenwelle*, Munich, 1975

Gisevius, Hans Bernd, *Adolf Hitler: Versuch einer Deutung*, Munich, 1963

Goebbels, Joseph, *Die Tagebücher 1924–1945*, ed. Elke Fröhlich, Munich, 1987

Gordon, Mel, *Sündiges Berlin – Die zwanziger Jahre: Sex, Rausch, Untergang*, Wittlich, 2011

Gottfried, Claudia, 'Konsum und Verbrechen: die Schuhprüfstrecke im KZ Sachsenhausen', in *LVR-Industriemuseum Ratingen – Glanz und Grauen: Mode im 'Dritten Reich'*, Ratingen, 2012

Graf, Otto, 'Über den Einfluss von Pervitin auf einige psychische und psychomotorische Funktionen', *Arbeitsphysiologie*, vol. 10 (1939), no. 6

Grass, Günter, *Die Blechtrommel*, Neuwied am Rhein/West Berlin, 1959

Guderian, Heinz, *Erinnerungen eines Soldaten*, Stuttgart, 1960

Haffner, F., 'Zur Pharmakologie und Praxis der Stimulantien', *Klinische Wochenschrift*, vol. 17 (1938), no. 38

Haffner, Sebastian, *Anmerkungen zu Hitler*, Munich, 1978

Halder, Franz, *Kriegstagebuch: tägliche Aufzeichnungen des Chefs des Generalstabes des Heeres 1939–1942*, 3 vols., ed. Hans-Adolf Jacobsen, Stuttgart, Arbeitskreis für Wehrforschung, 1962–4

Hansen, Hans-Josef, *Felsennest, das vergessene Hauptquartier in der Eifel*, Aachen, 2008

Hartmann, Christian, *Unternehmen Barbarossa: der deutsche Krieg im Osten 1941–1945*, Munich, 2013

Hassell, Ulrich von, *Die Hassel-Tagebücher 1938–1944: Aufzeichnungen vom anderen Deutschland*, Munich, 1999

Hauschild, Fritz, 'Tierexperimentelles über eine peroral wirksame zentralanaleptische Substanz mit peripherer Kreislaufwirkung', *Klinische Wochenschrift*, vol. 17 (1938), no. 36

Heinen, W., 'Erfahrungen mit Pervitin: Erfahrungsbericht', *Medizinische Welt*, no. 46 (1938)

Hesse, Reinhard, *Geschichtswissenschaft in praktischer Absicht*, Stuttgart, 1979

Hiemer, Ernst, *Der Giftpilz*, Nuremberg, 1938

Holzer, Tilmann, 'Die Geburt der Drogenpolitik aus dem Geist der Rassenhygiene: deutsche Drogenpolitik von 1933 bis 1972', inaugural dissertation, Mannheim, 2006

Ironside, Edmund, *Diaries 1937–1940*, New York, 1962

Jens, Walter, *Statt einer Literaturgeschichte*, Munich, 2001

Katz, Ottmar, *Prof. Dr. med. Theo Morell: Hitlers Leibarzt*, Bayreuth, 1982

Kaufmann, Hans P., *Arzneimittel-Synthese*, Heidelberg, 1953

Keller, Philipp, *Die Behandlung der Haut- und Geschlechtskrankheiten in der Sprechstunde*, Heidelberg, 1952

Kershaw, Ian, *Hitler 1889–1945: das Standardwerk*, Munich, 2008 (vol. 1: *1889–1936: Hubris*, London, 1998; vol. 2: *1936–1945: Nemesis*, London, 2000)

Kielmannsegg, Johann, Adolf Graf von, *Panzer zwischen Warschau und Atlantik*, Berlin, 1941

Klee, Ernst, *Das Personenlexikon zum Dritten Reich: wer war was vor und nach 1945*, Frankfurt am Main, 2003

Kocka, Jürgen and Thomas Nipperdey (eds.), *Theorie der Geschichte*, vol. 3: *Beiträge zur Historik*, Munich, 1979

Kosmehl, Erwin, 'Der sicherheitspolizeiliche Einsatz bei der Bekämpfung der Betäubungsmittelsucht, Berlin', in Gerhart Feuerstein, *Suchtgiftbekämpfung: Ziele und Wege*, Berlin, 1944

Kramer, Eva, 'Die Pervitingefahr', *Münchener medizinische Wochenschrift*, vol. 88 (1941), no. 15

Kroener, Bernhard R., 'Die personellen Ressourcen des Dritten Reiches im Spannungsfeld zwischen Wehrmacht, Bürokratie und Kriegswirtschaft 1939–1942', Rolf-Dieter Müller and Hans Umbreit, *Das deutsche Reich und der Zweite Weltkrieg*, vol. 5.1: *Organisation und Mobilisierung des deutschen Machtbereichs: Kriegsverwaltung, Wirtschaft und personelle Ressourcen 1939–1941*, Stuttgart, 1988

Leeb, Wilhelm Ritter von, 'Tagebuchaufzeichnung und Lagebeurteilungen aus zwei Weltkriegen: aus dem Nachlass', ed. with biographical notes Georg Meyer, in *Beiträge zur Militär- und Kriegsgeschichte*, vol. 16, Stuttgart, 1976

Lemmel, Gerhard und Hartwig Jürgen, 'Untersuchungen über die Wirkung von Pervitin und Benzedrin auf psychischem Gebiet', *Deutsches Archiv für klinische Medizin*, vol. 185 (1940), nos. 5. and 6

Lewin, Louis, *Phantastica: die betäubenden und erregenden Genussmittel*, Linden, 2010

Liebendörfer, 'Pervitin in der Hand des praktischen Nervenarztes', *Münchener medizinische Wochenschrift*, vol. 87 (1940), no. 43

Lifton, Robert Jay, *Ärzte im Dritten Reich*, Stuttgart, 1998

Liljestrand, G., *Poulsson's Lehrbuch für Pharmakologie*, Leipzig, 1944

Linge, Heinz, *Bis zum Untergang*, Munich, 1980

Long, Tania, 'Doctor describes Hitler injections', *The New York Times*, 22 May 1945

Luck, Hans von, *Mit Rommel an der Front*, Hamburg, 2007

Mann, Golo, *Deutsche Geschichte des 19. und 20. Jahrhunderts*, Stuttgart/Mannheim, 1958

Mann, Klaus, *Treffpunkt im Unendlichen*, Reinbek, 1998

———, *Der Wendepunkt*, Reinbek, 1984

Maser, Werner, *Adolf Hitler: Legende Mythos Wirklichkeit*, Munich, 1997

Meurer, Christian, *Wunderwaffe Witzkanone: Heldentum von Hess bis Hendrix*, Essay 09, Münster, 2005

Mitscherlich, Alexander and Fred Mielke, *Medizin ohne Menschlichkeit: Dokumente des Nürnberger Ärzteprozesses*, Frankfurt, 1978

Mommsen, Hans, *Aufstieg und Untergang der Republik von Weimar 1918–1933*, Berlin, 2000

Müller-Bonn, Hermann, 'Pervitin, ein neues Analepticum', *Medizinische Welt*, no. 39 (1939)

Nansen, Odd, *Von Tag zu Tag: ein Tagebuch*, Hamburg, 1949

Neumann, Erich, 'Bemerkungen über Pervitin', *Münchener medizinische Wochenschrift*, no. 33 (1939)

Neumann, Hans-Joachim and Henrik Eberle, *War Hitler krank? – ein abschließender Befund*, Cologne, 2009

Nöldeke, Hartmut und Volker Hartmann, *Der Sanitätsdienst in der deutschen U-Boot-Waffe*, Hamburg, 1996

Osterkamp, Theo, *Durch Höhen und Tiefen jagt ein Herz*, Heidelberg, 1952

Overy, Richard, J., 'German aircraft production 1939–1942', in *Study in the German War Economy*, Ph.D. thesis., Queens' College, Cambridge, 1977

Pieper, Werner, *Nazis on Speed: Drogen im 3. Reich*, Birkenau-Löhrbach, 2002

Pohlisch, Kurt, 'Die Verbreitung des chronischen Opiatmißbrauchs in Deutschland', *Monatsschrift für Psychiatrie und Neurologie*, vol. 79 (1931)

Püllen, C., 'Bedeutung des Pervitins (1-Phenyl-2-methylamino-propan) für die Chirurgie', *Chirurg*, vol. 11 (1939), no. 13

————, 'Erfahrungen mit Pervitin', *Münchener medizinische Wochenschrift*, vol. 86 (1939), no. 26

Ranke, Otto, 'Ärztliche Fragen der technischen Entwicklung', *Veröff. a. d. Geb. d. Heeres-Sanitätswesens*, vol. 109 (1939)

————, 'Leistungssteigerung durch ärztliche Maßnahmen', *Deutscher Militärarzt*, no. 3 (1939)

Reko, Viktor, *Magische Gifte: Rausch- und Betäubungsmittel der neuen Welt*, Stuttgart, 1938

Ridder, Michael de, *Heroin: vom Arzneimittel zur Droge*, Frankfurt am Main, 2000

Römpp, Hermann, *Chemische Zaubertränke*, Stuttgart, 1939

Scheer, Rainer, 'Die nach Paragraph 42 RStGB verurteilten Menschen in Hadamar', in Dorothee Roer and Dieter Henkek, *Psychiatrie im Faschismus: die Anstalt Hadamar 1933–1945*, Bonn, 1986

Schenck, Ernst Günther, *Dr. Morell: Hitlers Leibarzt und seine Medikamente*, Schnellbach, 1998

————, *Patient Hitler: eine medizinische Biographie*, Augsburg, 2000

Schmidt, Paul, *Statist auf diplomatischer Bühne 1923–1945*, Bonn, 1950

Schmölders, Claudia, *Hitlers Gesicht: eine physiognomische Biographie*, Munich, 2000

Schoen, Rudolf, 'Pharmakologie und spezielle Therapie des Kreislaufkollapses', in *Verhandlungen der Deutschen Gesellschaft für Kreislaufforschung*, 1938

Schramm, Percy Ernst, 'Adolf Hitler: Anatomie eines Diktators' (5th and last in the sequence), *Der Spiegel*, 10/1964

Schultz, I. H., 'Pervitin in der Psychotherapie', *Deutsche medizinische Wochenschrift*, nos. 51–2 (1944)

Seifert, W., 'Wirkungen des 1-Phenyl-2-methylamino-propan (Pervitin) am Menschen', *Deutsche medizinische Wochenschrift*, vol. 65 (1939), no. 23

Shirer, William L., *Aufstieg und Fall des Dritten Reiches*, Cologne/Berlin, 1971 [*The Rise and Fall of the Third Reich: A History of Nazi Germany*, New York/London, 1960]

Snelders, Stephen and Toine Pieters, 'Speed in the Third Reich: Methamphetamine (Pervitin) use and a drug history from below', *Social History of Medicine Advance Access*, 2011

Speer, Albert, *Erinnerungen*, Frankfurt am Main, 1969

Speer, Ernst, 'Das Pervitinproblem', *Deutsches Ärzteblatt*, January 1941

Steinhoff, Johannes, *Die Straße von Messina*, Berlin, 1995

Steinkamp, Peter, 'Pervitin (metamphetamine) tests, use and misuse in the German Wehrmacht', in Wolfgang Eckart (ed.), *Man, Medicine, and the State: The Human Body as an Object of Government*, Stuttgart, 2007

Störmer, Uta (ed.), *Am rätselhaftesten ist das Sein: Tagebücher von Burkhard Grell (1934–1941)*, Berlin, 2010

Sudrow, Anne, *Der Schuh im Nationalsozialismus: eine Produktgeschichte im deutsch-britisch-amerikanischen Vergleich*, Göttingen, 2010

Thukydides [Thucydides], *Der Peloponnesische Krieg*, Wiesbaden, 2010

Toland, John, *Adolf Hitler*, Bergisch-Gladbach, 1977

Udet, Ernst, *Mein Fliegerleben*, Berlin, 1942

Unger, Frank, 'Das Institut für Allgemeine und Wehrphysiologie an der Militärärztlichen Akademie (1937–1945)', medical dissertation, Hochschule Hanover, 1991

Wahl, Karl, . . . *es ist das deutsche Herz*, Augsburg, 1954

Wellershoff, Dieter, *Der Ernstfall: Innenansichten des Krieges*, Cologne, 2006

Wenzig, K., *Allgemeine Hygiene des Dienstes*, Berlin/Heidelberg, 1936

Yang, Rong, *'Ich kann einfach das Leben nicht mehr ertragen': Studien zu den Tagebüchern von Klaus Mann (1931–1949)*, Marburg, 1996.

Online materials

'Historische Begründung eines deutschen Chemie-Museums': www.
deutsches-chemie-museum.de/uploads/media/Geschichte_der_
chemischen_Industrie.pdf

Hitler's medication: http://www.jkris.dk/jkris/Histomed/hitlermed/
hitlermed.htm

http://hss.ulb.uni-bonn.de/2005/0581/0581.pdf

D. Additional Literature

Agamben, Giorgio, *Die Macht des Denkens*, Frankfurt am Main, 2005

Allmayer-Beck, Johann Christoph, *'Herr Oberleitnant, det lohnt doch nicht!': Kriegserinnerungen an die Jahre 1938 bis 1945*, ed. Erwin A. von Schmidl, Vienna, 2012

Beck, Herta, *Leistung und Volksgemeinschaft*, vol. 61, Husum, 1991

Bitzer, Dirk and Bernd Wilting, *Stürmer für Deutschland: die Geschichte des deutschen Fußballs von 1933 bis 1954*, Frankfurt am Main, 2003

Bolognese-Leuchtenmüller, B., 'Geschichte des Drogengebrauchs: Konsum – Kultur – Konflikte – Krisen', *Beiträge zur historischen Sozialkunde*, no. 1, 1992

Bonhoff, Gerhard and Herbert Lewrenz, *Über Weckamine (Pervitin und Benzedrin)*, Berlin, 1954

Bostroem, A., 'Zur Frage der Pervitin-Verordnung', *Münchener medizinische Wochenschrift*, vol. 88, 1941

Bracke G., *Die Einzelkämpfer der Kriegsmarine*, Stuttgart, 1981

Briesen, Detlef, *Drogenkonsum und Drogenpolitik in Deutschland und den USA: ein historischer Vergleich*, Frankfurt am Main, 2005

Buchheim, Lothar Günther, *Das Boot*, Munich, 1973

Clausewitz, Carl von, *Vom Kriege*, Neuenkirchen, 2010 [1832]

Courtwright, David, T., *Forces of Habit: Drugs and the Making of the Modern World*, Cambridge, 2002

Daube, H., 'Pervitinpsychosen', *Der Nervenarzt*, no. 14 (1941)

Davenport-Hines, Richard, *The Pursuit of Oblivion: A Social History of Drugs*, London, 2004

Quincey, Thomas De, *Confessions of an English Opium Eater*, London, 1821

Delbrouck, Mischa, *Verehrte Körper, verführte Körper*, Hameln, 2004

Dittmar, F., 'Pervitinsucht und akute Pervitinintoxikation', *Deutsche medizinische Wochenschrift*, vol. 68 (1942)

Dobroschke, Christiane, 'Das Suchtproblem der Nachkriegszeit: eine klinische Statistik', *Deutsche medizinische Wochenschrift*, vol. 80 (1955)

Eberle, Henrik und Matthias Uhl (eds.), *Das Buch Hitler*, Cologne, 2005

Fest, Joachim, *Der Untergang: Hitler und das Ende des Dritten Reiches. Eine historische Skizze*, Berlin, 2002

Fischer, Hubert, *Der deutsche Sanitätsdienst 1921–1945*, 5 vols., Osnabrück, 1982–8

Friedrich, Thomas, *Die missbrauchte Hauptstadt*, Berlin, 2007

Gisevius, Hans Bernd, *Bis zum bitteren Ende: vom Reichstagsbrand bis zum Juli 1944*, Hamburg, 1964

Goodrick-Clarke, Nicholas, *Die okkulten Wurzeln des Nationalsozialismus*, Graz, 1997

Görtemaker, Heike B., *Eva Braun: Leben mit Hitler*, Munich, 2010

Grass, Günter, *Beim Häuten der Zwiebel*, Göttingen, 2006

Greving, H., 'Psychopathologische und körperliche Vorgänge bei jahrelangem Pervitinmißbrauch', *Der Nervenarzt*, no. 14 (1941)

Haffner, Sebastian, *Im Schatten der Geschichte*, Munich, 1987

———, *Von Bismarck zu Hitler: ein Rückblick*, Munich, 2009

Hartmann, Christian, *Wehrmacht im Ostkrieg: Front und militärisches Hinterland 1941/42*, Munich, 2009

Herer, Jack and Mathias Bröckers, *Die Wiederentdeckung der Nutzpflanze Hanf*, Leipzig, 2008

Hitler, Adolf and Gerhard L. Weinberg, *Hitlers zweites Buch*, Munich, 1961

Iversen, Leslie, *Drogen und Medikamente*, Stuttgart, 2004

Jünger, Ernst, *Annäherungen: Drogen und Rausch*, Stuttgart, 1980

Kaufmann, Wolfgang, *Das Dritte Reich und Tibet*, Hagen, 2008

Keyserlingk, H. von, 'Über einen pervitinsüchtigen, stimmungsabnormalen Schwindler', *Deutsche Zeitschrift für gerichtliche Medizin*, vol. 40 (1951)

Klemperer, Victor, *LTI: Notizbuch eines Philologen*, Stuttgart, 1998

Kluge, Alexander, *Der Luftangriff auf Halberstadt am 8. April 1945*, Frankfurt am Main, 1977

Koch, E. and M. Wech, *Deckname Artischocke: die geheimen Menschenversuche der CIA*, Munich, 2002

Koch, Lutz, *Rommel: der Wüstenfuchs*, Bielefeld, 1978

Kohl, Paul (ed.), *111 Orte in Berlin auf den Spuren der Nazi-Zeit*, Cologne, 2013

Kuhlbrodt, Dietrich, *Nazis immer besser*, Hamburg, 2006

Kupfer, Alexander, *Göttliche Gifte*, Stuttgart, 1996

Kutz, Martin, *Deutsche Soldaten: eine Kultur- und Mentalitätsgeschichte*, Darmstadt, 2006

Langer, Walter C., *Das Adolf-Hitler-Psychogramm*, Munich, 1982

Läuffer, Hermann (ed.), *Der Spass ist ein Meister aus Deutschland: Geschichte der guten Laune 1933–1990*, Cologne, 1990

Laughland, John, *The Tainted Source*, London, 1998

Ledig, Gerd, *Vergeltung*, Frankfurt am Main, 1999

Leonhard, Jörn, *Die Büchse der Pandora*, Munich, 2014

Ley, Astrid and Günther Morsch (ed.), *Medizin und Verbrechen: das Krankenrevier des KZ Sachsenhausen 1936–1945*, Berlin, 2007

Maiwald, Stefan, *Sexualität unter dem Hakenkreuz*, Hamburg, 2002

Manstein, Erich von, *Verlorene Siege*, Bonn, 2009

Misch, Rochus, *Der letzte Zeuge*, Munich/Zürich, 2008

Neitzel, Sönke and Harald Welzer, *Soldaten: Protokolle vom Kämpfen, Töten und Sterben*, Frankfurt am Main, 2011

Overy, R. J., *Hermann Göring: Machtgier und Eitelkeit*, Munich, 1986 [*Goering: The 'Iron Man'*, London, 1984]

Paul, Wolfgang, *Wer war Hermann Göring*, Esslingen, 1983

Pauwels, Louis and Jacques Bergier, *Aufbruch ins dritte Jahrtausend: von der Zukunft der phantastischen Vernunft*, Bern/Stuttgart, 1962

Piekalkiewicz, Janusz, *Krieg der Panzer: 1939–1945*, Munich, 1999

Pynchon, Thomas, *Die Enden der Parabel*, Reinbek, 1981 [*Gravity's Rainbow*, New York, 1973]

Raddatz, Fritz J., *Gottfried Benn: Leben – niederer Wahn. Eine Biographie*, Berlin, 2003

Reese, Willy Peter, *Mir selber seltsam fremd: die Unmenschlichkeit des Krieges Russland 1941–44*, Berlin, 2003

Richey, Stephen W., 'The Philosophical Basis of the Air Land Battle: *Auftragstaktik, Schwerpunkt, Aufrollen*', *Military Review*, vol. 64 (1984)

Schlick, Caroline (ed.), *Apotheken im totalitären Staat: Apothekenalltag in Deutschland von 1937–1945*, Stuttgart, 2008

Schmieder, Arnold, 'Deregulierung der Sucht', in *Jahrbuch Suchtforschung*, vol. 2, Münster, 2001

Schmitt, Eric-Emmanuel, *Adolf H.: Zwei Leben*, Frankfurt am Main, 2008

Schmitz-Berning, Cornelia, *Vokabular des Nationalsozialismus*, Berlin, 2000

Schneider, Peter, *Die Lieben meiner Mutter*, Cologne, 2013

Schulze-Marmeling, Dietrich, *Davidstern und Lederball*, Göttingen, 2003

Schütte, Uwe, *Die Poetik des Extremen*, Göttingen, 2006

Sharp, Alan (ed.), *The Versailles Settlement: Peacemaking after the First World War 1919–1923*, 2nd edn, New York, 2008

Stehr, J., 'Massenmediale Dealerbilder und ihr Gebrauch im Alltag', in B. Paul and H. Schmidt-Semisch (eds.), *Drogendealer: Ansichten eines verrufenen Gewerbes*, Freiburg, 1998

Stern, Fritz, *Kulturpessimismus als politische Gefahr: eine Analyse nationaler Ideologie in Deutschland*, Munich/Bern, 1963

Theweleit, Klaus, *Männerphantasien*, Reinbek, 1982

Traue, Georg, *Arische Gottzertrümmerung*, Braunschweig, 1934

Twardoch, Szczepan, *Morphin*, Berlin, 2014

Van Crefeld, Martin, *Kampfkraft: Militärische Organisation und Leistung der deutschen und amerikanischen Armee 1939–1945*, Graz, 2009

Volkmann, Udo, *Die britische Luftverteidigung und die Abwehr der deutschen Luftangriffe während der Luftschlacht um England bis zum Juni 1941*, Osnabrück, 1982

Wegener, Oskar, *Die Wirkung von Dopingmitteln auf den Kreislauf und die körperliche Leistung*, Flensburg/Freiburg, 1954

Weiß, Ernst, *Ich: der Augenzeuge*, Munich, 1966

Wette, Wolfram, *Militarismus in Deutschland*, Darmstadt, 2008

Wisotsky, S., 'A Society of Suspects: The War on Drugs and Civil Liberties', in H. Gros (ed.), *Rausch und Realität: eine Kulturgeschichte der Drogen*, vol. 3, Stuttgart, 1998

Wissinger, Detlev, *Erinnerungen eines Tropenarztes*, Books-on-Demand, 2002

Wulf, Joseph (ed.), *Presse und Funk im Dritten Reich*, Berlin, 2001

Zuckmayer, Carl, *Des Teufels General*, Stockholm, 1946

References

1 Methamphetamine, the *Volksdroge* (1933–1938)

1. There are still some prescription drugs based on methamphetamine, e.g. in the USA (such as the ADHD medication Desoxyn). Still, methamphetamine is broadly regulated according to international drugs regulations, and in most cases not available on prescription, but only 'tradeable', as a source material for the manufacture of medication. In Europe there is no legal drug based on methamphetamine, only on similar products such as methylphenidate and dextroamphetamine.
2. Friedrich Dansauer and Adolf Rieth, *Über Morphinismus bei Kriegsbeschädigten*, Berlin, 1931.
3. In around 1885 the American chemist John Pemberton combined cocaine with caffeine to make a drink called Coca-Cola, which was soon sold as a panacea for all ills. Until 1903 the original Coke apparently contained up to 250 milligrams of cocaine per litre. Wilhelm Fleischhacker, 'Fluch und Segen des Cocain', *Österreichische Apotheker-Zeitung*, no. 26, 2006.
4. See 'Viel Spass mit Heroin', *Der Spiegel*, 26/2000, pp. 184ff.
5. See Werner Pieper's brillant anthology, *Nazis on Speed: Drogen im 3. Reich*, Birkenau-Löhrbach, 2002. Quoted on p. 47.
6. Michael de Ridder, *Heroin: vom Arzneimittel zur Droge*, Frankfurt, 2000, p. 128.
7. See Pieper, *Nazis on Speed*, pp. 26ff. And in this context also p. 205.

8. BArch-Berlin R 1501, *Akten betr. Vertrieb von Opium und Morphium*, vol. 8, Bl. 502, 15 September 1922.

9. Quoted from Tilmann Holzer, *Die Geburt der Drogenpolitik aus dem Geist der Rassehygiene: deutsche Drogenpolitik von 1933 bis 1972*, inaugural dissertation, Mannheim, 2006, p. 32.

10. Auswärtiges Amt, AA/R 43309, note by Breitfeld (opium adviser in the AAO, 10 March 1935). Quoted in Holzer, *Die Geburt der Drogenpolitik*, p. 32.

11. Even respected liberal historians were involved in a deliberate falsification of the official files concerning the period leading up to the war. See Hans Mommsen, *Aufstieg und Untergang der Republik von Weimar 1918–1933*, Berlin, 2000, p. 105.

12. Klaus Mann, *Der Wendepunkt*, Reinbek, 1984. Quoted from Mel Gordon, *Sündiges Berlin – Die zwanziger Jahre: Sex, Rausch, Untergang*, Wittlich, 2011, p. 53 [*Voluptuous Panic: The Erotic World of Weimar Berlin*, Port Townsend, 2008].

13. Pieper, *Nazis on Speed*, p. 175.

14. Fritz von Ostini, 'Neues Berliner Kommerslied', also known as 'Wir schnupfen und wir spritzen', *Jugend*, no. 52, 1919.

15. Kurt Pohlisch, 'Die Verbreitung des chronischen Opiatmissbrauchs in Deutschland', *Monatsschrift für Psychiatrie und Neurologie*, vol. 79 (1931), pp. 193–202, table II.

16. The NSDAP did not have a Party programme in the traditional sense, and never made a secret of its irrational approach. Its structures remained chaotic until the end. See Mommsen, *Aufstieg und Untergang*, p. 398.

17. Günter Grass, *Die Blechtrommel*, Neuwied am Rhein/West Berlin, 1959, p. 173.

18. The statement is by Gregor Strasser. Quoted from Dieter Wellershoff, *Der Ernstfall: Innenansichten des Krieges*, Cologne, 2006, p. 57.

19. Pieper, *Nazis on Speed*, p. 210.

20. Ibid., p. 364.

21. BArch-Berlin R1501/126497, Bl. 214, 215, 220.

22. 'Die Unterbringung dauert so lange als ihr Zweck es erfordert.' Quoted in Holzer, *Die Geburt der Drogenpolitik*, p. 191. See also 'Maßregeln der Sicherung und Besserung', in §§42b, c RStGB: *Unterbringung von straffälligen Süchtigen in Heil- und Pflege- oder Entziehungsanstalten.* This regulation remained in force until 1 October 1953.

23. *Reichsärzteordnung*, 13 December 1935. See also Pieper, *Nazis on Speed*, pp. 171 and 214, and Walter Martin Fraeb, *Untergang der bürgerlich-rechtlichen Persönlichkeit im Rauschgiftmissbrauch*, Berlin, 1937.

24. *Reichsärzteordnung*, 13 December 1935. See also Pieper, *Nazis on Speed*, pp. 171 and 214, and Walter Martin Fraeb, *Untergang der bürgerlich-rechtlichen Persönlichkeit im Rauschgiftmißbrauch*, Berlin, 1937.

25. Holzer, *Die Geburt der Drogenpolitik*, p. 179.

26. Ibid., p. 273.

27. BArch-Berlin R58/473, Bl. 22 (microfiche).

28. Quoted in Pieper, *Nazis on Speed*, p. 380.

29. Ibid., pp. 186 and 491.

30. Waldemar Freienstein, 'Die gesetzlichen Grundlagen der Rauschgiftbekämpfung', in *Der öffentliche Gesundheitsdienst*, vol. A (1936–7), pp. 209–18. See also Holzer, *Die Geburt der Drogenpolitik*, p. 139.

31. Ernst Gabriel, 'Rauschgiftfrage und Rassenhygiene', in *Der öffentliche Gesundheitsdienst*, Teilausgabe B, Bd. 4, pp. 245–53, quoted from Holzer, *Die Geburt der Drogenpolitik*, p. 138. See also Pieper, *Nazis on Speed*, pp. 213ff.

32. Ludwig Geiger, *Die Morphin- und Kokainwelle nach dem Ersten*

Weltkrieg in Deutschland und ihre Vergleichbarkeit mit der heutigen Drogenwelle, Munich, 1975, pp. 49ff. See also Rainer Scheer, 'Die nach Paragraph 42 RStGB verurteilten Menschen in Hadamar', in Dorothee Roer and Dieter Henkel (eds.), *Psychiatrie im Faschismus: die Anstalt Hadamar 1933–1945*, Bonn, 1986, pp. 237–55, here p. 247. One prime example of this is the case of the dentist Dr Hermann Wirsting, who was taken to Waldheim mental hospital in Saxony for compulsory therapy on 15 April 1940 and transported by ambulance to a euthanasia centre only a day later. Cf. Holzer, *Die Geburt der Drogenpolitik*, p. 262, and Henry Friedlander, *Der Weg zum NS-Genozid: von der Euthanasie zur Endlösung*, Berlin, 1997, p. 191.

33. Ernst Klee, *Das Personenlexikon zum Dritten Reich: wer war was vor und nach 1945*, Frankfurt am Main, 2003, p. 449.

34. BArch-Berlin NS 20/140/8, *Ärzteblatt für Niedersachsen*, no. 5, 1939, pp. 79ff. (Bruns, Erich). See Holzer, *Die Geburt der Drogenpolitik*, p. 278.

35. Quoted in Rudolph Binion, '. . . *dass Ihr mich gefunden habt': Hitler und die Deutschen. Eine Psychohistorie*, Stuttgart, 1978, p. 46.

36. Viktor Reko, *Magische Gifte: Rausch- und Betäubungsmittel der neuen Welt*, Stuttgart, 1938. Tellingly, here is a remark from Reko's fascistoid foreword, p. ix: 'In twelve selected chapters a number of intoxicating substances are described which, like coca a few years ago, threaten to make their way from the circles of inferior races into civilized peoples.'

37. Günther Hecht, 'Alkohol und Rassenpolitik', in *Bekämpfung der Alkohol- und Tabakgefahren: Bericht der 2. Reichstagung Volksgesundheit und Genussgifte*, Hauptamt für Volksgesundheit der NSDAP und Reichsstelle gegen den Alkohol- und Tabakmissbrauch, Berlin-Dahlem, 1939.

38. Erwin Kosmehl, 'Der sicherheitspolizeiliche Einsatz bei der Bekämpfung der Betäubungsmittelsucht', in Gerhart Feuerstein, *Suchtgiftbekämpfung: Ziele und Wege*, Berlin, 1944, pp. 33–42, here p. 34.

39. Pohlisch, 'Die Verbreitung des chronischen Opiatmissbrauchs in Deutschland', p. 72.

40. Ernst Hiemer, *Der Giftpilz: ein Stürmerbuch für Jung und Alt*, Nuremberg, 1937.

41. Quoted in Pieper, *Nazis on Speed*, pp. 364ff.

42. 45 per cent of doctors, a disproportionately large number, were members of the NSDAP. See Robert Jay Lifton, *The Nazi Doctors: Medical Killing and the Psychology of Genocide*, New York, 2000.

43. The preparation is still on the market today, advertised with its unique natural effective ingredient, Escherichia coli Stamm Nissle 1917, and is used in the treatment of chronically inflamed intestinal conditions.

44. Joseph Goebbels, leading article, *Das Reich – Deutsche Wochenzeitung*, 31 December 1944, pp. 1ff.

45. Erwin Giesing, 'Bericht über meine Behandlung bei Hitler', Wiesbaden, 12 June 1945, in 'Hitler as seen by his doctors', Headquarters United States Forces European Theater Military Intelligence Service Center: OI – Consolidated Interrogation Report (CIR), National Archives at College Park, Md.

46. 'Today as in 1914 the German political and economic situation – a fortress besieged by the world – appears to demand a quick military decision through destructive strikes right at the start of hostilities,' the committee chairman, Carl Krauch, said programmatically, anticipating the conception of *Blitzkrieg*. Quoted in Karl-Heinz Frieser, *Die Blitzkrieg-Legende: der Westfeldzug 1940*, Munich, 2012, p. 11.

47. Propiophenon, a waste product from industrial chemistry, was brominated, then turned through treatment with methylamine and subsequent reduction into ephedrine, which through reduction with hydrogen iodide and phosphorus became methamphetamine. See Hans P. Kaufmann, *Arzneimittel-Synthese*, Heidelberg, 1953, p. 193.

48. Reichspatentamt 1938: Patent Nr. 767.186, Klasse 12q, Gruppe 3, with the title 'Method for Manufacturing Amines'. One tablet contained 3 milligrams of active ingredient

49. Landesarchiv Berlin, A Rep. 250-02-09/Nr. 218, advertising printed matter, undated. See also Holzer, *Die Geburt der Drogenpolitik*, p. 225.

50. Quoted in Pieper, *Nazis on Speed*, pp. 118ff. That is 6 milligrams of methamphetamine distributed across the day – a dosage to which the body quickly becomes accustomed, which means that after a few days of use the effect is no longer felt as it was at the outset. The formation of tolerance leads to a so-called 'craving', the demand for a higher dosage to reattain the pleasant effects. If this pattern of consumption is allowed to get out of control, and the drug can no longer be given up without difficulty, addiction arises.

51. C. Püllen, 'Bedeutung des Pervitins (1-Phenyl-2-methylamino-propan) für die Chirurgie', *Chirurg*, vol. 11 (1939), no. 13, pp. 485–92, here pp. 490 and 492. See also Pieper, *Nazis on Speed*, p. 119.

52. F. Haffner, 'Zur Pharmakologie und Praxis der Stimulantien', *Klinische Wochenschrift*, vol. 18 (1938), no. 38, p. 1311. See also Pieper, *Nazis on Speed*, p. 119.

53. Stephen Snelders and Toine Pieters, 'Speed in the Third Reich: Methamphetamine (Pervitin) use and a drug history from below', in *Social History of Medicine*, vol. 24 (2011), no. 3, pp. 686–99.

... methamphetamine is extremely popular in this
... essional class. See also Hermann Müller-Bonn, 'Pervitin,
ein neues Analepticum', *Medizinische Welt*, no. 39, 1939, pp.
1315–17. Quoted in Holzer, *Die Geburt der Drogenpolitik*, p. 230,
and Pieper, *Nazis on Speed*, p. 115.

55. Cf. W. Seifert, 'Wirkungen des 1-Phenyl-2-methylamino-
propan (Pervitin) am Menschen', *Deutsche medizinische
Wochenschrift*, vol. 65 (1939), no. 23, pp. 914ff.

56. Erich Neumann, 'Bemerkungen über Pervitin', *Münchener medizinische Wochenschrift*, no. 33, 1939, p. 1266.

57. Fritz Eichholtz, 'Die zentralen Stimulantien der Adrenalin-
Ephedrin-Gruppe', in 'Über Stimulantien', *Deutsche
medizinische Wochenschrift*, 1941, pp. 1355–8. See also
Reichsgesundheitsblatt vol. 15 (1940), no. 206. On the instructions
of the Reich Health Office the manufacture of these high-
dosage chocolates was suspended. The Hildebrand company
also put on the market the caffeinated 'Scho-Ka-Kola' which
still exists today.

58. Fritz Hauschild, 'Über eine wirksame Substanz', *Klinische
Wochenschrift*, vol. 17 (1938), no. 48, pp. 1257ff.

59. Rudolf Schoen, 'Pharmakologie und spezielle Therapie des
Kreislaufkollapses', *Verhandlungen der Deutschen Gesellschaft für
Kreislaufforschung*, 1938, pp. 80–112, here p. 98. Quoted in
Holzer, *Die Geburt der Drogenpolitik*, p. 219.

60. See Otto Graf, 'Über den Einfluss von Pervitin auf einige
psychische und psychomotorische Funktionen', *Arbeitsphysiologie*,
vol. 10 (1939), no. 6, pp. 692–704, here p. 695.

61. Gerhard Lemmel and Jürgen Hartwig, 'Untersuchungen über
die Wirkung von Pervitin und Benzedrin auf psychischem
Gebiet', *Deutsches Archiv für klinische Medizin*, vol. 185 (1940),
nos. 5 and 6, pp. 626ff.

62. C. Püllen, 'Erfahrungen mit Pervitin', *Münchener medizinische Wochenschrift*, vol. 86 (1939), no. 26, pp. 1001–4.

63. Sebastian Haffner, *Anmerkungen zu Hitler*, Munich, 1978, pp. 31ff.

64. Golo Mann, *Deutsche Geschichte des 19. und 20. Jahrhunderts*, Stuttgart/Mannheim, 1958, p. 177.

2 *Sieg High!* (1939–1941)

1. Heinrich Böll, *Briefe aus dem Krieg 1939–45*, Cologne, 2001, p. 15.

2. Ibid., p. 16.

3. Ibid., p. 30.

4. Ibid., p. 26.

5. Ibid., p. 81.

6. Ibid., p. 22.

7. K. Wenzig, *Allgemeine Hygiene des Dienstes*, Berlin/Heidelberg, 1936, pp. 288–307.

8. Otto Ranke, '*Ärztliche Fragen der technischen Entwicklung*', *Veröff. A. D. Geb. d. Heeres-Sanitätswesens*, vol. 109 (1939), p. 15. See also BArch-Freiburg RH 12–23/1882, Ranke's speech 'Performance enhancement by medical means' at the foundation anniversary dinner of the MA, 19 February 1939, pp. 7ff.: 'Pervitin becomes particularly important in lengthy activity that is not physically exhausting, such as driving and flying for long distances, where sleep is traditionally the most dangerous enemy.'

9. BArch-Freiburg 12–23/1882, Radical inspectors, 4 October 1938.

10. BArch-Freiburg 12–23/1882, Ranke's lecture on stimulants, February 1940, never delivered, p. 6, and Ranke's report to

Lehrgruppe C about performance-enhancing substitutes, 4 May 1939.

11. When German troops marched into the Sudetenland in 1938 they had also had positive experiences with Pervitin. See BArch-Freiburg RH 12–23/1882, 'Reports on the use of Pervitin, here with unit N.A.39'.

12. BArch-Freiburg RH 12–23/1882, Ranke's speech 'Performance enhancement by medical means', p. 7.

13. Gottfried Benn, 'Provoziertes Leben: ein Essay', in Benn, *Sämtliche Werke*, vol. IV: *Prosa 2*, Stuttgart, 1989, p. 318.

14. BArch-Freiburg RH 12–23/1882, letter from the director of the Physiological Institute of Vienna University to Ranke, 8 December 1941.

15. BArch-Freiburg RH 12–23/1882, letter from Ranke to Lehrgruppe C, 4. May 1939.

16. BArch-Freiburg RH 12–23/1882, letter from Ranke to Generalarzt Kittel, 25 August 1939.

17. BArch-Freiburg RH 12–23/1882, report to Ranke about the use of Pervitin.

18. BArch-Freiburg RH 12–23/1882, Wehrphysiologisches Institut der Militärärztlichen Akademie, annex to report 214 a, 8 April 1940.

19. BArch-Freiburg RH 12–23/1882, report to Ranke about the use of Pervitin.

20. Ibid.

21. BArch-Freiburg RH 12–23/1882, report from Dr Wirth, concerning 'Use of Pervitin as a tonic', 30 December 1939.

22. As for example in the 20th Infantry Division. See BArch-Freiburg RH 12–23/1842, report from Staff Surgeon Dr Krüger.

23. BArch-Freiburg RH 12–23/1882, report to Ranke about the use of Pervitin.

24. Ibid.

25. BArch-Freiburg RH 12–23/1882, report from Senior Surgeon Grosselkeppler, 6 April 1940.

26. BArch-Freiburg RH 12–23/1882, report from Senior Staff Surgeon Schmidt to Ranke, 25 March 1940. See also BArch-Freiburg RH 12– 23/271, report from Ranke to Lehrgruppe C, 13 January 1940, and BArch-Freiburg RH 12–23/1882, report from Staff Surgeon Dr Krüger.

27. BArch-Freiburg RH 12–23/1882, 'Experiences with Pervitin and similar substances', army doctor AOK 6 (Haubenreisser), 15 April 1940.

28. BArch-Freiburg RH 12–23/1882, 'Experiences with Pervitin, Elastonon etc.', corps doctor, IV Army Corps (Günther), 8 April 1940.

29. Hanno Ballhausen (ed.), *Chronik des Zweiten Weltkrieges*, Munich, 2004, p. 27.

30. Golo Mann, *Deutsche Geschichte des 19. und 20. Jahrhunderts*, Stuttgart/Mannheim, 1958, pp. 915ff.

31. Bernhard R. Kroener, 'Die personellen Ressourcen des Dritten Reiches im Spannungsfeld zwischen Wehrmacht, Bürokratie und Kriegswirtschaft 1939–1942', in Rolf-Dieter Müller and Hans Umbreit, *Das Deutsche Reich und der Zweite Weltkrieg*, vol. 5.1: *Organisation und Mobilisierung des Deutschen Machtbereichs, Kriegsverwaltung, Wirtschaft und personelle Ressourcen 1939–1941*, Stuttgart, 1988, p. 826.

32. See Karl-Heinz Frieser, *Die Blitzkrieg-Legende: der Westfeldzug 1940*, Munich, 2012, pp. 11, 43 und 57.

33. Albert Speer, *Inside the Third Reich*, trans. Richard and Clara Winston, London, 1970.

34. BArch-Freiburg RH 2/768, files relating to Halder, Hans-Adolf, Bl. 6 (reverse).

35. BArch-Freiburg H 20/285/7, Wehrphysiologisches Institut, 16 October 1939, 'Concerning: "Pervitin"'. See also letter to Winkler, 16 October 1939, as well as RH 12–23/1644 and Ranke's war diary, entry for 4 January 1940.

36. BArch-Freiburg RH12–23/1644, Ranke's war diary, entry for 8 December 1939.

37. BArch-Freiburg RH12–23/1644, letter from Ranke to Zechlin, 24 January 1940. See also BArch-Freiburg RH 12–23/1882, Ranke's speech 'Performance enhancement by medical means' at the celebration of the founding of the MA, 19 February 1939, p. 5: 'I must confirm for myself and all my assistants that we have always hurled ourselves enthusiastically into our work when on Pervitin, and had a sense that even difficult work is accomplished more easily, and that the decision to take on difficult tasks is made very much more easily.'

38. BArch-Freiburg RH12–23/1644, Ranke's war diary, entry for 8 November 1939, p. 6.

39. Ibid., entry for 19 November 1939, p. 16.

40. Eva Kramer, 'Die Pervitingefahr', *Münchener medizinische Wochenschrift*, vol. 88 (1941), no. 15, pp. 419ff.

41. Liebendörfer, 'Pervitin in der Hand des praktischen Nervenarztes', *Münchener medizinische Wochenschrift*, vol. 87 (1940), no. 43, p. 1182.

42. Benn, 'Provoziertes Leben: ein Essay', p. 317.

43. BArch-Berlin R22/1475, Bl. 395, Conti to Reich justice ministry, on 21 October 1939.

44. BArch-Berlin R36/1360, 'To the honorary members of the former RfR', 19 October 1939.

45. Reichsgesetzblatt 1 (1939), p. 2176; Reichsgesundheitsblatt (1940), p. 9: 'Phenylaminopropan und seine Salze (z.B. Benzedrin, Aktedron, Elastonon) und Phenylmethylaminopropan und seine

Salze (z.B. Pervitin) sind durch die Polizeiverordnung des Reichsministeriums des Innern über die Abgabe von Leberpräparaten und anderen Arzneimitteln in den Apotheken dem jedesmaligen Rezeptzwang unterstellt.'

46. Leonardo Conti, 'Vortrag des Reichsgesundheitsführers Dr. Conti vor dem NSD-Ärztebund, Gau Berlin, am 19. März 1940, im Berliner Rathaus', *Deutsches Ärzteblatt*, vol. 70 (1940), no. 13, pp. 145–53, here p. 150.

47. Ernst Speer, 'Das Pervitinproblem', *Deutsches Ärzteblatt*, vol. 71 (1941), no. 1, pp. 4–6, 15–19, here p. 19. See also Tilmann Holzer, *Die Geburt der Drogenpolitik aus dem Geist der Rassehygiene: deutsche Drogenpolitik von 1933 bis 1972*, inaugural dissertation, Mannheim, 2006, pp. 238ff.

48. BArch-Freiburg RH 12–23/1575, letter from Conti to Handloser, 17 February 1940, and Handloser's reply to Conti, 26 February 1940.

49. 'By shifting the focus to the southern wing, the strong enemy forces to be expected in northern Belgium must be cut off and thus destroyed.' RH 19 I/41, Akten HGr 1: draft of a note by Manstein for the war diary, 17 February 1940, Anl. 51 (Bl. 174 f.); see also BArch-Freiburg RH 19 I/26, Notiz über Führer-Vortrag, Bl. 121 f.

50. Quoted in Frieser, *Die Blitzkrieg-Legende*, p. 81.

51. BArch-Freiburg, posthumous papers of Erich von Manstein, Notiz Nr. 32.

52. Anton Waldmann, unpublished diary, entry for 13 April 1940, 'Wehrgeschichtliche Lehrsammlung des Sanitätsdienstes der Bundeswehr'.

53. BArch-Freiburg RH 12–23/1882, 'Performance enhancement through medical means', as well as Ranke's lecture on stimulants, written February 1940 (not delivered).

54. Ibid., letter from the corps doctor, Gruppe von Kleist, Dr Schmidt, to Ranke, 15 April 1940.

55. Ibid., Army Medical Inspector, 17 April 1940, 'Re stimulants', including appendix 1 and appendix 2.

56. Ibid.

57. BArch-Frei burg RH 12–23/1884, 'Delivery of Pervitin and Isophen from the main medical depot to army and Luftwaffe'.

58. BArch-Freiburg RH 21–1/19, Ia/op Nr. 214/40, 21 March 1940, p. 2.

59. Karl Wahl, . . . *es ist das deutsche Herz,* Augsburg, 1954, p. 246. See also Wilhelm Ritter von Leeb, *Tagebuchaufzeichnung und Lagebeurteilungen aus zwei Weltkriegen. Aus dem Nachlass,* ed. with a biographical sketch by Georg Meyer, Stuttgart, 1976, in *Beiträge zur Militär- und Kriegsgeschichte,* vol. 16, p. 184.

60. According to Guderian, this was a 'turn of phrase that he himself used often'. See also Heinz Guderian, *Erinnerung eines Soldaten,* Stuttgart, 1960, p. 95.

61. Interview in *Die Zeit* magazine, 7 May 2015, p. 50.

62. Quoted in Frieser, *Die Blitzkrieg-Legende,* p. 114.

63. Ibid., p. 136.

64. The division consisted of just under 400 officers, 2,000 NCOs and about 9,300 soldiers.

65. BArch-Freiburg RH 12–23/1882; see, for example, the 'Outline of a report on experiments with stimulants', 23 February 1940, p. 2: '. . . the next night two tablets each were given to driver and co-driver, with the instruction to keep them in the fold of the field cap and take them as necessary, but no later than one o'clock in the morning'.

66. See also Frieser, *Die Blitzkrieg-Legende,* pp. 195ff.

67. Wolfgang Fischer, *Ohne die Gnade der späten Geburt,* Munich, 1990, pp. 62ff.

68. BArch-Freiburg N802/62, Guderian papers, 'From the 3rd report on the journeys of the commanding general during the French operation', Bl. 008.

69. Ibid., Bl. 010.

70. Marc Bloch, *Strange Defeat: A Statement of Evidence Given in 1940*, New York, 1968, pp. 93ff.

71. Quoted in Frieser, *Die Blitzkrieg-Legende*, p. 219.

72. Oral testimony.

73. Frieser, *Die Blitzkrieg-Legende*, p. 419.

74. This refers not only to the Second World War, but to the conventional waging of war even in the present day, in which tanks no longer play such a great part.

75. The so-called 'Rucksack Principle'. These first days of the campaign demonstrate the crucial extent to which a military operation is determined by supplies on a logistical level – the bottom level. See also, in this context, Johann Adolf Graf von Kielmannsegg, *Panzer zwischen Warschau und Atlantik*, Berlin, 1941, p. 161.

76. Quoted in Frieser, *Die Blitzkrieg-Legende*, p. 162.

77. BArch-Freiburg N802/62, Guderian papers, 'From the 3rd report on the journeys of the commanding general during the French operation', Bl. 007 u. Bl. 011/012.

78. Winston Churchill, *The Second World War*, vol. II, book 1, Stuttgart, 1948/9, p. 61 [London, 1949].

79. BArch-Koblenz N1348, letter from Morell to his wife, 3 June 1940.

80. Frieser, *Die Blitzkrieg-Legende*, p. 336.

81. Quoted in ibid., p. 326.

82. Churchill, *The Second World War*, p. 244.

83. Edmund Ironside, *Diaries 1937–1940*, New York, 1962, p. 317. Quoted in Frieser, *Die Blitzkrieg-Legende*, p. 325.

84. Franz Halder, *Kriegstagebuch: tägliche Aufzeichnungen des Chefs des Generalstabes des Heeres 1939–1942*, vol. 1, Stuttgart, 1964, p. 302. Quoted in Frieser, *Die Blitzkrieg-Legende*, p. 322.

85. Ibid.

86. BArch-Koblenz N1348, letter from Morell to his wife , 26 May 1940.

87. Ibid., 28 May 1940.

88. Ironside, *Diaries 1937–1940*, p. 333.

89. Hans-Josef Hansen, *Felsennest, das vergessene Hauptquartier in der Eifel*, Aachen, 2008, p. 81.

90. *Deutsche Wochenschau*, no. 22, 22 May 1940.

91. The Gestapo industriously collected information about Göring's addiction. See, for example, Albert Speer, *Erinnerungen*, Frankfurt am Main, 1969, p. 278.

92. *Berliner Lokal-Anzeiger, Zentralorgan für die Reichshauptstadt, Tagesausgabe Großberlin*, 1 June 1940, p. 1.

93. Quoted in Reinhard Hesse, *Geschichtswissenschaft in praktischer Absicht*, Stuttgart, 1979, p. 144.

94. Quoted in Dermot Bradley, *Walther Wenck, General der Panzertruppe*, Osnabrück, 1982, p. 146.

95. BArch-Freiburg RH 12–23/1931, *Bericht über die Kommandierung zur Gruppe Kleist*, 12 July 1940.

96. Ibid.

97. BArch-Koblenz N1348, letter from Morell to his wife, 3 June 1940.

98. Unpublished war diary of the Army Medical Inspector, made available by Dr Volker Hartmann, Bundeswehr Medical Academy.

99. BArch-Freiburg ZA 3/163, war diary of Otto Hoffmann von Waldau, head of the Luftwaffe leadership staff, March 1939 until 10 April 1942, entry for 25 May 1940. Cf. also BArch-Freiburg

ZA 3/163, Schmid, *Feldzug gegen Frankreich 1940*, and BArch-Freiburg ZA 3/58, USAF History Project, p. 16, in Ob.d.L./Führungsstab Ic, Nr. 10641/40 geh., *Überblick über den Einsatz der Luftwaffe bei den Operationen in den Niederlanden, in Belgien und Nordfrankreich*, 3 June 1940.

100. Heinz Guderian, *Erinnerungen eines Soldaten*, Stuttgart, 1986, p. 118.

101. 'Sturmfahrt bis zur Grenze der Schweiz', *Berliner Lokal-Anzeiger, Zentralorgan für die Reichshauptstadt, Tagesausgabe Grossberlin*, 20 June 1940, p. 2.

102. BArch-Freiburg RH 12–23/1931, 'Report on the commanding of the Kleist Group', 12 July 1940.

103. Ibid.

104. Ibid.

105. BArch-Freiburg RH 12–23/1882, letter from Senior Physician Dr Seyffardt, 'Re Vitamin abuse', to Senior Physician Dr Althoff, 16 May 1941, Feldpost no.: 28806.

106. BArch-Freiburg RH 12–23/1882, memo from Ranke, 25 April 1941.

107. BArch-Freiburg RH 12–23/1882, Ranke to staff medic Dr Scholz, 27 May 1941.

108. IfZArch, MA 617, Roll 2, see letter from Hamma company to Morell, 27 May 1941: substances naturally containing vitamins in the SRK distribution include rosehip powder, rye grains, aneurin and nicotine acid, flavouring agents include 'full milk powder, cocoa and some cocoa butter'.

109. Ibid., letter from the Hamma company to the pharmacist Jost, 29 October 1942.

110. BArch-Koblenz N1348, letter from Morell to his wife, 16 May 1940.

111. BArch-Freiburg R43, letter from the Hamma company to

the SS leadership headquarters/medical office, 26 August 1941.

112. The SS also used Morell's Vitamultin in the Russian war – see Himmler's confirmation of 12 January 1942 (IfZArch, MA 617, Roll 2): 'The Führer has ordered that the Waffen-SS units on the Eastern Front be issued with suitable vitamin preparations. The company HAMMA GmbH, Hamburg, has been commissioned to produce these vitamin preparations. You are reqested to support this company in every way with supplies of the necessary raw material and other forms of assistance, so that this order from the Führer can be put into effect within the due date. The *Reichsführer-SS*.'

113. BArch-Koblenz N1348, letter from Morell to his wife, 16 May 1940.

114. Letter from Theo Morell to Göring concerning Hippke, Records of Private Individuals (Captured German Records), Dr Theo Morell, National Archives Microfilm Publication T253, Roll 35. National Archives, College Park, Md.

115. BArch- Freiburg ZA 3/801, Richard Suchenwirth, 'Hermann Göring', unpublished study, pp. 42ff.

116. Anthony Aldgate and Jeffrey Richards, *Britain Can Take It: The British Cinema in the Second World War*, 2nd edn, London, 2007, p. 120.

117. Horst, Freiherr von Luttitz, quoted in *Schlaflos im Krieg*, documentary film by Pieken, Gorch and Sönke el Bitar, Arte, 2010.

118. From Johannes Steinhoff, *Die Strasse von Messina*, Berlin, 1995, pp. 177ff. Steinhoff, who reflects on his deployment in the Second World War, was in the 1950s one of those chiefly responsible for the construction of the Luftwaffe of the Bundeswehr. Later he became chair of the NATO Military Committee, before moving to the arms industry in the mid-

1970s. This account of the use of methamphetamine, dating from 1943, reads as if Steinhoff, who also took part in the Battle of Britain in 1940, is here describing his first and only use of the stimulant.

119. Ibid.

120. Ibid.

121. Theo Osterkamp, *Durch Höhen und Tiefen jagt ein Herz*, Heidelberg, 1952, p. 245. See also Speer, *Erinnerungen*, p. 272.

122. Wolfgang Falck, *Falkenjahre: Erinnerungen 1903–2003*, Moosburg, 2003, p. 230.

123. Richard, J. Overy, 'German aircraft production 1939–1942', in *A Study of the German War Economy*, Ph.D. thesis, Queens' College, Cambridge, 1977, p. 97.

124. BArch-Freiburg ZA 3/842, Göring to Lieutenant Colonel Klosinski, Commodore of K Unit 4, in autumn 1944, quoted from the record of the Suchenwirth's interview with Klosinski on 1 February 1957; see hss.ulb.uni-bonn.de/2005/0581/0581. pdf.

125. In the First World War not an unusual way of overcoming fatigue. In his lecture on stimulants, February 1940, not delivered (BArch-Freiburg, RH 12–23/1882), Ranke also goes into this issue, but rejects it for his own time: 'Stimulants are highly effective medications. Cocaine [. . .] is unsuitable for military use because of the addiction that arises, leading to severe physical and psychological damage.'

126. BArch-Freiburg ZA 3/326, typed report about the discussion with the Reich Marshal on 7 October 1943, 'Re: Home Defence Programme'.

127. Heinz Linge, *Bis zum Untergang*, Munich, 1980, p. 219.

128. Reproduced fom 'Udet Ernst, Spasspilot, Kriegsverbrecher und komischer Zeichner', in Christian Meurer, *Wunderwaffe*

Witzkanone: Heldentum von Hess bis Hendrix, Münster, 2005, essay 9, pp. 73ff.

129. German Information Office Berlin, 18 November 1941. Quoted in Ernst Udet, *Mein Fliegerleben*, Berlin, 1942.

130. See also BArch-Freiburg ZA 3/805, Richard Suchenwirth, *Ernst Udet: Generalluftzeugmeister der deutschen Luftwaffe*, unpublished study..

131. Methamphetamine is both distinctly more powerful than amphetamine, and demonstrably neurotoxic if used improperly (too high a dose, excessively frequent use). It reduces the formation and availability of serotonin and dopamine in the central nervous system, and can permanently change the neurochemistry of the body.

132. BArch-Freiburg RH 12–23/1884, letter from Conti, 20 December 1940.

133. BArch-Freiburg RH 12–23/1884, letter from Handloser, 20 and 29 January 1941.

134. Speer, 'Das Pervitinproblem', p. 18.

135. Holzer, *Die Geburt der Drogenpolitik*, pp. 242ff.

136. These are the official figures. But we must assume that the Temmler Works, without the knowledge of the Reich Health Office (RGA), which was attempting to collect data, was also delivering directly to the Wehrmacht. This might explain the discrepancy of 22.6 kilograms of Pervitin substances between the official figures of the Opium Office in the RGA and Temmler's 1943 sales statistics.

137. Holzer, *Die Geburt der Drogenpolitik*, pp. 245ff.

138. BArch-Berlin NS 20–139–6/Rundschreiben Vg. 9/41, NSDAP, Hauptamt für Volksgesundheit, 3 February 1941, Conti. Quoted in Holzer, *Die Geburt der Drogenpolitik*, p. 244.

139. RGBl.I, 12 June 1941, p. 328: '6. Verordnung über Unterstellung

weiterer Stoffe unter die Bestimmungen des Opiumgesetzes'.

140. Experienced medical officers such as Army Medical Inspector Anton Waldmann had already warned early on: 'The people are nervous, irritable. Stress levels elevated due to their extraordinarily heightened performance – but herein also lies the danger of a total sudden collapse, if we do not ease off and allow rest, sleep, recovery and success.' Waldmann, unpublished diary, entry for 1 November 1940, 'Wehrgeschichtliche Lehrsammlung des Sanitätsdienstes der Bundeswehr'.

141. Confirmation from the Reich Chemistry Office, 7 May 1941 to the Temmler company: 'In accordance with the decree from the Reich Defence Secretary, the Prime Minister, Reich Marshal Göring, about the urgency of the Wehrmacht manufacturing programmes', Landesarchiv Berlin, A Rep. 250–02–09 Temmler.

3 High Hitler: Patient A and His Personal Physician (1941–1944)

1. IfZArch, MA 617, Roll 2, text of a speech by Theo Morell, p. 4. Very much a child of his time, here he brings together two quotations assuming a classic paternalistic assignment of roles between doctor and patient: 'The relationship of trust . . .' comes from the book by the West Prussian doctor and medical writer Erwin Liek (1878–1935), *Der Arzt und seine Sendung* (1925), the last sentence quoted here from Bismarck's personal physician, Emil Schweninger.

2. Joachim C. Fest, *Hitler: eine Biographie*, Berlin, 1973, p. 535.

3. Ibid., p. 992.

4. *Der Spiegel*, 42/1973, p. 201.

5. Hans Bernd Gisevius, *Adolf Hitler: Versuch einer Deutung*, Munich, 1963, p. 523.

6. Ian Kershaw, *Hitler 1936–45: Nemesis*, London, 2000, p. 612 . Elsewhere, too, Kershaw is dismissive of Morell's importance: 'At any rate, Morell and his medicines were neither a major nor even a minor part of the explanation of Germany's plight in the autumn of 1944' (p. 728).

7. BArch-Koblenz N1348, Morell entry, 8 November 1944.

8. From the 'File on Professor Morell', Camp Sibert, 15 January 1946, Entry ZZ-5, in IRR-Personal Name Files, RG NO. 319, Stack Area 230, Row 86, Box 11, National Archives at College Park, Md.

9. Ibid.

10. Special Report 53 identifies as experts Prof. Dr Felix Haffner, director of the Pharmacological Insitute at Tübingen University, Prof. Dr Konrad Ernst, also of Tübingen University, and Dr Theodor Benzinger von Krebsstein: 'On 23 April 1947, these three scientists signed a written statement to the effect that from the existing files of information nothing could be found to point to the possibility that Hitler had often received narcotics.' Prof. Dr Heubner from the Pharmacological Institute of Berlin University was also contacted, as well as Prof. Dr Linz, director of the Opium Office in the Reich Health Office. Both denied that Hitler might have received narcotics in larger quantities. But there were also other voices: the criminal investigator Jungnickel of the drug squad in Berlin as well as Jost, owner of the Engel chemist's shop in Berlin-Mitte, and Prof. Müller-Hess, director of the Institute of Legal Medicine and Criminology at Berlin University, stated that it was very possible that Hitler had been supplied with opiates by his personal physician – but were

unable or unwilling to provide information about quantities and possible effects. In IRR Impersonal Files, RG No. 319, Stack Area 770, Entry 134A, Box 7: 'Hitler, poisoning rumors', XE 198119, National Archives at College Park, Md.

11. '. . . in order to provide further material for the debunking of numerous Hitler myths', ibid.

12. BArch-Koblenz N1118, Goebbels, posthumous papers, letter to Hitler, Christmas 1943.

13. Percy Ernst Schramm, 'Adolf Hitler: Anatomie eines Dikators' (5th and last instalment), *Der Spiegel* 10/1964.

14. Quoted in Ernst Günther Schenck, *Dr. Morell: Hitlers Leibarzt und seine Medikamente*, Schnellbach, 1998, p. 110.

15. BArch-Koblenz N1348, Morell's medical diary, 18 August 1941.

16. BArch-Koblenz N1348, Morell entry, 9 August 1943.

17. BArch- Freiburg RH 12–23/1884. See also Tilmann Holzer, *Die Geburt der Drogenpolitik aus dem Geist der Rassehygiene: deutsche Drogenpolitik von 1933 bis 1972*, inaugural dissertation, Mannheim, 2006, p. 247.

18. BArch-Koblenz N1348, Morell entry, 8 August 1941.

19. Ibid. On the composition of glyconorm see Morell's posthumous papers, in this instance his letter of 2 December 1944.

20. BArch-Koblenz N1348, Morell entry, 8 August 1941.

21. Morell even used leeches, a traditional domestic remedy that was supposed to hinder blood clotting and act as bloodletting on a small scale. Hitler himself tapped them out of the jar, and Morell used his fingers to put them under his patient's ear, as they kept slipping out of his tweezers. 'The one at the front sucked faster, the one at the back only very slowly,' he noted conscientiously. 'The one at the front fell off at first, let go at the bottom and dangled freely. The one at the back

sucked for half an hour longer, then it too let go at the bottom, and I had to pull it off at the top. The bleeding then went on for about two hours. Because of the two bandage strips the Führer did not go to dinner. Ibid., 11 August 1941.

22. Philipp Keller, *Die Behandlung der Haut- und Geschlechtskrankheiten in der Sprechstunde*, Heidelberg, 1952.

23. BArch-Koblenz N1348, Morell entry, 27 August 1941.

24. An overview with explanations about the individual medications that Hitler took can be found here: www.jkris.dk/jkris/Histomed/hitlermed/hitlermed.htm.

25. Quoted in Ottmar Katz, *Prof. Dr. Med. Theo Morell: Hitlers Leibarzt*, Bayreuth, 1982, p. 219.

26. Percy E. Schramm (ed.), *Kriegstagebuch des Oberkommandos der Wehrmacht 1940–1941*, vol. II, 1982, p. 673.

27. Ibid., entry for 21 October 1941, p. 716.

28. BArch-Freiburg RH 12–23/1882, Dr Otto Guther, 'Erfahrungen mit Pervitin', 27 January 1942.

29. This also applied to the navy; see the escape of the heavy cruiser *Prinz Eugen* from Brest harbour. There the warship had repeatedly been exposed to British bomb attacks. To prevent it from being sunk, with the concomitant loss of prestige, Hitler ordered a retreat, along with the equally affected battleships *Gneisenau* and *Scharnhorst*. The problem lay in the fact that they had to pass through the English Channel in order to reach the German Bight, almost a two-day journey away. In previous centuries no enemy fleet had managed to pass the British coast, over 300 miles long, unharmed. So the senior naval commander several times contradicted the order on the grounds that 'it was impossible to obey'. But when, on the night of 11 February 1942, Brest harbour was in dense fog and the crew of the British submarine that was watching the German

base went to sleep because they did not expect the fleet to leave at that time of day, the ships weighed anchor. This was followed by a forty-eight-hour flight on full alert, during which no one was allowed to sleep. All the men were permanently on their stations: in the gun towers, in the engine room, in the control room, on deck. 'In view of the fact that [. . .] a loss of concentration and performance on the part of any member of the crew could have had a damaging effect on the successful outcome of the enterprise, an order was issued to distribute Schokakola (1 pack per head) and Pervitin in tablets', according to the medical log of the ship's doctor of the *Prinz Eugen* for 12 February: 'Three tablets per head of fighting unit were issued.' At around midday the convoy passed Dover. Meanwhile the British had noticed what was happening right in front of their eyes. The coast artillery fired full blast, over 240 British bombers took off, but were held in check by 280 German fighter planes. All hands were deployed on the ships, on heavy guns, on anti-aircraft weapons. An amphetamine sea battle: 'The powerful stimulant effect of Pervitin on the central nervous system dispelled the need for sleep and the feeling of fatigue that were gradually making themselves felt,' Naval Senior Physician Witte reported. On the evening of 13 February the ships reached Wilhelmshaven. In England the penetration of the Channel was received as one of the greatest marine humiliations in the history of Great Britain. The successful operation brought the Germans one thing in particular: the summary of the medical report states that 'the supply of Pervitin to ships on operation was considered necessary. With a crew of 1,500 men a provision of about 10,000 tablets is required.' BArch-Freiburg RM 92-5221/Bl. 58–60, wartime log of the cruiser *Prinz Eugen*, 1 January 1942–31 January 1943, vol. 2: 'Secret Command matter – medical report on the cruiser *Prinz Eugen*'s breakthrough from the English Channel to the German Bight, between 11 February 1942 and 13 February 1942'.

30. The rule of thumb: methamphetamine intolerance appears after three doses of 10 milligrams (three to four Pervitin pills) after only two to three days in succession. None the less, each individual has a different tolerance threshold. Some need more even after the second application to achieve the initial effect; for others, a steady dosage can carry on for days without any noticeable decline in effect. Generally speaking, methamphetamine drowns out the natural limits of performance – warning signals from the body – through the artificial stimulation that it unleashes in the brain's nerve cells. Limits of both psychical and physical working capacity are no longer perceived, but extended further and further, even if rest has been required for some time. So the drug's profile fits the entire German action in Russia in exemplary fashion.

31. BArch-Freiburg Rh 12–23/1384, Army Directive 1942, part B, no. 424, p. 276, 'Combating the abuse of narcotics'. See also Holzer, *Die Geburt der Drogenpolitik*, pp. 289ff.

32. Franz Halder, *Kriegstagebuch: tägliche Aufzeichnungen des Chefs des Generalstabes des Heeres 1939–1942*, vol. 3, Stuttgart, 1964, p. 311.

33. Gisevius, *Adolf Hitler: Versuch einer Deutung*, p. 471. Quoted in Fest, *Hitler*, p. 647.

34. BArch-Koblenz N1348, letter from Morell to the cardiac specialist Professor Weber, 2 December 1944: 'Going for a walk had become quite an alien concept, as a daily period of a quarter of an hour in fresh air became the norm for many months.'

35. Quoted in Ernst Günther Schenck, *Patient Hitler*, Augsburg, 2000, p. 389.

36. IfZArch, MA 617, Roll 3. From a letter from Nissle, the inventor of Mutaflor, to Morell, 1 March 1943.

37. Albert Speer, *Erinnerungen*, Frankfurt am Main, 1969, p. 592.

38. IfZArch, MA 617, Roll 1, security measures for FHQ Werwolf, 20 February 1943.

39. Speer, *Erinnerungen*, pp. 256ff.

40. Quoted in Fest, *Hitler*, p. 660.

41. Speer, *Erinnerungen*, pp. 358 and 368.

42. Schramm, *Kriegstagebuch des Oberkommandos der Wehrmacht 1940–1941*, entry for 21 December 1942.

43. BArch-Koblenz N1348, Morell entry, 18 August 1942.

44. Haffner, 'Hitler, poisoning rumors', p. 110.

45. Fest, *Hitler*, p. 673.

46. Speer, *Erinnerungen*, pp. 345, 342 and 472.

47. Letter from the Engel-Apotheke to Theo Morell, 29 August 1942, National Archives Microfilm Publication T253/45.

48. BArch-Koblenz N1348, Morell entry, 9 December 1942.

49. Ibid., Morell entry, 17 December 1942.

50. Quoted in Werner Pieper, *Nazis on Speed: Drogen im 3. Reich*, Birkenau-Löhrbach, 2002, p. 174.

51. IfZArch, MA 617, Roll 1.

52. Morell, discussion memo, National Archives Microfilm Publication T253/45.

53. Ibid.

54. BArch R42/5281–5182, letter from 20 August 1942; see also BA R38/0156–0157, letter from 25 January 1943.

55. Communication from Reich Commissar Koch, 29 August 1942, National Archives Microfilm Publication T253/35.

56. IfZArch, MA 617, Roll 2, letter fom Morell to his wife, 22 September 1942.

57. Communication from Reich Commissar Koch, 29 August 1942, National Archives Microfilm Publication T253/35.

58. IfZArch, MA 617, Roll 2, letter from Morell to Koch, 22 September 1942.

59. See also letter to Dr Möckel of 1 April 1944: 'Your seminal academic work interests me, as does your love of drugs.' In this context see also Morell's letters to Koch, 14 and 17 December 1943, National Archives Microfilm Publication T253/35.

60. See Karl Schlögel, *Die Zeit*, 30 October 2014, p. 19.

61. Quoted in Schenck, *Dr. Morell*, p. 267.

62. Letter from Morell to Koch, 16 October 1942, National Archives Microfilm Publication T253/35.

63. Letter from Koch, 31 October 1943, National Archives Microfilm Publication T253/42. This concerned the abattoirs at Vinnytsia, Kiev, Proskurov, Berdychiv, Zhitomir, Dubno, Darnytsia, Kasatin, Kirovograd, Bila Tserkva, Nikolayev, Melitopol, Zaporizhia, Dnipropetrovsk, Poltava, Krementchuk, Uman, Korosten.

64. Quoted in Schenck, *Dr. Morell*, p. 253.

65. Philipp Vandenberg, *Die heimlichen Herrscher: die Mächtigen und ihre Ärzte*, Bergisch-Gladbach, 2000, p. 256.

66. Letter from Morell to District Magistrate Schuhmacher in Lemberg [Lwów], 12 December 1943, National Archives Microfilm Publication T253/35.

67. From an order from the Führer's Wehrmacht adjutancy: 'Anyone negligently or deliberately using fuel for non-war-deciding purposes will be treated as a saboteur of the war effort', National Archives Microfilm Publication T253/36.

68. IfZArch, MA 617, Roll 3, record of a discussion with Dr Mulli, 9 October 1943 at 22.35.

69. IfZArch, MA 617, Roll 3, letter from Hamma company to Morell, 5 February 1945.

70. See, for example, the letter from Morell to Reich Minister Ohnesorge, 11 February 1944: '. . . took the liberty of making the suggestion that the Führer would like to ask you to deliver a lecture', National Archives Microfilm Publication T253/41.

71. IfZArch, MA 617, Roll 3, letter from Mulli to Morell, 10 August 1943.

72. Letter fom Morell to Koch, 28 October 1942, National Archives Microfilm Publication T253/35.

73. Draft letter from Theo Morell, re manufacture of new medical products, 30 March 1944, National Archives Microfilm Publication T253/38. In this letter he also writes: 'So I had developed, using special ingredients, an injectable liver extract which is the first liver preparation to have no painful side-effects, and which has proved to be extraordinarily effective in experiments by clinicians of my acquaintance and among my friends, as well as in self-administered experiments. [. . .] I am forced to produce it myself, as specialities of equal value are no longer available on the market and I can no longer treat my patients – I do not need to mention the importance of their remaining in good health – in an orderly fashion if I do not produce and make available my own medications. [. . .] Bureaucratic difficulties must be differently overcome in the interest of the people's health and particularly of my patients.'

74. Goebbels, diary entry from 20 March 1942. Quoted in Peter Gathmann and Martina Paul, *Narziss Goebbels: eine Biografie*, Vienna, 2009, p. 95. By now Goebbels had also become so fond of the syringe that Dr Weber, Morell's assistant, observed:

'The Reich minister now has so many bumps that it's almost impossible to give him an injection.' Letter from Weber to Morell, 16 June 1943, National Archives Microfilm Publication T253/34. This also reports, among other things, that Goebbels suffered from severe headaches for three days after an injection of Morell's liver preparation.

75. BArch-Koblenz N1348, 'Order from the Führer to investigate a slivovitz test on methyl alcohol and other harmful substances', 11 January 1944. The written reply from the field laboratory on the same day: 'Smell and taste: like slivovitz. [. . .] On the basis of this examination, no health concerns about its use.'

76. Quoted in Ernst Günther Schenck, *Patient Hitler: eine medizinische Biographie*, Augsburg, 2000, pp. 389ff.

77. BArch-Koblenz N1348, Morell entry, 18 July 1943.

78. BArch-Koblenz N1348, Morell entry, 6 December 1943.

79. Quoted in Rong Yang, *'Ich kann einfach das Leben nicht mehr ertragen': Studien zu den Tagebüchern von Klaus Mann (1931–1949)*, Marburg, 1996, p. 107. Klaus Mann noted in his diary: 'Got some more Euka tablets in a chemist's, thanks to the stupidity of the pharmacist.' Quoted in Pieper, *Nazis on Speed*, p. 57.

80. BArch-Koblenz N1348, Morell entry, 18 July 1943.

81. Ibid.

82. BArch-Koblenz N1348, 'Special Entry', 18 July 1943.

83. The opioid oxycodon (oxycodone in the UK), the effective ingredient of Eukodal, is sold in the United States under the names 'Oxygesic' and 'Oxycontin', and in 2010, with a profit of 3.5 billion dollars, was ranked fifth among the most successful medicines. In Germany, oxycodon is known among other things as 'Oxygesic', and is the most regularly prescribed

opioid for oral use. There are currently 147 permitted medical products containing oxycodon, most in controlled-release formulations (a delayed absorption of the effective ingredient), not least for the treatment of chronic pains. The preparation called Eukodal, which Hitler was given for the first time in the summer of 1943, has not been on the German market since 1990.

84. William Burroughs, *Naked Lunch*, Paris, 1959, p. 65.

85. Speer, *Erinnerungen*, p. 119.

86. Quoted in Katz, *Prof. Dr. Med. Theo Morell*, p. 280.

87. Letter from Morell to Sievert, 26 August 1943, National Archives Microfilm Publication T253/45.

88. Letter from the pharmacist Jost to Morell, 30 April 1942: 'Since I need prescriptions as evidence of my cocaine sales and to enter them in the narcotics books, I politely request that you send 5 prescriptions according to the regulations of the BMG [Reich Opium Law] as soon as possible.'

89. Postcards from this period bear the inscription: 'The Führer knows only struggle, work and care. We want to take from him the share that we can take.'

90. According to Elias Canetti, *Crowds and Power*, trans. Carol Stewart, London, 1960, p. 295.

91. Joseph Goebbels, *The Goebbels Diaries*, trans. and ed. Louis P. Lochner, London, 1948, p. 342.

92. Letter fom Koch to Morell, 31 May 1943, National Archives Microfilm Publication T253/37.

93. BArch-Koblenz N1348, Morell entry, 7 October 1943.

94. Ibid., 21 November 1943.

95. Ibid., 27 January 1944.

96. Letter from a state official, Köglmaier, to Morell, 10 December 1943, National Archives Microfilm Publication T253/35.

97. In this context see also the 'Note on the reporting of illnesses by leading personalities' of 23 December 1942. Here it says: 'I not only release doctors, healing practitioners and dentists from their duty of silence towards my Commissar General Professor Dr med. Karl Brandt, but order them, once the hard-and-fast diagnosis has been made of a serious or grave illness in a leading person or one in a position of responsibility in the state, the Party, the Wehrmacht, the economy, etc., to inform me about such matters. Adolf Hitler.' Speer, *Erinnerungen*, p. 327.

98. See, for example, the letter from Frau von Kries, of the Wehrmacht adjutancy to the Führer, to Morell, 17 February 1943: 'We are running low on supplies and would therefore be grateful if you could help us out with some medication. *Heil Hitler!*' IfZArch, MA 617, Roll 2.

99. Letter fom Morell, 1 December 1944, National Archives Microfilm Publication T253/37.

100. Also exemplary in this respect is the letter from an old patient to Morell, from 14 April 1944: 'We speak of you and your wife very often, and these memories always cheerfully pep us up.' National Archives Microfilm Publication T253/38.

101. BArch-Freiburg RH 12–23/1321, carbon, PhIV Berlin, 20 December 1943, to the 'director of the service'. See also Holzer, *Die Geburt der Drogenpolitik*, pp. 254ff.

102. BArch-Freiburg RH 12–23/1321, B. 125a, signed Schmidt-Brücken and Wortmann, Staff Chemist.

103. '1 kg cocaine hydrochl. in original packaging from the manufacturers to be issued straight away to the Department of Counter-Intelligence ZF Vi C.' See BArch-Freiburg RH 12–23/1322, Bl. 123, Wortmann to the Central Medical Department, 22 May 1944, 'Secret'.

104. Verbal communication from Herta Schneider, quoted in John Toland, *Adolf Hitler*, Bergisch-Gladbach, 1977, p. 920 [New York/London, 1977].

105. BArch-Koblenz N1348, Morell entry, 9 January 1944.

106. Ibid.

107. Ibid., 29 January 1944.

108. BArch-Koblenz N1348, letter fom Morell to his wife, 16 May 1940.

109. In 1949 Erich von Manstein would be sentenced by a British military court for war crimes. After his release in 1953, as the only former Wehrmacht field marshal he unofficially advised the newly established Bundeswehr (the Army of West Germany) until 1960. In 1955 he published his memoirs, *Verlorene Kriege* – which deserve to be read critically – in which he attempted to justify his behaviour in the Russian war and shift as much responsibility as possible on to Hitler.

110. See 'Marshal von Kleist, who broke Maginot Line in 1940, seized', *Evening Star,* Washington D.C., 4 May 1945, p. 1.

111. Report by Hasselbach, 29 May 1946, p. 3, IRR-Personal Name Files, RG NO. 319, Stack Area 230, Row 86, Box 8, National Archives at College Park, Md.

112. BArch-Koblenz N1348, Morell entry, 14 March 1944.

113. From 'Life history of Professor Dr. med. Theo Morell', p. 6, IRR-Personal Name Files, RG NO. 319, Stack Area 230, Row 86, Box 8, National Archives at College Park, Md.

114. Letter from Dr Stephan Baron v. Thyssen-Bornemisza, 5 November 1943, National Archives Microfilm Publication T253/45.

115. IfZArch, MA 617, Roll 2, letter from Morell to Luise Funk, the wife of the Reich economics minister, 12 May 1944. There may have been another reason for the presence of the assistant.

Morell had, as Weber later put on record, wanted to 'build him up for Hitler, so that he himself would appear dispensable at the right moment and would be able to step down from Hitler's immediate circle. I would then have had to take his place.' However, Morell's exit strategy remained only an idea. Until his dismissal he never really tried to leave the innermost circle of power.

116. BArch-Koblenz N1348, Morell entries, 20 and 21 April 1944.
117. Since, because of the advance of the Red Army, no more livers were forthcoming from the Ukraine, Morell collected 'all the parasite and fluke livers' from Bohemia and Moravia. These were affected by different kinds of trematode worms such as the common liver fluke (*Fasciola hepatica*) and the lancet liver fluke (*Dicrocoelium lanceoluatum*). But that didn't bother Hitler's personal physician: see letter of 28 October 1944 to Morell from Hamma (T253/34), as well as Morell's letter to the Reich Minister of the Interior (T253/42): '. . . after the loss of the Ukraine we need a new source of raw material. For well-known reasons it is clear that the requisite amount of entirely suitable, healthy livers in the Old Reich cannot be made available. But so-called parasite livers or fluke livers are entirely suitable for processing into liver extract if certain precautionary measures are followed. This would have the merit of processing a hitherto worthless waste product into a valuable medication.' In this context see also BArch-Koblenz N1348, Morell entry, 20/21 April 1944.
118. BArch-Koblenz N1348, letter from Morell to the economics minister, Funk, 12 May 1944.
119. Quoted in Katz, *Prof. Dr. Med. Theo Morell*, p. 24.
120. Ibid., p. 161.
121. Goebbels, *The Goebbels Diaries*, vol. 9, April–June 1944, p. 405.

122. BArch-Koblenz N1348, Morell entry, 10 June 1944.

123. Ibid., Morell entry, 14 July 1944.

124. Ibid., Morell entry, 20 July 1944.

125. Erwin Giesing, 'Report about my treatment of Hitler', Wiesbaden, 12 June 1945, Headquarters United States Forces European Theater Military Intelligence Service Center: OI – Consolidated Intelligence Report (CIR), National Archives at College Park, Md, p. 10.

126. 'Adolf Hitler: Aufriss über meine Person', *Der Spiegel*, 24/1973, pp. 103ff.

127. Ibid.

128. Paul Schmidt, *Statist auf diplomatischer Bühne 1923–45*, Bonn, 1950, p. 582.

129. Gottfried Benn, *Sämtliche Werke*, vol. I: *Gedichte 1*, Stuttgart, 1986, p. 46.

130. Giesing, 'Report on my treatment of Hitler'.

131. Giesing recorded his treatments of Hitler in a yellow diary. Using a secret code, he wrote in Latin and used a combination of symbols that he had invented himself. See Toland, *Adolf Hitler*, p. 1013.

132. Giesing, 'Report on my treatment of Hitler'.

133. BArch-Koblenz N1348, Morell entry, 5 August 1944.

134. Giesing, 'Report on my treatment of Hitler'.

135. Ibid.

136. Apart fom Merck's Psicain, which was said to lead to cardio-rhythmic disturbances in susceptible patients.

137. Kershaw, *Hitler 1936–45*, p. 728: 'That Hitler was poisoned by the strychnine and belladonna in the anti-gas pills or other medicaments, drugged on the opiates given him to relieve his intestinal spasms, or dependent upon the cocaine which formed 1 per cent of the ophthalmic drops prescribed by Dr

Giesing for conjunctivitis, can be discounted.' It is not eye drops with 1 per cent cocaine, but nasal and palate swabs with a 10 per cent content that are the medical historical facts – which signifies a notable difference in the effect of the drug. Hitler's biographer Fest ignores cocaine completely, while the Hitler researcher Werner Maser does describe the applications in detail, although without drawing conclusions (Werner Maser, *Adolf Hitler: Legende Mythos Wirklichkeit*, Munich, 1997).

138. Schenck, *Patient Hitler*, p. 507.
139. See Giesing, 'Report on my treatment of Hitler'.
140. Ibid.
141. Toland, *Adolf Hitler*, p. 1022
142. Giesing, 'Report on my treatment of Hitler'.
143. Maser, *Adolf Hitler*, p. 397.
144. BArch-Koblenz N1348, Morell entry, 3 October 1944.
145. Nicolaus von Below, *Als Hitlers Adjutant 1937–45*, Mainz, 1980, p. 384.
146. BArch-Koblenz N1348, Morell entry, 23/24 September 1944. Cf. Morell's entry for 17 October 1943. The therapeutic daily dose is between 0.005 grams and 0.01 grams. So Hitler was asking for up to four times as much, which clearly exceeds the medical application and has strong psychoactive effects.
147. Speer, *Erinnerungen*, p. 362.
148. BArch-Koblenz N1348, Morell entry, 30 October 1944.
149. Ibid., 4 October 1944.
150. Quoted in the report by Giesing, p. 15, in 'Hitler, Adolf: A composite picture', Entry ZZ-6, in IRR-Personal Name Files, RG No. 319, Stack Area 230, Box 8, National Archives at College Park, Md.
151. BArch-Koblenz N1348. All quotations are from Morell's report

on his meeting with Ribbentrop, written in the Regina-Palast-Hotel on 6 June 1943.

152. BArch-Koblenz N1348, letter from Bormann, 26 June 1944.

153. Ibid.

154. BArch-Koblenz N1348, handwritten menu, 3 October 1944.

155. See G. Liljestrand, *Poulsson's Lehrbuch für Pharmakologie*, Leipzig, 1944.

156. Giesing, 'Report on my treatment of Hitler'.

157. Quoted in Katz, *Prof. Dr. Med. Theo Morell*, pp. 295 ff.

158. Giesing, 'Report on my treatment of Hitler'.

159. Morell's method was clearly inadequate. On the subject of the disinfection of syringes see 'Alkohol und Instrumentensterilisation', *Deutsche medizinische Wochenschrift*, vol. 67 (1941), which says: 'Alcohol is not to be employed in sterilizing needles.'

160. Giesing, 'Report on my treatment of Hitler', conversation between Giesing and Hitler, 2 October 1944.

161. Giesing, 'Report on my treatment of Hitler'.

162. Ibid.

163. BArch-Koblenz N1348, Morell entry, 8 October 1944, and BArch-Koblenz N1348, letter from Bormann to the Reich Press Secretary, 10 October 1944.

164. BArch-Koblenz N1348, Morell entry, 8 November 1944.

165. Ibid.

166. Ibid., 7 November 1944.

167. Letter to Bernhard Wenz, 23 October 1944, National Archives Microfilm Publication T253/36.

168. IfZArch, MA 617, Roll 1.

169. BArch-Koblenz N1348, Morell entry, 9 November 1944.

170. IfZArch, MA 617, Roll 3, Letter from Prof. Nissle to Morell, 1 March 1943.

171. IfZArch, MA 617, Roll 1.

172. Ibid.

173. BArch-Koblenz N1348, Morell entry, 8 December 1944.

174. Ibid., 3 November 1944.

175. Ibid.

176. IfZArch, MA 617, Roll 1.

177. BArch-Koblenz N1348, Morell entry, 9 November 1944.

178. IfZArch, MA 617, Roll 3, letter from Prof. Nißle to Morell, 1 March 1943.

179. IfZArch, MA 617, Roll 3, Morell entry, 1 November 1944.

180. Ibid., 30 October 1944.

181. Ibid., 31 October 1944.

182. Ibid., 8 November 1944.

183. Giesing, 'Report on my treatment of Hitler'.

184. BArch-Koblenz N1348, Morell entries, 18 July 1943 und 29 September 1944.

185. See Toland, *Adolf Hitler*, p. 1013.

186. BArch-Koblenz N1348, Morell entry, 30 September 1944.

187. Ibid., 21 November 1944.

188. Ibid., 24 November 1944.

189. Ibid., 27 November 1944.

190. Walter Benjamin, *On Hashish*, trans. Howard Eiland et al., Boston, 2006, p. 24.

191. Hermann Römpp, *Chemische Zaubertränke*, Stuttgart, 1939.

4 The Wonder Drug (1944–1945)

1. Richard Wagner, *Tristan und Isolde* (premiered 1865), act 3, scene 1 (Kurwenal).

2. Hans von Luck, *Mit Rommel an der Front* (3rd edn), Hamburg, 2006.

3. Roland Härtel-Petri, *Crystalspeed–Crystal-Meth: kristallines N-Methamphetamin: eine kurze Einführung*, Bezirksklinik Hochstadt, p. 50; see also H. Klee (ed.), *Amphetamine Misuse: International Perspective on Current Trends*, Amsterdam, 1997, pp. 181–97.

4. After the end of the war problems of addiction were hardly discussed. The effects on society in the 1950s have barely been addressed. See, for example, Billy Wilder's Berlin-set film *One Two Three*, in which the Coca-Cola manager played by James Cagney, C. R. MacNamara, 'only takes two Pervitin: "Today's going to be a tough day."'

5. Landesarchiv Berlin, A Rep. 250-02-09 Temmler.

6. BArch-Berlin R86/4265: on 17 January 1944 the Temmler company was given a new permit for Pervitin production there. In this context see also the letter from the patient Gorrissen to Morell from 8 November 1944, which sheds light on the mood of the elderly population in the Nazi state: 'Because I am very keen to have a general refreshment. Every time I want to go down to the town for treatment, for example (or even more important, when I have to come back up from town twelve minutes later), I first have to take between half and one tablet of Pervitin, which really peps up a weary body, but which equally you shouldn't take too often because otherwise you become "addicted" to it, as my GP tells me. You can imagine that these days more than ever it is no fun living on like a physical old wreck, when you still feel mentally on top form and think back on considerable levels of performance even ten years ago.' National Archives Microfilm Publication T253/38.

7. BArch-Freiburg RH 12–23/1930. The agenda of the meeting speaks volumes: '9.30, "Chemical construction and production

of performance-enhancing substances, particularly caffeine and Pervitin", Prof. Dr Schlemmer, Pharmaceutical Institute of Strasbourg University. 10.00, "The pharmacology of performance-enhancing substances", Staff Surgeon Dr Brok, Medical Academy of the Luftwaffe, Berlin. 10.20, "The clinical application of performance-enhancing substances", Senior Physician Prof. Dr Uhlenbruck.'

8. BArch-Freiburg RH 12–23/1611, Staff Surgeon Dr Soehring: 'Use of morphine–Pervitin in the transport of the wounded', 23 November 1944.

9. Ibid.

10. Interrogation report on one German naval POW, in Entry 179, Folder 1, N 10–16, RG No. 165, Stack Area 390, Box 648, National Archives at College Park, Md.

11. OKW 829/44.Geh., quoted in Pieper, *Nazis on Speed*, p. 142.

12. Walt Whitman, *Specimen Days & Collect*, Philadelphia, 1883, p. 80.

13. Nicolaus von Below, *Als Hitlers Adjutant 1937–45*, Mainz, 1980, p. 366.

14. Hartmut Nöldeke and Volker Hartmann, *Der Sanitätsdienst in der deutschen U-Boot-Waffe*, Hamburg, 1996, p. 211.

15. In Carnac, Orzechowski also encountered Ranke in October 1942. What they talked about is not recorded. Where Pervitin is concerned, in the late phase of the war Otto Ranke was far from prominent, and instead turned his attention to different areas of defence physiology. After the war he became professor of physiology at Erlangen University, where he died in 1959 of a heart attack. The word 'Pervitin' does not appear in the obituary published in the *Klinische Wochenschrift* (vol. 38 (1960), no. 8, , pp. 414–15).

16. BArch-Freiburg N906, unpublished war diary by Armin Wandel, 26 February–12 April 1944.

17. Ibid.

18. Cajus Bekker, *Einzelkämpfer auf See: die deutschen Torpedoreiter, Froschmänner und Sprengbootpiloten im Zweiten Weltkrieg*, Oldenburg/Hamburg, 1968, pp. 160ff.

19. BArch-Freiburg N906, From the 'Report on the state of health of the K-Command and hygiene of the individual fighter', secret commando file. Supplies listed were 'White bread sandwiches, gingerbread, chocolate, glucose, some fruit, warm coffee in Thermos flasks, additional preserved meat for *Seehund*.' The purpose of the deliberately poor nutrition was 'so that with an adequate supply of calories rectal tenesmus is avoided'.

20. BArch-Freiburg RM 103–10/6, medical war diary of the K-Group Command, 1 September 1944–30 November 1944, by Dr Richert, p. 5, Entry of 11 October 1944.

21. Ibid.

22. Admiral Heye wasn't shy when it came to evaluating the results of experiments on humans in concentration camps. Thus, for example, he borrowed ideas for the improvement of the winter clothing of his underwater fighters from Prof. Holzlöhner, who was responsible for the 'Kälteversuche' on inmates of Dachau, 'so that deployment even in low water temperatures is possible. As Prof. Holzlöhner has specialist knowledge concerning the question of preventing hypothermia, his advice on this issue has been requested.' BArch-Freiburg RM 103–10/6, medical war diary of K-Group Command, 1 September 1944–30 November 1944, by Dr Richert.

23. See also Anne Sudrow, *Der Schuh im Nationalsozialismus: eine Produktgeschichte im deutsch-britisch-amerikanischen Vergleich*, Göttingen, 2010.

24. Claudia Gottfried, 'Konsum und Verbrechen: die

Schuhprüfstrecke im KZ Sachsenhausen', in LVR-Industriemuseum Ratingen, *Glanz und Grauen: Mode im 'Dritten Reich'*, Ratingen, 2012, p. 48.

25. BArch-Freiburg RM 103–10/6, medical war diary of the K-Group Command, 1 September 1944–30 November 1944, by Dr Richert, entry for 16.–20 November 1944 as well as Richert's report on the experiments in Sachsenhausen.

26. Odd Nansen, *Day After Day*, trans. Katherine John, London, 1949.

27. BArch-Freiburg RM 103–10/6. medical war diary of the K-Group Command by Dr Richert.

28. Interrogation report on one German naval POW, p. 12.

29. With every successful mission a red stripe was added to the fin. Ibid., p. 5.

30. Nöldeke and Hartmann, *Der Sanitätsdienst in der deutschen U-Boot-Waffe*, pp. 214ff.

31. Ibid.

32. Ibid.

33. Ibid., pp. 216ff.

34. Ibid.

35. BArch RM 103/11, radio message from Heye, 3 April 1945.

36. 'US Report prepared by A. H. Andrews Jr., Lt Cdr. (MC) USNR, and T. W. Broecker Lieut. USNR', in RG No. 319, Stack Area 270, IRR Files, Box 612, National Archives College Park, Md.

37. Dachau, outside the gates of the Bavarian capital, was the first concentration camp to be built in Germany, in 1933. From the very first, National Socialist 'health leadership' would be spiced up with biological racism there. Nothing symbolized this more obviously than the 'Institute for Medical Herbal Studies and Nourishment' that Himmler, the head of the SS,

had set up here on the advice of his nutrition inspector, Günter Schenck. In Europe's largest herb garden, concentration camp inmates had to breed all the plant-based drugs and medical herbs that Germany *required* for the war. Almost all the *needs* of natural healing substances and spices for the Wehrmacht and the SS were grown, harvested, dried and packed in Dachau. Once again it was a question of import independence, as the leader of the Main Office for the People's Health confirmed: 'The high consumption of plant-based healing substances in war requires an organization which is at the given moment in a position to make up for the shortfall in drugs from abroad.' Fields of gladioli provided vitamin C, and even a pepper substitute was bred – Himmler proudly called it 'Dachau pepper'. The goal was, as Rudolf Höss – a *Rapportführer* in Dachau concentration camp and in May 1940 camp commandant in Auschwitz – explained, 'to wean the German people off foreign herbs and artificial medications that are damaging to the health and turn them towards the use of non-harmful, good-tasting spices and natural herbs' (Pieper, *Nazis on Speed*, p. 282). Everything German was supposed to become ostensibly more healthy while everything un-German was eradicated. Work in the Dachau 'plantage' was seen as heavy labour; the area, which directly abutted the main camp grounds, was substantially guarded and torture was common. Polish clerics were particularly badly abused for this forced labour; the herbs grew in blood, so to speak. For Himmler the 'herb garden' in Dachau was a major building block for the economic empire that he was trying to expand the SS into. Research and production fully exploiting the inexhaustible possibilities of the camp system were to turn his terror organization into a global player, with him as

CEO. It included several SS health firms such as the 'German Experimental Institution for Nutrition and Healing GmbH', 'Convalescent Homes for Natural Healing and Way of Life GmbH' and 'German Healing Agents GmbH', as well as the control of the mineral water market in occupied Europe; and, in Dachau, alongside the production of herbs and natural drugs there were also medical experiments on human beings. In the camp these were carried out principally by the Luftwaffe to find out at what altitude the organism collapses – and how immersion in ice-cold seawater could be survived. Prisoners were exposed to simulated altitudes in pressure chambers and plunged into icy baths. Biochemical experiments into the treatment of infected wounds and malaria experiments were also performed; the latter were to benefit the German settlers in the southern areas of the Soviet Union, in the Crimea and the Caucasus. The drug experiments also fell under the heading of this pseudo-scientific torture.

38. As early as 1938 Professor Ernst Holzlöhner, who ran human hypothermia experiments for the Luftwaffe from 1942, had tested the effects of narcotics and poison gas on the central nervous system of prisoners. This included the use of Pervitin, to discover how 'this affects the organism during a parachute jump' (Alexander Mitscherlich and Fred Mielke, *Medizin ohne Menschlichkeit: Dokumente des Nürnberger Ärzteprozesses*, Frankfurt am Main, 1978, p. 28).

39. Canetti, *Crowds and Power*, p. 284.

40. Harvard University/Francis D. Countway Libary of Medicine/ Henry K. Beecher Papers/H MS c64/Box 11, f75, 'U.S. Naval Technical Mission in Europe: Technical Report no. 331–45.'

41. Ibid.

42. These Luftwaffe experiments in Dachau formed the basic

capital that Hubert Strughold used as a pledge in his negotiations with the Americans. In the context of 'Operation Paperclip', along with Wernher von Braun, who had designed the prototype of the cruise missile in the form of the V2 rocket, he was among the pioneers of US space travel, such as the development of the Pershing II rockets, which would help to decide the Cold War for the USA at the end of the 1980s.

43. *Hitler's Table Talk, 1941–1944,* trans. Norman Cameron and R. H. Stevens, London, 1953, p. 288.

44. BArch-Koblenz N1348, Morell entries, 9 and 10 December 1944.

45. Ibid., 8. and 9 December 1944.

46. Ibid., 11 December 1944.

47. Quoted in Claudia Schmölders, *Hitlers Gesicht: eine physiognomische Biographie*, Munich, 2000, p. 210.

48. William L. Shirer, *Aufstieg und Fall des Dritten Reiches*, Cologne/Berlin 1971, p. 997 [*The Rise and Fall of the Third Reich: A History of Nazi Germany*, New York/London, 1960].

49. BArch-Koblenz N1348, Morell entry, 11 December 1944.

50. Ibid., 19 December 1944.

51. Ibid., 31 December 1944.

52. Joseph Goebbels, *Das Reich – Deutsche Wochenzeitung,* 31 December 1944, leading article, pp. 1ff.

53. BArch-Koblenz N1348, Morell entry, 2 January 1945.

54. Pieper, *Nazis on Speed*, p. 103.

55. 'Conditions in Berlin, March 1945', in SIR 1581–1582, RG No. 165, Stack Area 390, Row 35, Box 664, p. 1, National Archives at College Park, Md.

56. Hubert Fischer, *Die militärärztliche Akademie 1934–1945*, Osnabrück, 1985 [Munich, 1975].

57. BArch-Koblenz N1348., Morell entry, 17 February 1945.

58. These were not free of problems, as Morell now admitted – see his record of a conversation from 22 March 1945: 'Communication that new liver preparation in all ampoules toxic when tested in Olmütz. Distribution impossible under all circumstances.' A telegram from Morell to the Kosolup paint factories dated 18 March 1945 sets things out quite clearly: 'Ampoule testing in Olmütz showed all unusable as unsterile and hence toxic. Not to be used under any circumstances. Prof. Morell.' National Archives Microfilm Publication T253/39.

59. '. . . request permission to bring the Hamma hypophyse total extract on to the market. The preparation is to be distributed in dragees and ampoules.' Letter from Morell, 24 February 1945, National Archives Microfilm Publication T253/35.

60. 'At the beginning of 1945 the situation became somewhat tense with regard to alkaloids, the manufacturers being unable to produce sufficient quantities owing to the continual air raids', dated 10 April 1945. See also 0660 Germany (Postwar) 1945–1949, Bureau of Narcotics and Dangerous Drugs: Subject Files, 1916–1970, Record Group 170; National Archives at College Park, Md.

61. BArch-Koblenz N1348, Morell entries, 13 and 17 February 1945.

62. Bezymenskii, Lev, *Die letzten Notizen von Martin Bormann: ein Dokument und sein Verfasser*, Munich, 1974, p. 191.

63. BArch-Koblenz N1348, Morell entry, 22/23 March 1945.

64. Sebastian Haffner, *Anmerkungen zu Hitler*, Munich, 1978, p. 51.

65. BArch-Koblenz N1348, Morell entry, 5 March 1945.

66. *Der Prozess gegen die Hauptkriegsverbrecher vor dem Internationalen*

Militärgerichtshof Nürnberg, 14. November 1945–1. Oktober 1946, vol. 41, Munich, 1984, p. 430.

67. BArch-Koblenz N1348, Morell entry, 20 April 1945.

68. Letter from Morell to his chemist, Mulli, 20 April 1945, quoted in Schenck, *Patient Hitler*, p. 50.

69. 'Life History of Professor Dr. Med. Theo Morell', p. 6, IRR-Personal Name Files, RG NO. 319, Stack Area 230, Row 86, Box 8,, National Archives at College Park, Md.

70. Tania Long, 'Doctor describes Hitler injections', *The New York Times*, 22 May 1945, p. 5.

71. Copy of a letter from the Hamma company to the corporate tax office in Hamburg, National Archives Microfilm Publication T253/39.

72. Christian Hartmann, *Unternehmen Barbarossa: der deutsche Krieg im Osten 1941–1945*, Munich, 2011, p. 81.

73. BArch-Koblenz N1128, Adolf Hitler posthumous papers, Hitler's personal testament.

74. See Bekker, *Einzelkämpfer auf See*.

75. BArch-Koblenz N1348, posthumous papers of Theodor Morell. See Karl Brandt's report on Morell, 9 September 1945, p. 2.

Acknowledgements

1. Quoted in Johann Peter Eckermann, *Gespräche mit Goethe*, Frankfurt, 1987, p. 496.

Picture Credits

Index